BEHIND MUD WALLS

Seventy-five Years in a
North Indian Village

KARIMPUR

SITE OF WISER'S CAMP
1925-1930

POND

PRAKASH'S HOUSE
(Wiser's residence)

Brahman Section

Sweeper Section

Humble Lane

POND

N

TO KURAOLI

Bus
Stop

KHERA

KHAN
BAHADUR'S
SHRINE

Farmer Section

TO MAINPURI

Leatherworker
Section

0   250

FEET

Karimpur, circa 1970

Behind Mud Walls

Seventy-five
Years in a North
Indian Village

WILLIAM H. WISER

CHARLOTTE VIALL WISER

WITH CHAPTERS BY SUSAN S. WADLEY
AND A FOREWORD BY DAVID G. MANDELBAUM

UNIVERSITY OF CALIFORNIA PRESS

Berkeley, Los Angeles, London

UNIVERSITY OF CALIFORNIA PRESS
BERKELEY AND LOS ANGELES, CALIFORNIA
UNIVERSITY OF CALIFORNIA PRESS, LTD.
LONDON, ENGLAND

Library of Congress Cataloging-in-Publication Data
Wiser, Charlotte Viall.
Behind mud walls: Seventy-five Years in a North Indian Village / by
William H. Wiser and Charlotte Viall Wiser ; with chapters
by Susan S. Wadley and David G. Mandelbaum.
p.   cm.
Previously published: Behind Mud Walls, 1930–1960: with a sequel,
The Village in 1970 : and a new chapter by Susan S. Wadley,
The Village in 1984 / by William H. Wiser and Charlotte Viall Wiser,
with a foreword by David G. Mandelbaum, 1989.
Behind mud wall, 1930–1960 / William H Wiser
and Charlotte Viall Wiser. 1971.
Originally published: Behind mud walls / by Charlotte Viall Wiser
and William H. Wiser, 1930.
Includes bibliographical references.
ISBN 0-520-22710-7 :
1. India—Social life and customs. 2. Villages—India.
I. Wadley, Susan Snow, 1943–   . II. Wiser, William Henricks,
1890–1961. III. Title.
DS421.W73   1989
954.03'5—dc19   89-5166
CIP

LIBRARY OF CONGRESS CATALOG CARD NUMBER 63-19178
PRINTED IN THE UNITED STATES OF AMERICA
09   08   07   06   05
10   9   8   7   6   5   4   3

Contents

Foreword

The Wisers first came to Karimpur, a village east of Agra, to do a brief statistical survey. They remained for five years to write a human document. When their book appeared in 1930 it was one of the few accounts of village life in India as seen by sympathetic observers who knew the villagers as friends and neighbors.

Thirty-two years later, after a new generation had come of age, Charlotte Wiser wrote the additional chapters, telling of her return to her friends in Karimpur and of their lives in the new times. When first she saw the village, its older people had grown up in the nineteenth century, when imperial rule was firm, unchallenged, and quite distant from everyday village affairs. Its youngsters now will reach into another century and are already living in a time when the village is much more closely linked to the larger world. This augmented edition of the book is unique in that it shows the people of an Indian village as seen by the same friend after three decades.

The Wisers are to be counted among those missionaries

who have made notable contributions to anthropology. They knew well that anyone who works to help villagers must first understand what village life is really like if the work is to be effective. William H. Wiser, who died in 1961, wrote illuminatingly about the relations between families of different castes in his monograph, *The Hindu Jajmani System* (Lucknow Publishing House, 1936). He and Mrs. Wiser were among the pioneers in working out the approaches to village development which are today being used throughout India and beyond India. Their efforts in the India Village Service and in teaching about rural realities entered into the shaping of the great Indian government movement for community development.

That movement has brought changes into Karimpur whose full effect is only gradually being felt. Mrs. Wiser finds that in most outward aspects the face of village life is much the same as it was. The daily round is little changed as is the villagers' absorption with their fields and with the tight world of the village and neighborhood. The animals are still quartered in the house or compound. The tasks of the women have altered very little; they still spend long hours in the kitchen enveloped in smoke from the chimneyless hearth.

In deeper respects also, the foundations of village society have not been altered. The family is still the main center of each person's interest and has unquestioned first claim to his loyalty. If there is any choice between family obligations and personal or community advantage, the family comes first. Kinship ties count heavily, even to affecting army recruitment. Caste still separates one village group from another in social relations, and still provides the organizational frame for economic relations. The fundamental concept of society is an hierarchical one. Villagers are zealous to maintain, if possible to advance, their group's status. They must ward off any upward mobility by lower groups which might impugn their own social rank. All villagers can unite in common defense, as they did in protesting a tax assessment, but concerted action for village improvement is still apt to be thwarted by factionalism; if one side is for something, the other is likely to be against it.

Religion continues as a central fact of village life. Religious observances are part of one's daily life, indicate the main occasions in each person's life cycle, provide the principal markers of accomplishment in the yearly round. More than that, the main savor of village life comes in the setting of religion. Mrs. Wiser mentions taking a truckful of villagers to the nearest place of pilgrimage on the Ganges and notes, "I have never seen a happier crowd." Many others of the familiar, traditional ways continue to bring satisfaction and reward.

Yet the impact of the new ways is apparent and can be summed up in a sentence from the talk with a group of young men, "We have more to eat and more to sell." The villagers now raise hardier, more productive varieties of crops, and the animals are better than they were—a particularly noteworthy advance because, as the Wisers noted in 1930, improvement of the livestock was basic to the improvement of village economy. Farming has become more productive and less uncertain through the use of fertilizers, improved implements, tube-well irrigation. Better roads and bus service have made marketing trips to town easier and more frequent. Transportation greatly improved with the increase of bicycles in the village from two to fifty-six. Owning a bicycle brings some prestige to a villager; more importantly it is a machine that is of considerable economic importance.

A main advance has been in medical care. It was the simple, yet effective, medical aid which the Wisers gave that opened doors to them when they first came to Karimpur. Medical and hospital services outside the village were not then trusted. Now all who are sick are taken to town for medical treatment if they can afford it. Malaria has been much reduced, though other public health measures have not yet taken hold. The net result of better health care and more food is clearly demonstrated by the growth of Karimpur's population from 754 to 1129 in the three decades, an increase of 49 percent. This increase slows the benefit of the other gains, because the same lands must now be made to support all these additional people, half as many again as there were thirty years ago.

New crops, new techniques, population spurts have all affected village life before these decades, indeed long before this century. But never before have they come so rapidly and with such cumulative effect. An important element in the new wave is a social invention in public administration, the Community Development Program. It is a novel kind of bureaucracy for India, dedicated to culture change, designed to provide communication between village and research station Its officers do not have to cope with the usual tasks of maintaining society and government; the established governmental organizations do that. It attracts into its ranks many among the educated who sincerely want to devote themselves to helping their countrymen. The people of Karimpur know the program through their *gram sevak*, "village companion," the official who is at the base of the bureaucracy's hierarchy and on whom the success of the program in any one village largely depends.

Karimpur's village companions have achieved marked success with their farming demonstrations, but have been able to accomplish much less where their suggestions for change touched domestic routine and relations among people. The slower response in matters of social organization is not unusual in the history of mankind—social patterns are generally less amenable to change than technological patterns. Social improvements desired by many villagers and by officials alike are not yet within grasp, but the villagers' view, as Mrs. Wiser communicates it, is undespondent: "All are surprised that so much has been done in so short a time."

One of the first measures to stir the village after independence was land reform, the transfer of ownership from a relatively few large landowners to more of the villagers. Not all in Karimpur have benefited from the legislation; it has brought on an increase of wasteful litigation; there still are large flaws in the program, yet, on the whole, it has given an incentive to produce more from the land and thus to raise the standard of living of the family. Contrast the earlier reaction to a new kind of plough which Dr. Wiser urged the villagers to adopt, with the present use of an improved implement. In the last chapter of the 1930 edition, their response is quoted: "We were sorry to disappoint you, but we could not risk such an expensive and doubtful experiment, when the benefits would most likely not stay with us." In 1962 factory-made ploughs were accepted implements, with twenty-six being used to cultivate the village lands.

Technical improvements often raise social problems which require the development of adaptive social inventions. The tube wells installed in Karimpur by the government have been a great boon. But they require a tube-well operator who is a government employee and so was not under the social control of the villagers. Yet his control of the water gave him great power over them and, under the prevailing social conditions, he was likely—whoever he might be—to use that power to augment unofficially his small official salary. To protect the villagers' interest, a water control board of six men of this village has been established, including the president of the village council.

The new village council, the *gram panchayat*, is a key element in Karimpur's development. Elected periodically, endowed with legal and fiscal powers, expected by the government to take the lead in self-help and by the villagers to tap governmental bounty, it is a social device completely different from the traditional *panchayat*. In Karimpur, as in most villages, power did not shift greatly when an elected council was introduced. The outstanding leaders of the new council

are mainly the sons and nephews of the powerful elders. But
Karimpur profited by the election of an unusually fine council
president who has been able to devote most of his energies
to the work of the council with results beneficial to the whole
village.

Yet the new social forms require a social substructure
which has not been firmly established. The council president
indicated this when he told Mrs. Wiser: "There is not one
member of the *panchayat* whom I can trust to carry through
a job." The villagers' prevailing fear and distrust of each
other, rooted in experience and buttressed by poverty, was
noted in the earlier chapters, and had not decreased much
when the later chapters were written. Trust and mutual confidence are found in the family, in the circle of related families
of the caste, even between families of different caste who
have traditional association. But there is little tacit reliance of
one person upon another on the basis of both being fellow
villagers working for the common good of the community.

The common good is well understood when all approach
the gods together in cooperative rites, or when all close ranks
to ward off alien intrusions, but it is not clearly understood—
and this can be seen in the legislatures of great nations as
well as in village councils—that each may prosper best when
all in a community prosper together. There is rather the idea
that the good things of the village are forever fixed in amount,
and each person must manipulate constantly to garner a
large slice for his own. Hence the characteristic maneuver,
which the young men mentioned to Mrs. Wiser, of bribes
and counterbribes to the record keeper over a sliver of land.
When one man does achieve a larger slice, he is thereby seen
as a threat by those who have been superior in status to him;
his rise is interpreted as diminishing them in the all-important
social hierarchy. So they cannot usually rest easily until he is
somehow diminished.

The Wisers do not hide these seamier sides of village life

but describe them for what they are, the outcome of social conditions rather than of the machinations of evil men. As friends, they know the worth and the talent of the villagers, and they are confident that the debilitating social conditions can in time be changed.

Mrs. Wiser now finds that in Karimpur change is in the breeze, the young men are on the move. The school is a principal factor in this. While a casual visitor might find the school far from adequate, with less than a third of the children in attendance and teaching facilities poor, Mrs. Wiser observes it from the vantage of thirty-five years of village improvement, and the promise of much better schooling to come.

There may be an allegorical meaning in the contrast between the earlier and the later discussion of mud walls. In 1930 the villagers said that these walls were a necessary part of each home's defenses, a barrier against the outer world, especially against those covetous officials who came to extort. Paradoxically, a dilapidated mud wall offered better protection because it suggested that those who lived behind it were not worth exploiting. In 1962 the young men stated that what they wanted most of all were walls of baked brick for their houses. No longer did they feel a need to build barriers which had constantly to be repaired—but not too well—after every rain. Now they do not fear that solid walls will attract the notice of predators. They want them, not for better hiding, but for better living.

These young men of Karimpur see village life as more open, with more good things possible, than did their fathers. They seem to have caught some of the fundamental optimism of the Wisers. The Wisers brought to Karimpur an optimism which runs deep in their faith and their country, that if men are under yokes which they do not want to bear, they can cast them off. This hopeful approach has not been absent in India but it has often been subordinated to a less buoyant view. The optimism of the Wisers' faith has been justified by what Mrs. Wiser observed on her return: "We now see what for many years we had hoped for"; and of government officials: "I am greatly encouraged not only by what government representatives are accomplishing, but even more by their methods."

Much, very much, remains to be accomplished in Karimpur, as in many other Indian villages, before its people have the basic decencies they want for their children. The Wisers have sketched the villagers, their aspirations, their handicaps, soberly yet hopefully, in simple human terms, yet with a perceptiveness not often found in more sophisticated studies or in journalistic reports. In the microcosm of Karimpur we see enacted one of the greatest movements of our times. This edition of the book should not only enlighten students of village life, it should also give encouragement to India's people and well-wishers.

DAVID G. MANDELBAUM

University of California,
Berkeley, January, 1963

Preface to the 2000 Edition

I first went to Karimpur, a village some 150 miles southeast of New Delhi, India, in 1967, as a graduate student in anthropology. I have been going back ever since—for a year in the 1970s, another year in the 1980s, and almost yearly for the past decade. Karimpur is now my second home, and the family with whom I stay my second family. More important, Karimpur has now been studied for almost seventy-five years.

The changes that have taken place since William and Charlotte Wiser began studying in Karimpur in 1925 are both enormous and small. For many of Karimpur's inhabitants life hasn't changed much, despite the increasing connections with a wider community and the forces of globalization. Moreover, there is a growing disparity between the better-off (for no one in Karimpur is rich, and very few would qualify for middle class) and the very poor since the Wisers first wrote about this community in the 1920s.

While those with land certainly felt richer and more powerful in the 1920s, through the 1960s their lifestyle differed little from that of the poor. In the 1920s, everyone's home was made of adobe bricks (mud walls). The children of both the better-off and the very poor, both male and female, frequently died, often in infancy. Their sons, but never their daughters, went to school. The women of all caste groups and economic levels married while young, often by eleven or twelve years (though the actual marriage ceremony did not mark living with the husband's family or the consummation of the marriage, which usually took place in a separate ceremony called *gauna* three or four years later, after the girl reached puberty). Everyone rode in bullock carts; even bicycles were a rarity. And almost everyone lived off the land, either as primary tenant, sharecropper, or laborer.

Now, increased medical care means that children are surviving, though girls are at greater risk than boys. In fact, the disparity between male and female survival is greater now than before: whereas in the 1920s both male and female children had only a 50 percent chance of surviving to age five, in the 1990s, girls are most likely to die in infancy and early childhood, while their brothers reap the benefits of better-quality medical care (table 1). This increased survival has had a major effect on family size and population growth (table 2), especially among the poor, who are least likely to use birth control.

The mud walls of the 1920s are now regularly replaced by brick, especially among the wealthier families. In the 1920s, 21 percent of the men and 4 percent of the women were literate. In the 1960s, few girls were in school, and almost none went beyond fifth grade. Now girls from the richer families regularly go to high school, and some obtain B.A.s. These wealthier families have close to 100 percent literacy for both men and women, while one of the poorer castes has no literate women and yet others are still sending less than a third of their daughters to primary school.

In a major shift for all groups, by the 1990s, the average age of marriage for girls was over sixteen, but the landowning families with better-educated daughters often wait until the girl is twenty or more. However, the transition from daughter to wife is more abrupt, as the ceremony of *gauna* has been almost eliminated because of the older age of the brides and the expense of holding a second ceremony. Further, dowry is required in most marriages, whereas previously the poor married their daughters without dowry, sometimes even receiving a bride price.

Although many farming families still keep bullocks to work their fields, long-distance travel is now by tractor, bus, truck, or motorcycle. Yet here too the disparity between the better-off and the very poor is increasingly marked, as the richer families purchase modern modes of transportation, while the poor continue to walk or cycle. And while some sons of wealthier families are moving into the urban lower, middle class, many sons of the poor find themselves in urban slums, unable to find decent jobs.

So while the better-off farming families (usually high caste) of Karimpur feel that they have lost political power in India's democratic state, they have been able to access modern goods and services whereas the poor have not. Increasingly, then, the lifestyles of the better-off and very poor are diverging. This duality—of increased globalization and the separation of richer and poorer—presents a challenge to this community, and to thousands of others, in the twentieth century. In the following chapters, representing the 1920s, the 1960s, the 1980s, and the 1990s, the Wisers and I detail some aspects of this transformation of one village in northern India.

Susan S. Wadley
November 1999
Syracuse, New York

Preface to the 1989 Edition

In 1967, at the invitation of "Dadi," as Charlotte Wiser was known in Karimpur, I went to live in her house with Prakash's family as my hosts for a year of doctoral dissertation research. I returned again in 1974 when Bruce W. Derr did his doctoral research on Karimpur. In 1984 I returned once more with my family to study men's and women's life histories and social change. Karimpur was once again my home, and I have visited it almost yearly since 1984.

Given the historical depth represented by the work of the Wisers, Derr, and myself, it seems inevitable that yet another edition, with yet one more sequel, of *Behind Mud Walls* should appear. For in fact the fifteen years from 1970 to 1984 produced many changes in Karimpur, changes that can shed light on broader social processes in South Asia and elsewhere. In one brief chapter I have tried to outline these changes. A few summary comparative statistics are found in the appendix, and a bibliography lists the published writings on Karimpur by the Wisers, Derr, and myself.

Treading in the Wisers' footsteps, as I have done in Karimpur
and in academia for some twenty years, is not always easy. Their
insights and humanity have been hard to follow, and I hope that
I have done them and my friends in Karimpur justice. I might
note that in Karimpur itself, the personalities of the Westerners
are conflated and confused, so that I am often mistaken for Dadi's
granddaughter, and any denials of a kin relationship are not heard.
Moreover, there is now a local legend about the "Rani" who
comes to Karimpur periodically to help the poor and ill there,
a legend with which I was unfamiliar until it was told to me by
a servant in the Superintendent of Police's house, his wife having heard it from her servants.

None of this would have been possible without the hospitality
of the family of Prakash, a pseudonym given by the Wisers. (I
have retained their pseudonyms in all my writings on Karimpur
so that there is some consistency in naming from one text to
another.) To them, a heartfelt thank you.

Research assistance to Bruce Derr and myself in 1984 was
ably provided by Umesh Chandra Pandey, Nanhe Khan, Ant
Ram Dhimar, and Monisha Behal. Shona and Leela provided
light-hearted distractions and no serious illnesses: their diaries
continue to remind me of the amusing incidents of that year and
the ease with which they absorbed Indian culture, where I had
had to "learn" it. Funding in 1967–69 was provided by the National Science Foundation, in 1974–75 by the American Insti-
tute of Indian Studies, and in 1983–84 by the U.S. Department
of Education (Faculty Research Abroad) and the Smithsonian
Institution. I am grateful to all of these for their help.

Susan S. Wadley
May 1989
Syracuse, New York

Preface to the First Edition, 1930

When we came to Karimpur five years ago, to make a survey of the social, religious, and economic life of a fairly typical North India village, we were bent upon gathering facts by the most direct methods possible. But our new neighbors were not prepared for anything so rapid or impersonal. They refused to help us by any route other than the leisurely one of friendship. The result was that we became engaged in numerous neighborly activities which often led us out of sight of our survey, but which we could not conscientiously refuse. We had learned from our neighbors that the road of friendship and service is courteous and just, if not the most efficient. Those who expected a routine survey—as we did when we started out—gave us up long ago as hopelessly enchanted. But the information collected with the help of our village friends, is a document which we hope will be of some value as source material.

Many of our experiences along the way have been too personal to have a place in a survey. Yet they are too revealing to be discarded. We have set some of them down in this volume for the friends, both Indian and foreign, who have asked us repeatedly to share our village experiences with them. This informal presentation may be more interesting, and perhaps more helpful, than the detailed information of a survey. We have limited ourselves to those experiences which helped us most to understand our village neighbors, and those which were most challenging. We have included the latter that they might in turn challenge the young men and women, many of whom we know, who because of special training and gifts, or because their fathers own villages, are peculiarly fitted to serve village folk if they choose. As in other countries, interest in rural problems is growing rapidly in India. Since our coming to Karimpur, a number of training schools and institutes for prospective rural workers have sprung up; and there have been an increasing number of speeches and articles on the needs, the conditions, and the handicaps of the peasant. We want to use whatever influence and knowledge we have to encourage a healthy growth of interest based on careful study rather than on sentiment.

A mistake which most of us have made when we have gone straight from our town environment to the village is that we have expected villagers to react like college graduates or sophisticated town dwellers. We have criticized them when they have fallen short of our expectations, while the fault lay with us. Gradually we have learned what others before us have learned, that the ordinary village farmer is the victim of circumstances, not the master. His life is pervaded and pressed down by his fears of the forces which control him. Before we can do much to help, we must consider the source, the power, the utility or harmfulness, of these forces. The maladjustments which many of us have caused in the past, when we were sincerely trying to help, have been due to our consideration of the villager as a free individual, and our oversight of the circumstances which dominate his life.

Although this book is much more personal than our survey, still we have striven to keep it impartial. We have written nothing we would hesitate to write about our own community or our own family. When one of us has been tempted to wax romantic or condemnatory, the other has followed after with a firm blue pencil and has cut down effusions to prosaic facts. We realize that conditions vary greatly in living, as in language or diet or architecture, in different parts of the country and sometimes in different areas of the same province. All we can say is that we know these things to be true of our village. Friends in nearby sections of this province have said that some of our experiences are so much like theirs that they might be their own; whereas a friend from Madras remarked that if he did not know us so well he might doubt our veracity! Whether the material herein presented be of interest because of its contrast or its similarity, we hope that it will be provocative of further observation and thought and service.

We acknowledge our thanks to the friends and relatives who have made our prolonged stay in the village possible. We are grateful to our Mission for being so long-suffering while we made no apparent progress. We also wish to thank the friends who have criticized this material and helped make it more readable. And we express our gratitude to our village neighbors, who have been hospitable, generous, and sympathetic, even in times when we have been most trying.

CHARLOTTE VIALL WISER
WILLIAM H. WISER

American Presbyterian Mission,
Mainpuri, U. P. India, May, 1930

Behind Mud Walls
1930–1960

Music is and was a primary form of recreation in
Karimpur. Here a group of men have joined William
Wiser for an afternoon of music. In addition to his
violin, a drum and harmonium are present. (1920s)

BEHIND MUD WALLS
1930–1960

with a sequel:
The Village in 1970
and a New Chapter by Susan S. Wadley:
The Village in 1984

CHAPTER I

Friend or Foe?

We sat on the running board of our car, and contemplated the village across the, road. We had chosen Karimpur as being reasonably typical of the villages in our section of the United Provinces. We had secured credentials from higher quarters, and had been officially introduced to the *patwari*, the village accountant in the employ of the government. We had found an old mango grove, and therein had set up tents for our helpers, ourselves, and our two small sons. Now we were ready to study the village. But would the village permit itself to be studied? Certainly it gave no sign of welcome.

The irregular high, rain-furrowed mud walls which faced us might have been mistaken for a deserted fortress. No door-yards, no windows were there to give glimpses of family life. Nothing but blank walls and more walls, so joined that it was often difficult to tell where one man's house ended and his neighbor's began. Dark doorways, patted into shape by hand, were the chief indications of separate dwellings. Directly opposite the entrance to our grove was a high-arched doorway, once imposing, now about to collapse. Behind it were more blank walls. The only other breaks in the weather-beaten barrier were narrow lanes leading back into the village. These too were bordered by walls. A welcome variation in the picture was the pond which separated half of our grove from the village. It had been dug to furnish mud for walls and was now filled with water from the recent rains. On it two white geese drifted, making trails through the green scum. At one side a small semicircle of clear water indicated that here the washerman beat the village clothes. Beyond the far end of the pond we could see carpenters at work in a lane. A few extraordinarily thin cows wandered in from the fields and disappeared through the dark doorways, or down the narrow lanes. After some time a woman emerged from one of the doorways, a water jar on her head and another on her hip. She slunk close to the wall and hurried around a corner as though afraid of attracting our attention. We wished we could take upon ourselves the guise of lean cows. How else were we to pass the barriers? It began to rain, a cold, autumn rain. We retired to the dining tent for a conference on methods of approach.

Our assistant brought in the news that after observing our camp, and considering the various rumors that had arrived in advance, the leaders of the village had concluded that the Sahib must be the settlement officer come to check landholdings and revise rents. They knew that he was not the district magistrate nor a deputy; neither was he a police official. There had been missionaries here before, and he might be classified as such. But he had secured land maps of the area and had access to records of landholdings. Who would want these but someone interested in taxes? Our assistant had tried to assure them that we were here on a helpful mission. But rumor was against him. They would watch and learn for themselves. They were running no risks with unlabeled strangers.

Less sophisticated members of the community, especially the women, were more than suspicious. They were terrified lest we approach them or their animals or their children. It was obvious that no one was pining for our acquaintance. And yet our work depended on the cooperation of these, our neighbors. We had to win their confidence and friendship, or roll up our tents and move on.

Early the next morning, a tall figure carrying a closely wrapped bundle appeared from the corner of the village where untouchables lived, and ventured across the muddy road. He was a Christian. He had heard somewhere that we were missionaries, and he knew from experience that missionary visitors in tents were not to be feared. He brought his baby, suffering from dysentery, for treatment. We had a medical kit for family emergencies from which we gave him medicine for the baby, along with a bit of homely advice on feeding. As he recrossed the road, neighbors peered from several doorways, waiting to see him or his child collapse, as they have laughingly confessed to us since.

As soon as our first caller had departed, the Sahib made his first trip into the village. He had chosen the least personal item on our list—the testing of the water of the then eighteen village wells. He followed the line of walls which faced our camp until he reached the first well. He might not have recognized it as a well had not a woman been stooping over it, drawing up a clay jar filled to the brim with water. There was no curb to protect the well or to save children from falling in. Yet well accidents, we learned, were rare. As the woman raised her carefully covered head and spied the Sahib, she snatched her water jar and her baby, and escaped. Across the narrow lane from the well, a goldsmith sat on his mud veranda blowing through a long brass tube into the embers of his miniature clay furnace. He puffed on as though unaware of the presence of a stranger. Beyond the well a group of carpenters were fitting spokes into the solid hub of a cart wheel.

They salaamed dutifully, and one of them offered to draw water for the sample bottle. If the Sahib had let a jar down into the well himself, he would have polluted its water. They were obviously worried by his visit, and relieved when he moved on.

The second well, still further down this outer lane, was reserved for Brahmans. All around it Brahman farmers were chopping fodder and feeding their animals in the leisure of a rainy morning when fields do not demand watering. Here, too, there was no gesture of welcome beyond perfunctory salaams. Polite monosyllables were apparently the limit of their vocabulary. Their welcome was very unlike the cordiality to which we were accustomed from Indian friends in Mainpuri. Even the dogs yapped and the donkeys escaped as fast as their hobbles would allow.

The search for other wells led the Sahib down twisting narrow lanes through the heart of the village. More walls, broken only by irregular doorways, lined these lanes. An occasional high, gaily decorated gateway, topped with protecting grass eaves and bordered by smoothed walls, indicated the coming of prosperity to some household. But most of the walls were sadly eroded. Where families had dwindled to numbers too small to maintain earlier pretensions, sections of the outer walls had been allowed to crumble. And where families had died out, the Sahib looked through gaping doorways at rough mounds of earth where secluded courtyards once had been. In other sections, particularly down what we later called Humble Lane, walls were more neighborly, and women visited in the lane while their children made mud carts. All vanished at the sight of the stranger. Thus the Sahib went the round of the wells—the shepherds' well, the wells used by farmer castes, the Muslims' well, the wells reserved for the various craftsmen, and those for the serving castes, the leather workers' well, and the wells of other untouchable groups. While waiting for someone of proper caste to produce a jar with which to draw

water for his sample bottles, the Sahib explained to the men
who salaamed him that he was interested in studying the village water supply and that he hoped to correct any deficien-
cies which might be the cause of ill-health. Everywhere his
explanations were greeted with noncommittal monosyllables.
His bottles were filled with well water for testing, but the
experiment had failed as a friendly overture.

The *patwari* provided us with the names of the four men
who could help us most, if they chose. The Sahib called on
these and was greeted with hospitable offers of milk, fuel,
and even beds. But to his intimations of a social survey, there
was a guarded response. We had not before realized how difficult it would be to explain the purpose of a study to a practical villager. The same difficulty has since arisen in trying to
explain political events. After hearing an explanation of do-
minion status, the villager will ask, "How will it benefit me?
Will it give me full ownership of my fields? Will I get consolidated holdings? Will I get canal water? Will we get a decent road through the village? Will some of us get jobs?"
Such questions challenge one's theories. And they must be
answered honestly before one can win the questioner's support. Our introduction from district officials could secure for
us every physical comfort but not the cooperation we desired.
Experience has taught the villager to conceal his wealth and to
avoid any revelation of his true status, lest it be used later to
his disadvantage. A direct question at once rouses his suspicion. And without his confidence we could hope only for
distortions of the truth.

We set ourselves the task of turning opposition into confidence, and fear into friendship. We had not known it, but
the Christian father with his child was our first step. His baby
did not die, as anticipated by neighbors, but improved. On
the following morning we found three daring fathers with ail-
ing children at our tent door. On the following day there were
ten, then twenty, then fifty. Half of the office tent was trans-

formed into a dispensary. The previous summer in the hills, the Memsahiba had heard a lecture on medical helps for those working in villages. The notes from this lecture were brought out and used until the pages were in tatters. Our medical supplies were rapidly exhausted and had to be replenished by frequent trips to town. We acquired another tent to be used as a dispensary, and established a young villager in it with instructions for simple treatments, while we occasionally withdrew to the office for study.

At times the survey threatened to be swamped by prolonged hours of amateur medical service. But these hours served our purpose as few activities could have done. Fathers, and the few mothers who dared come, became communicative, voluble. Opportunities for questioning rapidly increased, although weariness and pity for unnecessary suffering often blotted out our desire to seek information. First aid and home nursing had not appeared in our survey schedule or budget. But they proved our greatest asset—and expense. They will remain necessary items in any effort at village service, until village folk learn to protect themselves from the preventable diseases which now travel freely from town to town and house to house.

The District Medical Officer, at first amused, later keenly interested, drove out to our camp on Sunday mornings for special cases. On one visit he removed a disfiguring tumor from the side of a small girl's nose. Her parents refused to send her to the hospital, and yet they begged us to help her. We turned our baby's play pen upside down under a mango tree and used it as an operating table. The doctor's assistant gave the anesthetic and the Memsahiba acted as nurse. Gasoline was the antiseptic wash, and tire-mending solution was painted over the wound afterward. The operation was successful, and has become one of the village legends. In our second year the Medical Officer was unable to continue his services. But he had visited us often enough to disprove to the villagers many of the rumors of hospital terrors. Since then one of our Mission doctors has made fortnightly visits to our village—at great personal inconvenience—first from Kasganj and now from Fatehgarh, each about forty-five miles away.

Although after our first test case the dispensary continued to draw our neighbors to us, they were still unwilling to have us come to them, inside their homes. Someone had to be desperate to risk this, and the desperate one was a Brahman tortured by maggots up his nose. A fortnight after our arrival a youth came with the request that the Memsahiba come to see his father. As she followed him through the village she realized that she had much to do to win friends. Children running gaily out of doorways shrieked and disappeared. The women who peeped out did not smile in welcome. She was invited to enter a doorway higher and wider than most doorways in the village. It was set in an entrance white-washed into startling contrast to the crumbling mud walls which flanked it. On either side of the doorway was a vertical row of niches painted a vivid blue; and above it, broken bits of mirror plastered into the mud were glittering in the sunshine. Inside, she was led across a long narrow room with emptied clay troughs ranged along one side. The earth floor was littered with cow dung not yet gathered up by the women of the family. Beyond this room she entered a large courtyard deserted save for stacks of fodder and neat mounds of dung cakes. The walls had not been built up nor mud plastered for many seasons. The Memsahiba learned later that few families could boast this extra courtyard for the animals. It was evidence of the high position once held by this household, now transferred to more thrifty neighbors.

Beyond this courtyard in a long narrow room like the one first entered, she found the patient on a rope-strung cot. Close beside him a calf was tied. He had been ill for weeks and had not been moved during that time. Neither had the quilts which served him as bedding been changed. He was buried under a thick quilt with not a hair nor a toe exposed. Thus he escaped the flies and wasps which swarmed about him. When he pushed back his covering the stench was nauseating. His son and his brother fled. The much-worn lecture notes supplied instructions for treatment, and with their help and a pair of tweezers the Memsahiba attacked the maggots. As one after another was drawn out the men returned, fascinated, and three women came slowly from the inner family courtyard with their noses carefully covered. The Memsahiba asked the brother of the patient to fan away the flies while she worked. He shouted the order to someone else. The fan appeared as she was about to depart. Several visits with tweezers and a strong prescription, disposed of the maggots.

The Brahman was exceedingly grateful both for relief from the maggots and for the prescribed change of clothes and bedding. He was dying from syphilis, and the maggots had been an added torment. When we learned later that his body was being burned, we expected to hear that the Memsahiba had caused his death by her inauspicious presence. But not even his son intimated this. It had been his fate to die, and maggots and memsahibas were irrelevent.

The story of the maggots spread. The faces which looked out from the shadows as the Memsahiba passed were less hostile. When daily visits to the house of the sick Brahman were almost over, there came a smothered call of "Memsahiba" from a doorway. She responded gladly. Inside the family courtyard, behind the long narrow stable room she found a group of women hovering over a wailing baby. She did her best to help. On her second call in this home the women were sufficiently relieved of worry over the child to turn their attention to her. And the questions began—shy but direct. How many sons had she? Did she nurse her own babies or turn them over to a wet nurse as they had heard? Did she prepare the Sahib's food with her own hands? Neighbor women congregated on the roof of the storeroom at the side of the courtyard. One or two descended by the courtyard ladder to join the questioners. Every question had to be repeated and every answer gone over many times in many forms before comprehension dawned. One neighbor appointed herself interpreter, announcing that she had once talked with a foreign woman and could understand the Memsahiba's English—and the Memsahiba had been using her most grammatical Hindustani. Someone called down from the roof inviting the Memsahiba next door. Next door the same questions were gone over, with more added.

On the following day there was a further invitation with calls to neighbors still farther on. The Medical Officer's impromptu nose operation had been made on the girl of the headman of the village. This gave the Memsahiba an invitation to his home. And when once accepted there, she was accepted by the village. Sometimes she was called to see ill mothers or babies. Often it was curiosity developing into a desire for friendship which prompted the women to send for her. Questions became increasingly personal, until there was little left to excite curiosity. Mutual adjustments in vocabulary and pronunciation made conversation more natural. The strain of unfamiliarity gradually relaxed until here, behind uninviting mud walls, the Memsahiba found herself among friends who were ready to ask her help in time of need, and who in turn were ready to help her to understand their ways and their lives. A notebook and pencil would have alarmed them into speechlessness. Any information to be recorded had to wait until she returned to camp.

In those early days we made a rule for ourselves never to enter a house until some member of the household first invited us to come in. The hospitality with which we have consistently been met has rewarded us for keeping this rule at times when our desire to see and hear tempted us to intrude. Holding to it during our five years in the village, we now go freely and naturally into any but two or three homes,

the Sahib stopping at the men's quarters and the Memsahiba
going among the women. By continually demonstrating our
desire to be neighbors we finally made it clear that there was
only goodwill in our camp. We might be foolish in our ques-
tionings, but not malicious. As good neighbors we were accessible at any time to those in need. When two men once
came to ask our help at midnight, our helpers tried to send
them away. Their reply was comforting: "We know that if
the Sahib hears our voices, he will not turn us away."

We shared our car in season and out of season. Whenever
we passed any of our neighbors trudging to or from Mainpuri we offered them a lift. At first some of the older men
were reluctant. But now the slowing of the engine is a signal
for any Karimpurite to start running down the road and climb
in, or perch on the running board if there is no more room inside. When we return to the car after it has been standing outside our Mainpuri bungalow, or a bazaar shop, we are never
surprised to find village friends waiting patiently beside it.
They take for granted that we will have room for them somewhere, for the drive home. During the first year whenever the
car stirred, village youngsters came flying. They swarmed
over every available bit of running board and fender, shouting and singing, and holding on tight while we carried them to
the first mile post. Now that the car is a part of everyday
village life, the rides to the mile post occur only when a
crowd of youngsters happens to be on hand looking for something to do. They, like the grownups, take for granted that
the ride is theirs for the asking. When eighteen small boys
and girls board an already loaded car, the occasion is hilari-
ous—for all but the driver.

Just as we shared the car, our small sons shared their
carts and tricycle, and the games which could be played in
the sunshine. We depended on the sun and profuse use of
disinfectants to save us all from smallpox, and the boys from
ringworm and other skin infections accepted as inevitable in

the village. The article which we shared most gladly was soap. We were relieved to find that caste rules forbade the sharing of our food. At least here was a limit set for us without any breach of neighborliness.

One night when the village singers, accompanied by the village band, were energetically entertaining themselves, the Sahib got out his violin. It had always been popular with city friends and might be equally so here. When he offered to join the band he was accepted politely, but reluctantly. However, when they realized that there was no trick in his offer and no intention of laughing at their music, they welcomed him with enthusiasm. The band was composed of an old hand-bellows harmonium, manipulated by one of the goldsmiths, a *dholak* (a small barrel-shaped drum which is struck sharply and rhythmically with the fingers at one end and the palm of the hand at the other), a pair of long iron tongs fitted with a ring of iron to be jangled, and a pair of castanets two inches in diameter. A violin was a welcome addition, especially when the player could carry any of their tunes. Thereafter, when special guests were to be entertained, the Sahib was called over to the village to assist. On such occasions, players and audience were packed close together on the floor of the goldsmith's workshop, or on the headman's veranda. The performance lasted until the singers, usually one of the village elders or his satellites, had exhausted their repertoire and voices. Due to his success with the violin, the Sahib was invited to join wedding parties going from the homes of our leaders to other villages. He traveled, slept, and ate with the bridegroom and his relatives, and left them with nothing to suspect or fear.

For the sake of those who still persisted in associating us with the evil eye, we tried to keep nothing hidden. In camp this is easily accomplished. Our cooking has always been done in the open where any passerby might stop and observe. Our boys' baths are open to inspection at any time. When youngsters peer into the dining tent at meal times, we do not drive them away. Their own home training usually sends them scampering from the food of another. And if some child has no such scruples, there are sure to be others present to remind him. They have watched us wash dishes, and have marveled at our loaves of bread and cakes. Even oranges, grown a few miles away, are regarded as curiosities. Our sleeping room is our retreat when curtains are drawn. But even its contents are familiar to the boys and girls. There is nothing concealed and therefore nothing to fear. Our office with its typewriter is as lasting a mystery as any. Here we often let the children come, and any grown-up is free to enter and stand over us or squat comfortably beside the desk. The flaps are seldom down. A friend accustomed to locked doors in a large city once visited our camp. After two days of un-exclusive living, she exclaimed "I don't see how you stand having them on top of you all of the time. I'd go wild."

When we first pitched our camp beside the village we took for granted that we would study village life disinterestedly and move on. But something far different has happened. The villagers refuse to believe that we might move on, and press us to build a bungalow to establish our permanence. We have lost the disinterested attitude to such an extent that we can-not plan our own future, apart from the village. When we came back for our second camping season, missionary friends warned us that the village folk would very likely resent our return. Curiosity was gone, and our welcome would probably go with it.

Our experience has been to the contrary. Each year has bound us closer to the life of the community. Some of our neighbors have grasped the idea of our survey and are will-ing to cooperate in its preparation. Others have accepted us simply as friends. They urge us to stay and take our place among them. Their difficulty is in finding the place. Every member of village society has his special function, and the maintenance of the group depends on the proper functioning of each member. No one can be carried along who does not contribute. And what is our particular contribution? They have tried to make it medical service, and this is satisfactory as long as cases are simple. But when there is serious trouble we call in, or go to, a doctor. Some of our staunchest friends among the village elders have expressed their annoyance at our limitations. We have a dispensary. Then why run off to someone else when we could function best? They have finally accepted our service as a form of village last resort, or emergency bureau. They know that when the village prescriber can do nothing more for a sick child, or a spirit controller fails to cure a buffalo, they can fall back on us to secure the proper help. If the police watchman goes too far in his oppressions, the Sahib will speak for them. If there is some difficulty with records, the Sahib will consult the proper authority. We may study if we choose, but these other irregular services are our real share in the common burden. They justify our retaining a place in the village regime.

In our district a man does not speak of his wife as "my wife," or "Mrs. Ram Lal," but as *mere ghar ki* ("of my house"). In the same way he may refer to other members of his immediate family or to anything belonging to his household as "of my house," or simply "of the house." Our village friends now speak of us as "the Sahib and Memsahiba of our house," "the small sons of our house," and even, "the car of our house," thereby drawing us into their village family. Once we were regarded as foes. Now our appearance in a village lane neither rouses hostility nor excites curiosity. We are simply members of the village family performing our tasks, even as the carpenter and the farmer perform theirs.

CHAPTER II

The Leaders

The leaders of our village are so sure of their power that they make no effort to display it. The casual visitor finds little to distinguish them from other farmers. They dress as simply and cheaply as their neighbors, and do no more shouting or scolding; they work as faithfully as any in their fields; the walls enclosing their family courtyards may be high but are no better kept than those adjoining them, and their entrances are often less elaborate. And yet when one of them appears among men of serving caste, the latter express respect and fear in every guarded word and gesture. The serving ones have learned that as long as their subservience is unquestioned, the hand which directs them rests lightly. But let there be any move toward independence or even indifference. among them, and the paternal touch becomes a stranglehold.

Rights and privileges which would be in the hands of the landlord, were he to reside in the village, are retained by the small group of leaders. The ordinary villager looks to them for their wells. The waterways to his fields must pass through their land. His animals graze on areas under their control. He borrows their bullocks in times of need. He has the privilege of collecting fuel from their land. Wood for house and implement repairs, and even the wood for burning his dead, must be begged from one of them. Money for weddings is borrowed from them. Employment in slack times for some, and full-time employment for others, is supplied by them. Women of the serving classes find part-time work in their homes. Carpenters, potters, cotton carders, and others who serve all castes, are dependent on their leaders, since it is through their particular village leader that they obtain work. On each festival day, representatives from dependent families visit the homes of leaders who patronize them, and receive cakes and sweets from the womenfolk. Thus, in every detail of life the leaders have bound the village to themselves. Their favor may bring about a man's prosperity, and their disfavor may cause him to fail, or may make life so unbearable for him that he will leave the village.

In our village the economic power of the leaders is strengthened by their religious and social influence as Brahmans. The right of Brahmans to dictate may be challenged in the cities, but in villages like ours their control is absolute. Their birth as Brahmans is evidence of their superiority. Many an important decision in a humble section of the village waits on their divinely guided sanction. Although they occupy themselves as farmers and grain lenders, two or three of them are called upon to officiate as priests in ceremonies of grave importance to villagers. As with their economic power, they find it unnecesary to proclaim their authority as Brahmans. But if anyone fails to recognize the existence of this authority, he is reminded of it so effectively that he does not err again.

We had been in the village almost a year before we observed our leaders in action. Three miles across the fields from us there is a small hamlet. Its head man is a grain lender of wealth, but of lower-caste standing than the Brahman leaders of our village. Several years ago he built a small temple in the fields about two miles out of our village. The building of the temple was an act of religious merit. To add to the merit, he holds an annual fair in the grove beside the temple, thus making sure that its patron deity is worshiped at least once a year. This fair has become quite an event in the hot season calendar of our village and the hamlets round about. On the day appointed, women and children and a few men leave their offerings of marigolds or *pice* before the painted god just inside the temple door, and buy and sell in the grove outside. At dusk most of the women and children go home; the menfolk after completing their evening chores, walk out to the temple and gather in the theater set up in a field beside the grove. A small tent serves as dressing room for the actors, and a canopy marks the theater. Under it a large sheet is spread on the ground for the audience, and near the center there is an uncurtained platform on which the drama is staged.

One night in June we sat in our car, in the dark coolness outside the canopy, watching the performance. Parts of the *Ramayana* were being recited and acted by a traveling troupe. There were signs of uneasiness in the section where two of our Karimpur leaders, Brahmans, sat. The restlessness increased until it was difficult to see or hear what was going on, on the platform. Someone came and spoke excitedly to our host, the builder of the temple, who was standing beside the car. He became agitated. The confusion grew until the players were drowned out. Shortly, our Karimpur leaders rose and departed. Every man and boy from our village followed them out.

With the exit of three-fourths of the audience, the performance went flat. We soon slipped away, and gave some of our Karimpur neighbors a lift while they explained. The host at the fair was of lower caste than our Karimpur leaders. His nephew chose to exhibit himself in his importance and finery by sitting on the edge of the platform. By so doing he deliberately committed a caste outrage. The Brahman leaders, not he, should have had the higher seat. When his uncle had been warned, and was unable to move him, the insulted leaders gave the signal and walked out, knowing that their Karimpur delegation would follow.

A drama is a rare treat to the men of our village. And yet they left it without question. They had hurried through their work and walked out to the temple for a night's diversion.

And here they were walking home again. They expressed no resentment toward the leaders whose offended honor obliged them to miss the drama. Their complaints were against the youth who had precipitated the trouble. Needless to say, this erring nephew was absent from the dramatic performance the following summer.

What happened to the host and his nephew at the fair might happen to any of us if we should antagonize the leaders, deliberately or unwittingly. We ourselves had an initiation which made us realize how they could handicap us, if they chose. On our first Christmas in Karimpur we had a big party for the village children, with stories, games, and small gifts. At the close, there was a peanut scramble which caused much hilarity. Nothing was said against the party.

Our friendly relations with the village continued. By the time the following Christmas came we knew the children and their interests better, and had a program carefully planned. The hour for the party came and passed. Another hour. Two. Village folk are very casual in their regard for time. But when small boys are more than two hours late at a party something is wrong. We finally sent our assistant over to the house of the head man. There he found several leaders together, with crowds of boys sitting in the lanes around them. No sign of impatience abroad. He asked the eldest leader why the boys were kept at home. The leader explained that caste boys of the village could not accept peanuts which the

Sahib or any of his untouchable servants might have touched. The simplest way of refusing the nuts was to stay at home. No fuss, no protest, but quiet refusal of cooperation. Our first inclination was to give up the Christmas party. But the youngsters were patiently waiting across the road, while fun and gifts waited with us. We sent word, "No peanuts," and the children came thronging. Our Christian neighbors, untouchables, had a feast of peanuts that Christmas and so had we. Since then we have been spared the added expense of a scramble. The whole affair was a trifle, but it served as a warning. If we want to help the humble, we must do it with the good will of their present leaders. If we antagonize them, they may do us personally no harm, but they can hurt those whom we are trying to help—just as they kept the children from our Christmas festival.

A later incident in Karimpur revealed the absoluteness of the power of leaders such as ours, who combine in themselves the rights of high birth and economic power. The trouble started on a warm moonlight night in harvest season. Farmers were lying on their partly threshed mounds of grain in a grove, swapping stories before they slept. A *kachhi* (a lower-caste farmer) was asked to tell the version of the birth of Rawan, which he had once heard. He told of a Brahman who was married by an evil goddess to a girl of washerman caste (an untouchable group). The Brahman husband tried to destroy her, but after her rescue and many adventures, he was remarried to her without recognizing her. They had one son. Some years later, the Brahman went off for ten years as a *sadhu* (ascetic). On his return, he approached his wife nine times. The tenth time he came to her as a donkey, and while he was in this guise, Rawan was conceived—the Rawan who stole Sita from Rama and carried her off to his home in Ceylon.

The story, with its repeated ridicule of a Brahman and its association of a Brahman with the hated Rawan, infuriated a Brahman farmer-priest lying on his grain pile nearby. The insult to his caste increasingly angered him during the night, till he decided to take revenge. In the morning he collected his Brahman friends, and the band approached the *kachhis* armed with *lathis* (long poles with heavy tips). On their way they stopped at the house of the village head, also a Brahman, with the request that he accompany them. As far as caste and numbers were concerned, they needed no added strength. But he was the man from whom all of the *kachhis* got their necessary advances of food and money. The particular *kachhi* who told the story was deeply in debt to him. The Brahmans asked him to refuse all future credit, in case the *kachhis* failed to make a satisfactory settlement. If he withdrew his credit, the other influential men of the village would stand united and refuse theirs. Thus armed, the Brahman leaders went to the *kachhis* assured of success. The latter had already helped the offender to escape. They made no effort to defend themselves against the crowd which threatened them. Instead they begged forgiveness, and agreed that when the story teller returned he should accept a beating from the insulted high-caste neighbor. There was no choice for them between this and ruin.

If we were to limit our experiences to our own village, we should be tempted to interpret leadership as being synonymous with caste prestige. If caste precedence and economic power rest in the same men, their leadership is assured. If the two qualities are separate, villagers follow the man who can grant or withhold their daily bread. Ordinarily, we find this power resting with the Twice-Born. But in one village which we recently visited, an *ahir* (one of the lower castes) was influential enough to be made village head. A short time before our visit, he had been annoyed by the master of the village school, financed and directed by the District Board. This school was in the Brahman quarter of the village. The *ahir* headman set up an independent school in a house which he owned, and attracted to it—or forced—fifty of the sixty pupils of the District Board School. No doubt he will eventually disband his personally financed school. But he has succeeded in spoiling the year's record and work of the district schoolmaster, and hastened his transfer. Incidentally, he has impressed the men of his village with his power to make or destroy.

He who would help any one group or all groups of the village, cannot afford to ignore the power of present leaders. If he sees little hope of securing justice or improved conditions through them, and has sufficient financial support, he can replace them. But he must make the substitution complete. By securing for himself the position of economic master, as he would in case he became the landlord or financing agent, he can transfer all rights and duties of leadership to himself. A missionary in Moradabad has done this with marked success. He has freed his people from the all-encompassing indebtedness to the old leaders by transferring their dependence at every point to a cooperative society under his direct guidance. They still acknowledge a leader; they have been led so long that they would flounder if suddenly obliged to act on their own responsibility and make important decisions unguided. But their new leader is concerned with their welfare and the development of their independence, rather than their subordination. Though nominally a cooperative society, this method makes heavy demands upon the time and finances of the leader. Further, it requires the personal supervision of a number of highly qualified coleaders. But it is the fairest and surest form of replacement.

Partial replacement is much more doubtful and may prove harmful to those whom it aims to help. Like leaders everywhere, village leaders are jealous of their power. If they find someone attempting to usurp their rights, without paying the price, their suspicions are naturally aroused. If they discover that a villager is being drawn away from them at any one point, they become antagonistic toward the agency which is drawing him, and eventually devise means of forcing him back. This accounts for the failure of many a cooperative credit society which has reached past the leaders and made up its membership from dissatisfied followers. A villager accepts financial help from such a society. He pays up his old debts to his leader, and promises to incur no new debts except to the society. But he must still turn to his old leader for many favors such as grazing ground for his animals, water for his fields, and perhaps employment for his sons. Then some urgent need for money arises, which he finds is beyond the scope of the society. He turns to the old leader, whose rules for loans are more flexible. He thinks that he can pay up and still carry on as a member of the society. But the leader's grip has tightened and will not let him go. He is drawn back into the old order, and the service of the cooperative society has been frustrated.

Where cooperative societies have been introduced with the support of established leaders, their chances of success have been much greater. Leaders who are approachable and who have had a chance to discover what cooperation can do for them and their followers together, have not only helped but in some cases have themselves developed the work of the societies. The rural reconstruction and the better living societies of Benares District which include a whole village in a group, have served well, with the support of existing leaders. These societies have not limited themselves to credit nor any one phase of agriculture but have fostered the development of the community as a whole, helping and strengthening, whether through adult education, better marketing, improved sanitation, or other service which may be performed cooperatively.

This or a similar method of cooperation, which includes rather than replaces existing leaders, is most desirable, if the leaders are willing to cooperate. By sharing with them what we have learned of community welfare, we can help them to a more altruistic application of their power. They cannot be expected to change from selfish motives to community interest immediately. But when once they do care for the well-being, rather than the subservience of their dependents, they can do much more than we, as outsiders, can hope to do. We have seen this demonstrated by one of our leaders whose zeal for public service is outstanding.

The average farmer in our village listens with interest to an explanation of the advantages of a new variety of seed. But he would not risk trying it unless his leader had first tried it, or at least sanctioned it. He might be an enthusiastic observer of the demonstration of a Persian wheel—a large wheel for raising water, fixed vertically with a number of buckets at its circumference—but he could not afford to buy one without a loan from his leader. And he would not think of asking for a loan until his leader had himself installed a wheel. He knows that if he should presume to outshine his leader in any detail, social or economic, he would be brought down forcibly to his proper station. It is his lot to wait for the signal to advance. More, he has learned from experience that the cool judgment of his leader can save him from the mistakes into which his own gullibility is apt to plunge him. We can help these simple village folk most if we first win the confidence and approval of their leaders, even though in so doing we are obliged to grant advantages to the leaders which seem beyond their deserts.

The official revival of the authority of the village *panchayat* (assembly of arbitrators) is an acknowledgment of the power of the leaders. *Panchayats* have been adopted in several areas after other experiments in village service have been tried out. The *panchayat* requires the maximum cooperation of the leaders. They come into it as representatives of the village, and while acting on the *panchayat* they are expected to consider the order and well-being of the community rather than personal ambitions. The Magistrate of Muttra District recently wrote: "Personally I regard the *panchayat* as the unit of our administration through which there is most hope of making progress in the rural area. I make a point, therefore, of keeping in personal touch, so far as possible, with each village *panchayat*, and I direct Deputies and *Tahsildars* to do the same."

In Karimpur there is as yet no government-recognized *panchayat*, according to the United Provinces Village Panchayat Act of 1920. But the leaders often confer as a self-appointed *panchayat*. They try to settle boundary disputes or other quarrels which are not serious enough to warrant police interference or court expense. If invited to attend these meetings, the outsider with unselfish motives can do much to raise standards of justice. A man once complained of the judgment against him approved by a member of our *panchayat* who he felt should have supported him regardless of principle. The *panchayat* member defended himself by saying: "What could I do with the Sahib sitting right there?" There is always the danger of powerful factions controlling the village *panchayat* for evil, and our mistrust of certain leaders made us hesitate to press for government recognition.

One leader in particular had a record of abuse and extortion. He showed no consideration for the men whom chance brought under his control, but used them ruthlessly for the increase of his own wealth and power. Such a man would be a danger to the community if made an official representative of the village. When his name appeared among others as a member of the possible official *panchayat*, disapproval came from all groups. Men who, we thought, would be afraid to murmur against him, opposed his appointment openly. Then we made an interesting discovery. Those who had been wholly dependent upon him and had suffered from his oppression, were gradually and quietly transferring their allegiance to other leaders. The other leaders, welcoming any increase of their own power, encouraged the change at every possible point. The more he threatened, the more the others invited, until the only dependents left to him were men from hamlets outside the village boundaries. Almost imperceptibly a momentous change in village leadership had been effected by humble folk, without any stir or any pretense of independence. If we follow their honest choice we are pretty sure of finding the leaders who are most just.

The burden of village responsibility rests on the leaders just as family responsibility rests on the head of the house. The moment a villager finds himself harassed by a landlord seeking payment of rent arrears or by the police implicating him in a dacoity (robbery) case, he comes to his leader, as a son to his father, expecting the necessary help, financial or otherwise. Like a father, the leader intercedes and makes whatever settlement is demanded on behalf of his dependent. It may demand days away from pressing field work, interviewing officials, and attending court. It may necessitate the expenditure of a considerable amount of rupees. But the leader gives and does all ungrudgingly as part of his responsibility. When we are tempted to criticize leaders, we should remind ourselves of the innumerable times when they have shouldered burdens which most of us would be tempted to throw back upon the man who incurred them.

When we first came to Karimpur a villager was a villager to us with no particular distinction between those who led and those who followed. In our efforts to make friends, we accepted any opportunity in any group. But when actual study began we found ourselves repeatedly brought back to one or another of the accepted leaders. We could not make progress without their cooperation, and they were not inclined to cooperate. They had much more to lose from interference or exposure than the ordinary villager. Before they stirred, we had to convince them that we were here to observe impersonally and not to destroy their position. When they chose to be friendly they showed us their best, most lovable selves.

And we learned what they could do if this side of them were to predominate over the jealous guarding of power.

The head of the village has been our willing counselor and has come with equal readiness to ask our counsel. After the operation on his daughter's nose, his faith in us was established, and since then our friendship has been strengthened through work together. He has often asked the Sahib to criticize him if his treatment of others seemed at any time to be unworthy of a "follower of God." He lends money and grain, but his rates are not exorbitant. He keeps records of payments, and as yet we have not heard him accused of the unfairness ordinarily ascribed to his kind. He demands payment in full, but no more than a businessman might in any community. His uprightness has made it easier for us to cooperate with him. But it has denied us the experience of encountering the selfish type of village head who is to be found in many places. His younger brother is sharper in his dealings and more conscious of his importance. It was he who instigated the departure from the dramatic performance at the temple.

Next door to the village head lives a man equally deferred to, but for a different reason. He has an undefined cordial relationship with the subordinate police officials who occasionally visit the village. They gather on his broad stoop with its partially thatched roof whenever the report of some misdemeanor has reached them. Accused and accuser are summoned, and witnesses, if any can be found. Trailing after them comes a crowd of interested spectators. The investigation proceeds informally, with unsolicited information and suggestions from the side lines. Before the officers leave with their report, they can count on a hearty farm meal prepared by the women of the family. Being host to representatives of the law in this way lends enviable prestige, while the opportunity for a quiet word with the guests as they dine, adds power to prestige.

This particular leader was hospitable toward us, but made it evident that he had no desire to go beyond the formalities. We had been in the village several months when he sent word that he was ill unto death. There was nothing we could do for him. As a last resort, he allowed himself to be taken to the Mission hospital in Fatehgarh, because there he would be on the banks of the Ganges if he should die. Weeks of skillful treatment saved him, and it was a great day for the village when we brought him home. His gratitude to the Mission doctor changed his attitude toward us. There has been no wavering in his friendliness since, although our contacts are strictly social.

One leader who took us and our study as a great joke, was won by the violin. In his youth he was the village clown and as yet has had no successor. He is present at every musical bout, and decides who shall sing and who shall not. At first, in his enthusiasm over the violin, he came to our camp at any hour (convenient or otherwise) announcing that he wanted to hear some music. When he found that the Sahib did not comply, he resigned himself to getting all he could on nights set aside for music. He still refuses to take our work seriously, but he laughs at us as friends and not as undesirable outsiders. And he makes no effort to interfere.

Another accepted leader expressed his friendliness by allowing his youngest son to work with us. He always invited us to his house for special functions, and we found him a gracious, though reticent host. As in former instances, it was a serious illness which brought us closer to this leader and his family. The lovable old gray-haired man became very ill with pneumonia. The Sahib nursed him constantly and brought the District Medical Officer out to see him, but all efforts failed. We lost a friend whom we wished we might have known longer. At the cremation, which the Sahib attended, one of the elders was heard to say: "Others come and make profession of friendship, and go away. Our Sahib shares our happiness and our troubles, and does not desert us. He demonstrates his friendship." It is not difficult to work with men when this is their attitude toward us.

In cultivating the good will of leaders and trying to develop their better qualities one is in constant danger of being monopolized by them. We who are interested in helping high and low alike dare not yield to their more lavish entertainment or flattery. The leader regards the rest of the village as existing for his convenience. It is difficult for him to understand how an outsider can be as interested in a potter or a sweeper as in himself. When we pass the house of a leader, he is sure to ask "Whither bound?" If we say, "To the house of Tori the *dhanuk* (an untouchable)," he lifts his eyebrows and asks, "Why?" If it is a personal call he expresses his disapproval, sometimes with an air of suspicion. If we are going to visit the sick, he nods his head in understanding. This is part of our village function. If we were limited to the point of view of the leaders we would find little need for village reconstruction. Through them we serve the village, but through them we cannot know the village.

CHAPTER III

Those Who Follow

There are men whose standing according to caste is as high as
that of the leaders. But they are content to go their own un-
obtrusive way, working their own land with one or two hired
helpers, asking no favors and granting none. Their voices are
seldom heard outside of their own fields or cattle rooms.
When problems arise, each of them turns helplessly to the accepted leader most closely related to him, relying on his
judgment and strength. In return, when there is dissension in
the village, each leader knows which of these men will follow
him without question. We may not see these followers for
months. But eventually a land dispute or illness brings one
of them to us, usually with his chosen leader as spokesman.
For a period we are closely associated, consulting records and
officials, or keeping watch beside a sick child. In these
times of trial we have found them to be like hard-working,
home-loving peasants anywhere, with the difference that in
them is a distinct consciousness of high birth.

Between these Brahmans and the next group of farmers lie

the two great divisions, *kshatriya* and *vaisya*, including many castes, pictured as the arms and body supporting the Brahman head. These divisions are represented by only a few families in Karimpur. Below them are the *sudras*, the feet. Chief in number and importance among *sudras* in our village are the *kachhis*, farmers who work on land which they rent for their own use or which they rent on shares with Brahmans. They have been brought up, like their forefathers, with the assurance that their mission in life is to till the soil and to accept the will of their superiors. They live in a little colony of joint-family enclosures apart from the rest of the village. As soon as one of their boys can lift a head load of grain or drive a bullock, he is expected to help. From then on he carries his full share until old age entitles him to partial rest. Severe illness may grant him a respite, but as soon as he can move, he must resume his duties. At the time of writing, one of the men has a badly damaged knee for which the doctor prescribes rest. His wife has fever, and her new baby is suffering from lack of nourishment. But they feel they cannot slacken. Their added burden must not fall on other members of the joint family already working to the limit of endurance.

They have their own group leader who presents their difficulties to the men higher up. His friendship was won by the doctor at the Mission hospital at Kasganj who removed cataracts from both his eyes. Since the restoring of his sight he has been one of our most loyal supporters. And his confidence has spread to the whole group. We have served in all of their homes in times of desperate need—they never complain or ask help unless the need is desperate. Often they let sickness go unreported until a rainy day lightens field work and gives them time to think of their families. Our contacts with them have strengthened our respect for their tirelessness and increased our desire to help them more constructively.

In addition to the *kachhis* there are eleven castes in Karimpur counted as *sudras*. None are as self-sufficient as the *kachhis* who have before them the hope that they or their sons may some day pay off their heavy debts to village leaders. The other *sudras* accept indebtedness and obligations to *jajmans* (patrons) as the order of life. When we first came to Karimpur we regarded the carpenters (one of the *sudra* castes) as independent craftsmen. They work in the lane that runs in front of their row of houses, making and repairing the carts, plows, and other implements of the farmers. Later as we stood watching their work, we overheard patrons ordering—not asking—them to make new handles for tools or to complete some house repairs. We realized that they were not independent, as we had thought. To get their payment, which for carpenters is fixed, they must go daily to the fields of their patrons during the harvest season to receive their share of the crop. The shares are given out more as donations than as payments due, and place upon the recipient an obligation which he can never quite repay. Among the carpenters we have found some of the cheeriest, most natural friends. Their houses are on our side of the village, and when one of them chops a finger with his adze, he comes over at once for first aid. We fought through days and nights for the life of the baby son of one of them, now the sturdiest among those whom mothers like to call "the Memsahiba's children." A good friend in the States sent money for a brace for a carpenter's lame daughter. It was a real test of their faith in us for them to let us put this weird contraption of leather and steel (which many villagers still hesitate to touch) on the child. The growing son of one of them came to us every day for months for the dose of cod-liver oil which helped build up his emaciated body. Now at ten he has begun his apprenticeship in earnest and laughs with us over his early fears of the Sahib and his nasty medicine. The old mother of one of the men was relieved of cataracts by the Mission doctor in Kasganj and considers herself our most special and necessary friend. We have given them all of our carpentry work and have added the construction of wooden models of village carts and implements, to occupy their slack seasons. When the car was wrecked, two carpenters straightened the twisted frame, while the village tailor patched the canvas top. The result amused our city friends, but greatly increased village pride in the car.

The other *sudras* are much more dependent than the carpenters. They not only go to the harvest fields for the semi-annual dole, but their women and children visit the houses of the great on festival days, standing patiently at the door until the women of the household toss them their portion of special cakes or sweets. They have earned what they receive, but this method of payment lends it the guise of just one more favor.

Whenever we turn from the proprieties of the homes of leaders to enter what we call Humble Lane, we are surrounded by *sudra* friends. At first they were loath to welcome us. Interpreting every incident of life in terms of spirits, chiefly evil, they saw only danger in our advent. But when we succeeded in helping the tailor's wife through a serious illness, and when the veterinary surgeon whom we called was able to save the buffalo of the grain-parcher's widow, they dared to return our greetings. By the end of our first year their expectations of us were far beyond what we were able to deliver. We have spent some of our most unhappy hours among them, when some avoidable illness has brought one of their bread winners to the point of death. Some of our gayest moments have been among them, when the women dramatically related the latest scandal, or the youthful *kahars* (carriers) staged some uproarious farce. Our sons love the industry and democracy of Humble Lane. They never tire of the whirl of the potter's wheel and the magic which changes the mound of clay into saucers or jars. While a parcher boy roasts our peanuts and grain they squat with other children of the village, listening to the laughter and popping corn, and watching the leaves in the furnace. In this community of *sudras*, men and women spend their lives performing the tasks to which they were born.

Some are tailors, some potters, some grain parchers, some oil pressers, and many are personal servants and farm hands. Their lot is to supply the wants of their farmer patrons. If the patrons are satisfied with them, they are content. They accept whatever each day brings, leaving plans and responsibilities for the morrow in the hands of their patrons. When receiving a payment of bread or grain, they go through the formality of complaining mildly. But it would not occur to them to ask for better conditions or freedom. In hot weather they suffer from lack of protection against the heat, and in the winter months they suffer from exposure to the cold. Their clothes are worn, filthy, and tattered, but there is food for the morrow. Jewelry and wedding garments are stored away for the next wedding or fair. Theirs is the cheerfulness that goes with cupboards always almost bare. There will never be abundance, so why struggle? They know that as long as there is grain in the storehouses of their patrons they will not starve. They may go further into debt, but debt is a familiar associate. Only if the patron is ill unto death, or if a series of calamities threatens his storehouse, is there real anxiety.

In a village not far away, a wealthy farmer ignored his responsibility to the families depending on him. It was a bad season, and prices were high. He decided that he would take his grain to the city to sell it at a high ready cash profit, rather than hold it in his storehouse to be loaned out to his people. When the first cart was loaded, his dependents realized that they were about to be robbed of their food supply. A crowd of them waylaid the carts a short distance out of the village, unloaded the grain, and distributed it among themselves, keeping a careful account of every pound. This record, with the usual promises to repay, was presented to the thwarted patron. He took the case to court. His followers were warned not to repeat the offense but were not punished. The court could not but recognize the justice of the action taken by the villagers, although it was obliged to give a formal reproof.

At the end of Humble Lane are the two well-kept houses of Muslim bangle sellers. Beyond them are cluttered the dirty, crowded huts of other Muslims—*fakirs*. When we asked a Muslim official why these Muslims were the dirtiest, poorest people in the village, he disclaimed them, as not being pure Muslims but converts from among low-caste Hindus. Another Muslim, a petty official, explained that these village Muslims, due to their dependence on Hindu patrons, have lost their identity as Muslims, and cannot be considered representative of their religion. Even our Muslim cook scorns them, and hastens to disown them as his brethren. He bought goat meat from them twice before learning from his *maulvi* in the town that none of them are qualified to butcher. He has not touched their meat since. And the experience made him suspect that they were not proper Muslims. Later he discovered that Hindus of the village smoked the *chilam* (the funnel-shaped red-clay tobacco pipe found in every home) with them. No Hindu as conservative as those of Karimpur would share his pipe with any but accepted Hindus. The officials and the cook are in agreement that weak men will do anything for money. The only money—or food—at present available for these Muslims is in the hands of Hindu masters. Therefore, they have made themselves as much Hindu and as little Muslim as possible.

They do not concern themselves with the more personal Hindu observances, especially those related to the preparation of food and the cleanliness of the body. But they celebrate the Hindu festivals as thoroughly as do their *sudra* neighbors. On the night of *Diwali,* the Feast of Lights, they illuminate their roofs and wall niches with the little saucers of mustard oil. At the time of *Karua Chaut,* when Hindu wives seek the favor of the gods for the prosperity of their husbands by fasting and by special drawings on their walls, the Muslim women do likewise. They are no more vague about the meaning of their activities than are the low-caste Hindus around them. Above all, they are careful never to miss the festivals which hold a promise of sweets to be handed out by patrons. No one claims them, or troubles to set standards for them either in religious observances or in daily living. No one shows any interest in them beyond the unskilled services which they have to offer. They do what is demanded of them and relish all the fun that can be squeezed from meager, sordid lives. They are a gay, happy-go-lucky crowd, when not in desperate need or suffering.

Among these varied groups of farmers and menials, there are a chosen few set aside as ambassadors to spiritdom, or shamans, known as *bhagats*. In ordinary life, *bhagats* perform the tasks assigned to the caste groups to which they happen to belong. But they are set apart from ordinary men, because they are imbued .with the power of appeasing certain deities. They practice a few austerities, and in moments of ecstasy are able to torture their bodies without consciousness of pain. Their task is to placate offended gods and goddesses and to release the victims of spells cast by capricious spirits. The special ailments of women are regarded as within the scope of their ministrations. The daughter-in-law who has no children seeks the guidance of one of them; their exorcisms are invited when a baby is ill; boils and aching joints are treated by them; when an animal is sick, or a buffalo fails to give milk, the owner sits beside a *bhagat* who is in a trance and relates the trouble. The *bhagat*, acting as medium for the goddess, tells him what penances she demands before the trouble can be alleviated.

One of our *bhagats* is a stocky, good-natured goatherd. We often meet him on the road to Mainpuri, carrying jars of goat's milk to customers in the town, or returning in haste to graze his animals. We always give him a seat on the running board where, braced by the luggage carrier, he squats and balances his jars. None of us dares to hold or touch a jar because our touch would contaminate the milk. On these trips he has become very friendly and communicative. It does not hurt his pride to bring his own ailments and those of his family and friends to us. He has supplied us with milk for the past three years, and we have never had reason to register the common complaint of watered milk.

Another *bhagat* is a tall, gentle carpenter. When his baby was ill, he spoke to us, but encouraged no treatment. It was in May, and we were staying in our Mainpuri bungalow. His wife brought the baby to us late one night as we were leaving the village and announced: "It was I, and not the father who bore this child. And I am going to keep him with the Memsahiba till he gets well." The *bhagat* protested mildly, reminding her that he would have no one to prepare his food. But with a defiance quite amazing in a woman of our village, she clambered past her husband into the car. Since that time the *bhagat* father has depended on us to help in all his family difficulties. He himself went to our Mission hospital in Kasganj for a serious operation. For some time afterward he impressed his friends with the account of his sensations in going under an anesthetic.

There are other *bhagats*, some more and some less friendly, but none antagonistic. They are sincere in their belief that they are chosen agents of the gods. If they were consciously deceiving, they would be jealous of the success of our doctor friends. As it is, they regard doctors as co-workers. We have tried never to laugh at their methods. But on every occasion when we are working together, we draw their attention to the existence of cause and effect, until they themselves are beginning to question some of their practices. We can leave the raillery to their own neighbors. It was a surprise to us to see the *kahars*, the village's best actors, in a burlesque on *bhagats*, ridiculing their weaknesses, especially in relation to women.

Supplementing the *bhagats* are the men known as *hakims*, who prescribe complicated mixtures of herbs for the cure of diseases. To mention an ailment in the presence of one of them is like pressing a button. Instantly there pops out a list of ingredients with details of grinding and sifting and brewing. One of them is the elderly farmer whose sight was restored by our Mission doctor. He visits us regularly, suggesting treatments in case one of our own family is not well, and feeling free to praise or condemn any of our activities. He considers himself our guide and preserver. He brings numbers of sufferers to us for help, complicating mat'ers by prescribing his own treatment along with ours. His intentions are good. If there are two kinds of treatment, the chances of cure must be twice as great. The other *hakim* is one of the oil pressers, whose father was reputed for his success in medicine. The son occasionally carries with him the imposing volume of prescriptions inherited from his father, and spends much time searching for the mixture which seems most suitable for the case in hand. He has always been curious about our medicines, and comes over to the dispensary tent to watch the visiting doctor. We encourage his observations, and have gradually won his confidence. He was much afraid of ridicule in the early days. It was more than a year before he shyly produced his inherited volume, still longer before he brought to light the bottles and jars of medicated oils which he brewed a decade ago, and which are yearly becoming more valuable as fever reducers and liniments.

We realized from the beginning that if we were to give what we had to give to sufferers in the village, we must do it with the cooperation and not against the antagonism of these two *hakims*. Whenever we are called to a serious case, we know that already one of them—most often the oil presser—has been called. There he sits beside the patient, watching and waiting for our suggestions. The adoption of our advice or

treatment depends on his word of approval or doubt after we
have gone.

After our doctor from Kasganj left India, another friend, a
woman doctor from Fatehgarh, forty miles away, succeeded
him. Recently she was in the home of a man suffering from
loathsome ulcers. She lanced and drained quantities of pus
from his leg while he shouted and the women of the household screamed. The oil presser watched with growing admiration. When she had finished he said, "Now look at the other
leg." It was covered. The patient objected, but the oil
presser remained firm. He had been alone on the case for
months, and appreciated the doctor's arrival. The patient's son
also pleaded. But still the oil presser insisted, "Let her see it,"
and removed the covering. The sick man's expression revealed
his horror at this betrayal. But the oil presser had seen our
doctor clear up ulcers and boils before. Afterward, both the
man and his family were happy that the illness had been
treated, but at the moment the slightest sign of unfriendliness
or suspicion toward us on the part of the oil presser would
have been welcomed by them as a signal to stop the doctor.
With him on the doctor's side, they had not the courage to
oppose.

Although the *bhagats* and *hakims* have become physical and
spiritual advisers to their own low-caste neighbors, and sometimes to the accepted leaders, their offices in no way conflict
with those of the priests. Some leaders retain for themselves
the priestly duties associated with birth, marriage, and death.
They share these rites with *brahmans*, or *maulvis* in the case
of Muslims. Their ceremonies follow the prescribed order
and take place at times appointed by the sacred laws. They
leave any impromptu, irregular services to the less dignified,
more ecstatic *bhagats*.

Both *hakims* and *bhagats* enjoy authority in their own peculiar fields. But they do not presume to carry it over to any
other relationships. When not in action prescribing or inter-

preting, they are like all other followers, watching their sheep and goats, repairing plows for patrons, or faithfully performing whatever tasks are assigned them. A *bhagat* may be called upon to drive out the evil spirit which has taken possession of the victim of a snake bite. As soon as this exalted service is completed, he may be called by his patron to some ignoble chore. He goes to it without any resentment at being thus debased, and without any assumption of superiority carried over from his association with deities. The oil presser *hakim* may be found at the bedside of a man of high caste dictating his treatment, and a few moments later peddling oil through the village. Each knows his appointed place in the village regime and has no thought of employing his special trust to change the status quo in his favor.

Those who laid down the rules for Hindu society, settled beyond all doubt the religious, social, and economic standing of every person. It is not for any man to choose what he will be. His birth fixes his station. And nothing that he can do will alter the plan. We who are outside the order are amazed at the contentment of all those within it, until we comprehend its strength and all-pervasiveness. Orthodox members of the order are shocked by the reformer who preaches workers' rights. Orthodoxy rides high in villages, especially in those like ours, dominated by Brahmans. On one occasion, when a high caste, unorthodox friend of ours spoke to a group of our villagers about the justice of granting some rights to untouchables, a high-caste villager spoke up: "Then why were we born farmers, barbers, tailors, carpenters, potters, and the rest?" This attitude, that each man has been created by God to fill a certain position in the great religio-socio-economic order, fosters contentment, or at least resignation. While such an attitude holds, the village leaders are sure of the unquestioning loyalty of those who follow.

The Untouchables

Still lower than the *sudras* in the Karimpur social scale are the untouchables. Although barred from the four great divisions which include all of the accepted castes—the *brahmans, kshatriyas, vaisyas,* and *sudras*—they have a carefully graduated caste system of their own. A leather worker and a sweeper are both untouchables. And the leather worker would not degrade himself by eating or drinking with the sweeper, nor would he consider marrying his daughter to the sweeper's son. Highest among the untouchables of Karimpur is the *dhobi,* whose appointed task is to wash the skirts and scarves, the shirts and loin cloths, of the villagers.

His position in the village is more like that of a *sudra.* But he is an untouchable, according to the traditional law. The rock on which he beats the villagers' garments is at the edge of the pond beside our grove. There he stands on sunny mornings, knee-deep in the water, swinging each garment above his head, thumping it down on the rock, then splashing it about in the pond, and wringing it into a tight wad. Meanwhile, other members of the family spread the washed clothes out on the parched, dusty ground to dry, in a pattern like that of an enormous patchwork quilt. Thanks to the sun, the garments which he gathers up from the ground and returns to his village neighbors are much fresher, though perhaps more battered than they were when he took them away a day or two before. He washes the clothes of high-caste families regularly. Housewives of lower castes complain that he often neglects their washing, if not reminded. The lowest of the untouchables must keep their own garments clean. He refuses to touch them.

The *dhobi* who worked here when we first came was far from blessed. He was deaf. He had four daughters and a widowed sister-in-law who died of tuberculosis two years ago. Girls can deliver clothes, and spread them out to dry, but they are not good at beating, and cannot buy and sell cow-dung cakes—the subsidiary industry which keeps many *dhobis* from poverty. Without a son he could not keep pace with the demands from all sections of the village. Neither could he feed his family on the grain and bread handed to the girls as payment. He gave up and withdrew to the home of relatives in another district.

When the housewives of the village refused to do the family washings in their courtyards any longer, three leaders went from here to negotiate with the *dhobi*. A more satisfactory arrangement was made, and he returned. This is the one method by which a village workman may gain the consideration which he desires. No threats, no disturbance. He simply absents himself until his services are more actively appreciated. The risk of such a move is demonstrated by the sequel to the *dhobi's* return. He found the new arrangement too much like the old to be worthwhile, and again retired to the village of his relatives. This time someone suggested another *dhobi*, and a younger man was found who wanted more work than he was getting in his father's village. He was invited to come here, with a payment offer a trifle better than that of the former washerman. If the new man and his wife are able to hold their employers to their agreement, the standard of the Karimpur *dhobi* will have advanced a step. No one seems to know or care about the old washerman. He is with relatives, and relatives can be counted on to share their food and labors. The change has come about informally, and without the noise of battle. But it is the outcome of many serious conferences of the leaders and their relatives and friends. The advent of a new washerman not even remotely related to the family which has served the village for generations has furnished housewives with gossip for months.

The *chamars* (leather workers) live a furlong from the rest of the village in a clutter of huts enclosed by mud walls. Both huts and protecting walls are as weather-beaten and neglected as the *chamars* themselves. We have not made much progress in friendliness with them, chiefly because of the inconvenience in reaching them. It is always easier to stop in houses of older friends along the way. Also, the patients whom they have called us to see have been past the point where we or our doctor could help. Their aloofness up to the present time is a reminder of the attitude of the whole village in the early months of our residence.

The *chamar* is less independent than the washerman or the potter or any other workman who serves many masters and thus is not wholly dependent on the pleasure of one. Each *chamar* with his family is bound to one *jajman* (patron). Although he receives a wage, his position is akin to that of a bondsman. In the village he is regarded not as an individual, but as so-and-so's *chamar*. Outside of the intimate affairs of family life, his time and his services and his sons' time and services are in the hands of his master. His wife too must be ready to help in the fields or at the heavier tasks in the house of the patron, whenever sent for. The patron's work and interests come first. If there is any time left over, the *chamar*

and his sons spend it on the plot of land granted him as payment for his services. He makes no plans and undertakes
nothing that requires time or money without the consent of
his patron.

One *chamar* boy began attending our night school without
consulting his patron. The latter happened to be visiting us
one night and looked with interest into the tent where boys
were struggling with Hindi. Suddenly his face hardened, and
he called his *chamar* out. He reminded the boy sharply that
there was still plenty of work for him to do—and it was then
after 9 p.m. The boy hurried off to his master's house. He
has not attended school since.

There is little opportunity for the *chamars* to work at their
traditional trade. When an animal dies in the village, they
are allowed to remove the skin. They cure the hides by a simple process, and sell them to *chamars* in town. They make
and mend the leather bags used in lifting water from the wells
for irrigation. From time to time they sew a patch on someone's shoe, with scarcely more than a "thank you" for the trouble. This is all incidental to their work as farm hands. But
the stigma of handling leather still clings to and labels them
as untouchables. They are not only cut off from villagers of
caste by the usual barriers of food and water, but are forbidden to share the friendly pipe.

A *sudra* from Mainpuri once visited his relatives in Karimpur. The *chamar* boy who accompanied us to Karimpur as
messenger boy and chief keeper of the car, happened to go
to the well where the town *sudra* was smoking with his relatives. Upon his arrival, the *sudra* said: "Nowadays there is
none of the old foolishness of refusing to smoke with *chamars*.
Here is this boy who has never done any leather work. Come,
let him smoke with us." The red clay pipe was passed around,
and our young *chamar* friend was included in the circle.
Then the city *sudra* left. The *chamar* boy was enjoying the
thrill of sharing a caste pipe and wanted to continue. But

as soon as their city relative was safely down the road, the *sudras* broke the pipe. Their hour of folly was over.

Prem, this messenger boy of ours, rides a bicycle—a rare feat in the village—and is so thoroughly related to the car and ourselves that his untouchable state is overlooked, except in the serious matters of food and drink, and smoking. In his home village, with his own people, he observes all the limitations of his birth. But here in Karimpur he has not associated himself with the *chamars*. He has adapted himself to the new freedom, without a blunder to remind himself or others of his customary place. One day an elderly village Brahman sat beside the Sahib in the front seat of the car. They stopped before the *chamar* huts to call for a woman to be taken to the hospital. While two *chamar* men lifted the woman carefully into the rear seat, our Brahman friend nearly went through the front glass in his effort to avoid their touch. The touch would not have been contaminating, like that of sweepers, but it was highly undesirable. Then when the car started, he made a place at his feet for Prem, our *chamar* boy, to perch, leaning against his knees. He chose to overlook the fact that Prem was on exactly the same level as the men whom he had been assiduously avoiding.

On another occasion this same boy was walking from Mainpuri out to our camp. A cart passed him on the road, and one of its two occupants offered him a ride. The speaker was a Brahman of Karimpur. The second man, a Brahman of another village, demurred, "But is he not a *chamar?*" The first man agreed that Prem's people were *chamars,* but added that Prem himself could hardly be called one in our village. He explained: "Here he has become watchman of the *Sahib's* car, and that is a job which has no caste." No further objection was raised, and Prem was taken in. He boasted to us of the ride when he got home, and remarked with satisfaction that it would never have happened in the vicinity of his father's village.

The *dhanuks* live at the corner of the village farthest from our camp. A series of encounters with members of the group have brought us much closer to them and their households than to the *chamars*. The women are the midwives of the village. Where the Memsahiba has been called in to help at a confinement she has worked with one of them. At other times she has followed after them with a doctor, trying to undo some of their damage—the result of well-intentioned but ignorant activity. One of the midwives, herself on the verge of confinement, was very ill with penumonia. The doctor prescribed constant care. Neither one of her caste nor untouchable neighbors were willing to come in and touch her. Her own sister had been called but had not arrived. If anything was to be done for her, the Memsahiba would have to do it. She nursed her for days, the midwife's husband taking his weary turn at night. Neighbor women would come in to observe, and to tell the woman how sorry they were that she was dying. But they could not help her. To their surprise, she recovered.

Later the husband, as good a type of country bumpkin as our village can produce, was knocked unconscious by the horizontal beam of a sugar press. After a day in the fields, he had been doing night duty, feeding cane into the press. He evidently had dozed and failed to duck his head as the bullocks swung the beam around to the side where he crouched. His fellow workers came to us, sure that his injury was fatal. The Sahib, armed with spirits of ammonia and antiseptic, applied first aid. A few days rest, and faith in our assurance and dressings gave him strength to return to his employer.

Like the *chamars*, the *dhanuks* are the drudges among farm hands. Each man is attached to some patron whom he serves at all tasks and in all seasons. A small plot of land granted by the patron claims any time he has for himself. The profession of the *dhanuk* women degrades them, if further degradation is possible. Everything to do with a birth is unclean, and these women who touch the new baby and mother are thereby rendered unclean. At the same time their work makes them freer and more sophisticated than their menfolk, because it gives them an entree in homes of high as well as low castes. They carry their freedom with a cool boldness that makes their position enviable among women limited to single courtyards.

The only untouchables in our village who are still strictly untouchable are our coreligionists, still known to the villagers by the old untouchable name of *bhangi*. Early any morning the men of this group may be found herding their swine along the roadsides and open spaces which border the village. These areas serve as village latrines for men and children, and for the women who do not observe *purdah*. The swine are the conservancy department, prompt and thorough in their service. During the remainder of the morning, the *bhangi* men loiter along the roads with their swine, keeping them from cultivated fields and guiding them to any stray refuse. Toward noon they drive the animals home, and spend the rest of the day lying about on their rope cots. Occasionally one of them makes a basket for sale or goes on an expedition to sell pig bristles. Just before festival days, several of them present themselves at the doors of their patrons, each with a long broom made of lentil stalks. They sweep the lanes and any other open spaces around the patrons' storehouses, raising clouds of dust to impress the world in general, and patrons in particular, with their industry. If any bad news must be sent by a patron to relatives in other villages, a *bhangi* acts as messenger. If extra help is needed at harvest time, *bhangis* may be called upon to help carry sheaves from the fields. These and other desultory jobs fall to them. But the greatest activity occurs when there is a feast in our village or in any village within convenient reach. It may be a wedding or the special reciting of religious poetry. The occasion does not matter. Where there is a feast, there the *bhangis* collect—not to share, but to gather up and eat the scraps left on the leaf plates of the party. What they cannot eat at the time, they carry home to be dried and kept for lean days.

To the wives of these men fall the most unpleasant tasks in the village. Each woman makes daily visits to the homes of her more conservative employers, where the women are kept in such strict *purdah* that they do not go to the fields to relieve themselves. In each house she slinks into the privy beside the courtyard or on the roof, keeping herself out of everyone's way. She gathers the excreta from the earthen floor into her basket and carries it, along with other household refuse, to the fields. Once a week she is admitted to the family courtyard of each of these homes. Members of the family keep themselves and their vessels carefully aloof while she scrapes clean the corner of the courtyard set aside for bathing and for the washing of cooking utensils. She brushes the scrapings into her basket, then cleans the drain which runs from this washing square along the edge of the courtyard, through the wall and into the lane outside. In some houses instead of flowing into the lane, the water from the drain empties into a large clay jar embedded in the outermost wall. The sweeper woman dips the water from this jar out into the roadway with a scrap of broken clay jar, and carries the objectionable residue to the fields. She goes into still other houses for the drain cleaning, houses where the women go to the fields twice daily and therefore have no privies, but where they are glad to pay a couple of unleavened cakes weekly to spare themselves the need of getting their hands into the slime of the drain.

We had known of the existence of untouchability before we came to the village. But when we found ourselves next door to it, we were distressed by its actuality. We have learned that it is possible for forty human beings to live on the edge of a village of almost eight hundred, go through the village daily to free it from the most disagreeable of its filth, help in the harvest fields, collect food at the doors of the more prosperous homes, buy spices and oil at the small shops, and regard the village in every way as home, yet never touch nor be touched by anyone belonging to the village.

Before we had time to learn who belonged to what group, we were constantly made aware of the presence of an untouchable by the way in which villagers behaved when one appeared. They shouted threats at any *bhangi* who dared approach while they talked with the Sahib. They were dumbfounded when the Sahib treated the *bhangi* with the same consideration as he did them. They tried to warn our boys from the touch of *bhangi* children, and were at first annoyed, then resigned, when the boys could not see any reason for fear. One day the Memsahiba stood on the threshold of a high-caste courtyard taking leave just as a *bhangi* girl came in to clean the privy. The girl came close and took the Memsahiba's hand. There was sudden confusion in the group inside the high-caste doorway. Children were pushed back to a safe distance, women tightened their draperies about them, and the wife of the head of the household screamed at the Memsahiba and the girl. When her protests became coherent, the Memsahiba realized that in touching the girl she had committed a terrible faux pas. The housewife drove the girl away, and gave the Memsahiba a lesson in untouchability. After it was over, the Memsahiba remarked that she went into the home of this girl and others of her group, as freely as into those of caste people, her hostess was horrified. But she finally compromised thus: "If you insist, you may do as you please when out of our sight. But when you are in our homes, we beg you to spare us this embarrassment."

The men and children of the village are with us more than the women, and have become accustomed to seeing us with untouchables as with others. We are casteless and can mingle with all. But as for themselves, the touch of a *bhangi* would be pollution. One holiday as we were returning from

the untouchable quarter to our camp, a crowd of village children descended upon us ready to play. As the leaders of the
group reached us and were about to capture us, someone who
had seen us leave the house of an untouchable shouted,
"*bhangi.*" Immediately the children stopped. The warner
went on to explain to them that we had just been with untouchables, and that they would have to wait until we had
bathed. The children danced around us, begging us to hurry
and bathe so that they might share their game with us. But
they made no further attempt to touch us until later in the
day.

Although occasioned by the work of scavenging which
bhangi men and women are expected to do, untouchability
has attached itself to the group as a whole. Not only are they
untouchable during the hours or during the years when they
are engaged as scavengers, but from the time they are born
until they die. They become so accustomed to being creatures to be avoided that they feel no resentment. Many a
time when we have winced under the scorn or rebuff which we
have suffered because of the *bhangis* we had in our tent or in
our car, we have observed that those who gave rise to the
scorn accepted the situation complacently. It is only when
the comparative freedom of the city or school has given them
a new attitude toward themselves that they become sensitive
to their position.

These untouchables were baptized as followers of Christ
about ten years before we came to Karimpur. We were prepared to find them Christian in every way, but soon realized
the unfairness of our expectations, as no one had had time
to give them regular teaching since their baptism. Every village contact was on the old basis. They called themselves
bhangi or Christian, whichever seemed expedient. And they
saw nothing unethical in the variation. We were shocked
when we found that a man coming for medical treatment
reported himself as a Christian to us one day, and as a *bhangi*

to our village helper the following day. Gradually we realized that we were alone in the use of the title, "Christian." When we remonstrated with those who applied the old title, they smiled tolerantly, and avoided the subject. Later, when our Hindu assistant, who had spent years among Christian boys in a Mission school in town, prepared the village census, with a section for *bhangis,* and none for Christians, we grasped the extent of imperviousness to change.

Our attitude toward the group was confused by their baptism. If they proposed to live as *bhangis,* why defame the name of Christ? Then as we saw more of the degradation thrust upon them under the old regime, we understood this reaching out for compassion. We gave them all of the time that we could, sharing with them Christ's message of comfort and courage which seemed to have been intended for men just like themselves. But their idea of what we should do for them was quite different. Like the low-born of any community, they were clever at currying favor. To us they proclaimed their Christianity and played on our sympathies. They took for granted that when they accepted baptism, all Christian missionaries automatically became their patrons. Never before had a missionary been as accessible as the one now living across the road. While still clinging to their old patrons, they took on the new. On Sunday evenings when the men attended religious services, they nodded their heads and agreed vigorously with all that the Sahib said. Hardly was the final prayer ended when they introduced some relative who was involved in a lawsuit. If the Sahib would only give them fifty rupees, and appear at court, the case would be easily won. They dealt lightly with the merits of the case and assured us that the Sahib's rupees and presence were really what were needed to secure justice.

If we had supported all the litigation to which we were invited by our Christian brethren during our first six months among them, we would have been bankrupt both as to time and money. There were other requests—favors from official friends, or money for the marriage ceremonies of a daughter far too young to be married under Christian law. When the Sahib felt obliged to refuse these requests, the brethren were deeply hurt. Any patron would have welcomed such opportunities—opportunities of drawing them more deeply under obligation to him.

We had no desire to place them under obligation to ourselves or to anyone else. In our ignorance of the offices of a patron, we were irritated by their constant, petty claims upon us. As the working of the patronage system gradually became clearer through all of our village contacts, we were more patient with these men who had lived by it always. Meanwhile, they had begun to comprehend that becoming followers of Christ was not related to the business of winning favors And we approached a better mutual understanding.

Their untouchability and their vague reaching out for something better, challenged us. Just as it would have been easy to be monopolized by those at the top of the social scale, so it would have been easy to devote ourselves to those at the very bottom. This we could not do. Instead we brought a teacher-pastor to live among them. For several months, he and his family shared the small room and courtyard of one of the Christians. Later, his neighbors built him a little place of his own. His night school, and still more his home, have been the hoped-for stimulus. Boys and girls, and a few men and women are learning to read and write—a privilege which they always regarded as far removed from them. The Christian homes are happy and clean, and those who live in them are self-respecting in spite of the work to which they must go each day.

The fact that they were untouchables had always been regarded as evidence of their transgressions in an earlier existence. The next incarnation might carry them still lower. From that dread they have now been released. Every evening a little group sits before the pastor's door, singing *bha-jans* (hymns), which they once assured us they never could learn. On Sunday evenings, not just the men as in the early days, but men, women, and children gather together. In hot weather they sit on the ground under a big *neem* tree. In cold weather, they gather around a miniature bonfire in someone's long, narrow front room. The meetings no longer end in discussions of lawsuits, but in a simple ceremony of giving. One representative from each household comes forward with a gift of grain as a part of the family's share in the support of their teacher-pastor. And as each one pours his grain out on a cloth spread upon the ground, he offers a short prayer.

Sanu, the teacher-pastor who has done so much for our people, was himself an ordinary village Christian until four years before he came to us. He herded his swine, and idled, while his wife cleaned privies. He expressed a desire to learn, and was sent to a training school where he started out with his primer. His wife read her primer, too, while nursing her baby and watching her two children through the classroom door. Neither of them was brilliant, but both were faithful in their studies and in their efforts to cast off their old careless, dirty ways.

When they came to us they were clean, and they did not fawn. They had been away from their untouchable life such a short time that it was not awkward for them to live among untouchables. Their clothes and their food were as simple as the clothes and food of those around them. But there was the difference in essentials which helped raise the standards of their neighbors. A few months ago the pastor's brother died; the responsibility of retaining the ancestral rights granted by the family patron rested on him. His relatives urged him to return to his home village to live, for the sake of holding the rights. They saw nothing difficult in his giving up his pastoral work and reverting to the old leisurely *bhangi* status. But he saw many difficulties. He talked with us of what the change meant: giving up his independence and acknowledging allegiance to masters who regarded and treated him as an untouchable. He knew what had happened to others. He recalled a schoolmate who had returned to his ancestral village and who had been told by his patron that as a Christian he could expect no food, favors, or rights. As a *bhangi* he was entitled to all of these.

The Christian considered his family. Behind him were his *bhangi* forefathers who had served the forefathers of his patron, and in whose steps everyone expected him to follow. Before him were his own children, looking to him for the support which depended on whether he ingratiated or antagonized his patron. Expediency framed his declaration: "Sir, I am your *bhangi*." Might he, Sanu, yield in the same way? He would be going home with the avowed purpose of claiming the rights granted his forefathers as *bhangis*, and passed on to him as a *bhangi*. Moreover, not only the attitude of his patrons, but that of all the members of his village, and the carrying on of his traditional function would persist in pressing him back into the old mold.

As he struggled to make his choice between the old status of *bhangi* with its bondage and its comfortable assurance of daily bread, and the new life of pastor with its high purpose, its freedom, and its risks, his wife made her plea. During the four years in the training school and two years as pastor's wife she had been released from the revolting work which never allowed her to forget that she was despised among women. She could make herself go back to it, as a dutiful wife. But to drag her three beloved baby daughters into it was more than she could endure. So, for the sake of their children, we think that they will continue in their present work—if relatives do not become too importunate. When relatives enter the field, we cease to conjecture.

Rabindranath Tagore has written beautifully of men and women like our untouchables, in "The Scavenger":

Why do they shun your touch, my friend, and call you
unclean
Whom cleanliness follows at every step making the earth
and air sweet for our dwelling and ever luring us back
from return to the wild?
You help us, like a mother her child, into freshness and
uphold the truth, that disgust is never for man.
The holy stream of your ministry carries pollutions away
and ever remains pure.
Once Lord Shiva had saved the world from a deluge of
poison by taking it himself.
And you save it every day from filth with the same divine
sufferance.
Come, friend, come my hero, give us courage to serve man,
even while bearing the brand of infamy from him.

If there were more who felt as Tagore does and as other
great minds of the nations do, it would not be difficult for men
to perform this service and still stand straight among other
men. But the village wills that they accept their infamy and
keep their little world clean without the knowledge that they
are heroes. If they suspected it, they might become dissatisfied. Dissatisfaction might lead to a change in the existing
order. The retainers of the existing order know that as long
as there is no change their power is assured. They have no objection to the change in personal living such as Sanu has
wrought among the *bhangis*. It might even result in their being more thorough in their functioning as scavengers. But
their ideas and amibitions must not clash in any way with
those which their patrons have assigned them. If this occurs,
pressure must be brought to bear to keep them in their traditional compartment.

Only recently a high-caste man of our village mocked at
our hopes for the untouchables: "You may think they are
Christians," he laughed. "Well, they are *bhangis*. And as
long as they are *bhangis*, they can stay in this village and do

the work of *bhangis*. But let them deny to us that they are *bhangis*, and out they go." The stranglehold.

Unless the new generation of leaders has the courage to face the consequences of greater tolerance, there is little to tempt the more ambitious members of these depressed groups to remain in the village. To improve himself economically, the untouchable is almost obliged to leave home.

Three Christians have already gone from our village to the greater freedom and opportunities of the city. But each one has left his wife behind to carry on her work and thus retain a claim to the rights of the family in all that the patron is expected to give. This is the adventurer's insurance. He can return at any time and lean on his patron, if he is willing to pay the price. The arrangement is far from ideal and threatens disaster to family unity. But we cannot say "stay," while we know that the stranglehold exists.

In our efforts to get the Christian men to occupy themselves with something more arduous and profitable than swine, we suggested farming. We knew of former *bhangis* who were farmers in another district. But straightway we trampled on the same old idea of fate—allotted tasks. An old *kachhi* friend exclaimed to the Memsahiba: "What is this the Sahib is try-to get the *bhangis* to do—work on the land? But that is *our* right. We were born to work on the land. They were born to clean up village filth. No one has the right to change this order established by God." He had nothing to lose or gain by the work suggested for the *bhangis*. He was simply try-ing to set us straight. The Christians themselves did not en-courage the idea. One of them undertook to farm a small plot on shares with a young Brahman who was an outcaste among his own kind. But the other Christians maintained that farming was not their work, even though they recog-nized the inadequacy of their existing tasks. Furthermore, two of them had tried cultivation on a humble scale, and found it discouraging. They had subrented a field of lowest-grade soil from a Brahman and had watered it from a natural pond. The caste people refused to have their wells used by untouchables for irrigation. After they had worked the land for two years and made it more fertile, others decided that the field was worth having, offered a slightly higher rent for it—and got it. After much endeavor, we had reached the point of arranging to buy the pair of bullocks necessary for the new farming venture, when the Christians became involved in a quarrel with a Brahman over the trespassing vagaries of their swine. Their bullock money went into the payment of a fine. And the joke was on us, at least until another sowing season arrives.

Whenever we have tried to secure for untouchables some social or economic benefit which seems to us the reasonable right of any member of the community, we have come into conflict with the wills of some of our best friends. Our latest endeavor has been in education. Muni, our pastor's only son, is nine years old. The father expressed the hope that his son might have advantages greater than his own. The first logical step was to get the boy started in regular school work. We consulted the master of the District Board School in our village. He said that if we would wait until the beginning of a new term, we could enter Muni in the school. When the new term opened we sent Muni. The master had been with Christian boys in a town school, and saw nothing heretical in the presence of a Christian. But to the village boys Muni was a *bhangi*.

At noon of the first day, all the older boys took their books and slates home, and refused to return to school. The smaller children returned. But at the close of the afternoon session, when their parents became aware of what had happened, they were thoroughly bathed. On the following day a few children from the lower castes answered the roll call. From then on, all fifty were absent, and Muni remained the lone pupil.

Knowing how cruel boys can be, we sent our eldest son, Arthur, just Muni's age, along with him as bodyguard. Arthur was friendly with the whole village and we felt sure that no one would molest Muni with him as escort. But there was no teasing, and no attempt to stop him. The village youngsters, free from school, reveled in their unexpected holidays. When we went into the village our friends were as cordial as ever. The school was not mentioned.

A month passed. The Sahib was the first to introduce the subject one evening while with a group of leaders. He asked why it would not be possible for this boy, with no taint of the *bhangi* about him or his parents, to learn along with more fortunate children? The boy had expressed his willingness to sit apart from the others. He was not going to school for the purpose of touching them. He could learn without touching them, just as all of his untouchable neighbors did everything else without touching any member of the village.

Then the village leaders expressed their feelings. The government had no right to upset the established order by allowing children from any caste or untouchable group to attend school. And the Sahib was making a great mistake in giving a *bhangi* the notion that he could learn. If the boy must be taught, let him learn from his own father. Or let there be a separate school for such boys. The Sahib's explanations were heard, but were considered unsatisfactory.

The son of the headman was sitting near the group. He had passed the classes included in the village school and was now enrolled in a school in town. "Have you been attending the town school?" The Sahib asked. The boy said that he had. "And Christian boys attend the town school?" The boy admitted that they did. The headman nervously tried to change the subject, but the Sahib was relentless. "And you sit with them in classes and play games with them?" he persisted. The boy confessed that he did.

Among those who heard, some were incredulous and others

were shocked. This then was the price of higher education. However, the headman was prepared. He explained that when villagers go to town or to fairs or on trains, they put themselves into the hands of others, and are not responsible for any defilement. But here in the village they are responsible for their own contacts and those of their children. No *bhangi* should become a regular pupil in the Karimpur school.

The Sahib consulted the members of the District School Board. They had already received a petition from our village friends that Muni be put out, and had replied that legally a child of any caste or creed might attend a government-supported school. Most of the members of the board were friends of ours, and were likewise friendly toward our democratic principles. But they could not force parents to send their children to school. If the parents of the Karimpur area boycotted their school much longer, it would have to be closed. They did not want this to happen any more than we did. One friend of many years of experience, advised us to give up our stand.

The villages of our district were not yet ready for such a radical move. Untouchable children had begun attending other schools in the district. They had had no one of influence to back them, and after a few weeks of enthusiastic school attendance, they were suddenly absent. No one quite knew why. Evidently the old forces were brought to bear effectively. Even though we might succeed in giving our protege a chance in school while we were in the village, he would be forced out as soon as we left. The Sahib persuaded a Swarajist Brahman friend to visit the village. He tried patiently to reason with his fellow Brahmans. But they were unmoved. His position confused them. Here was a man who did not favor the present government, yet who agreed with the government in the erroneous idea that all should have equal opportunities. Moreover, he was a Brahman. Yet he said there was no harm in exposing one's children to the company of an untouchable. They concluded that there was no good in education after all. One of the elders declared that when he was ten he could have knocked over the whole crowd of present-day schoolboys in one husky push. Another reminded his brethren that from their village four young men (all Brahmans) had become schoolteachers. All four had died while still young.

This was conclusive evidence against education. Yes, it would be well for them all if the school were closed. But later, away from the ears of leaders, a father approached the Sahib with the assurance that if he could persuade the two most powerful leaders to send their boys back to school, most of the other parents of the village were prepared to follow. They could not make the break without their leader's sanction.

Three months have now passed. The school board has kept the school going, although only three caste boys have returned, and they surreptitiously. The latest proposal—that a separate entrance, and a low-walled enclosure be provided for untouchable pupils—has been turned down. Our leaders, even the most unselfish among them, cannot risk this weakening of the old structure. They are reproachful, feeling that we in our stubborn ignorance have spoiled the school. But we regard ourselves simply as the advance guard of a movement which is sure to reach our district, as it has the most progressive parts of the country. If we can somehow persuade our friends to accept the change which is being wrought, gradually and civilly, they will be spared a painful shock when compulsory education descends upon them.

CHAPTER V

Occupants of the Front Room

When the cattle come home in the evening, our village lanes are transformed into stables. City visitors who go through the village with us at this hour step gingerly over streams of urine and piles of dung while picking their precarious way around and behind munching buffaloes and bullocks. After dark, when nights are cold, the animals are led into the cattle room, the front room of every farm house. If the men of the family have no room for themselves apart from the courtyard where the women stay, they sleep on their rope-strung cots or beds of straw, among the cattle. On suffocating summer nights, both master and animals sleep in the lane outside the door.

The farmer is more with his bullocks than with the human members of his family. He takes for granted that if we are ready to nurse his wife and children in times of illness, we will give the same care to his animals. When a cow is the only cow and a pair of bullocks are the only bullocks a family owns, and when they occupy the front room or share the family courtyard, they are distinctly members of the household. We have tried to accustom ourselves to their importance and propinquity. We still find it disconcerting while leaning over a patient to have a buffalo a few feet away shaking its head, glowing with its bulging, red-rimmed eyes, and snorting at the intrusion of our strange paraphernalia—even though it is tied. As for prescribing for animal ailments, we registered blank. When Tori came to us one night, wringing his hands, and begging the Sahib to come and help his buffalo about to die, the Sahib confessed his inability to help in such a situation. Tori described the buffalo's condition. But it was unintelligible to the Sahib.

His protests of ignorance were in vain. The importunate Tori insisted: "If you will only see the buffalo, you will be able to do something." The Sahib unwilling, and overcome by his sense of helplessness, was led by lantern light to the lane in front of Tori's house where the animal lay, suffering from what the Sahib learned later was a hernia. All were expectant when the Sahib arrived—they did not know then as they do now how little he knows about the care of animals. The Sahib suggested that the animal be taken to the District Veterinary Officer, six miles away. But all protested that it could not survive such a trip. The only alternative was to get the Veterinary Officer to Karimpur. The Sahib volunteered to bring him in the car. A sigh of relief passed through the group. The Sahib found the Veterinary Officer awaiting the arrival of his supervising officer. After some hesitation he came, with an aide and his instruments.

The lane was turned into an operating theater. Rice straw was spread on the ground. The buffalo was tied, thrown, bound, and sat upon by eight strong men. A carpenter was commandeered to be assistant surgeon. The Sahib held the lantern. Needle after needle broke as the doctor tried to bind the tough skin together over the bit of protruding intestine. But persistence won. During the succeeding four years the buffalo has amply rewarded her owner for his importunity on that memorable night.

The experience was the first of several which impressed upon us the necessity of including animal husbandry in any effort at village service. We have regretted our own inability to meet the need. Fortunately, we have had a District Veterinary Officer who has been willing to cooperate. In times of emergency he has been most helpful. When rinderpest was playing havoc with the cattle of the district, he informed us that there was danger to the cattle of Karimpur. He offered to supply the antirinderpest serum free if the Sahib would advise the villagers to have their cattle inoculated. We had been reading government bulletins on the effective immunity and the negligible after effects of this inoculation, and were prepared to support it. The officer brought his bottles of serum, and the Sahib accompanied him through the village and the fields. Farmers working their bullocks at the wells were doubtful, but the Sahib accepted full responsibility and agreed to pay fifty rupees in case of any ill effects. In this way he was able to secure the cooperation of all whom they met. The Veterinary Officer inoculated more than two hundred of our village cattle in two days. Even the *bhagat* who propitiates spirits which may reside in animals, brought his cattle to be inoculated. The *patwari* who is supposed to report every epidemic to the proper authorities to be checked, arrived on the scene after the work was finished. He had not been interested in the fate of the cattle, and for the first time in his career there was someone in the village with interest and power enough to secure official aid without his intervention. The Sahib, in his desire to help his farmer friends, had not thought of the *patwari* until the latter came hurrying with apologies and his diary. He begged the Veterinary Officer to note in his diary that he—the *patwari*—had rendered every assistance necessary. This request was made in the presence of the Sahib and was refused, much to the consternation of the *patwari*.

Only a few farmers aspire to own two pairs of bullocks.

The ordinary man contents himself with one pair. They plow his fields, help sow his seed, send water to his crops from the wells during the dry months of both winter and summer, press his sugar cane, and carry to market any produce he may have to sell. If he loses one of them, he must borrow an animal from one of his neighbors. But borrowing is uncertain. When he needs the help of bullocks most, his neighbors are all using theirs. If he cannot borrow, and cannot face the burden of the purchase of a new animal, he must sacrifice his holdings and work only a small plot by hand, or take a chance at hiring himself out to others more fortunate.

The villager depends on a cow or a buffalo for his milk supply. He prefers a buffalo, because it gives more milk and its milk is richer in the fats which go into *ghi* (clarified butter). If a buffalo is beyond his means, he invests in a cow. If he is too poor for a cow, he gets a goat or two. It is not so much the milk that he wants as the *ghi* made from it. He and his family drink very little fresh milk lest they cut down the quanity of *ghi*. The whole milk is boiled, set, and churned daily. The butter is accumulated for a week and clarified. It is the only animal fat used in the diet of the villagers except in the few cases where meat is used. The buttermilk from each day's churning is used freely in a number of important dishes, adding to their flavor and nutrition. During a great part of the year it constitutes the farmer's early morning meal. The discontinuance of the milk supply is very upsetting. Water may replace buttermilk, and mustard oil may replace *ghi*. But water is a poor substitute. Mustard oil, in many dishes, is distasteful to those accustomed to *ghi*. It is considered unworthy of the special delicacies associated with festivals and the entertainment of guests. If an animal stops giving milk for no accountable reason, its owner consults a *bhagat*, that he may make the necessary reparation for any offense against the gods. Recently a *bhagat* told one such owner that if he would feed five Brahmans on an auspicious date, he would again have milk. The owner gave the unceremonious reply that he would feed the Brahmans after the gods had renewed his milk supply, and not before. Far worse than being without milk temporarily is the loss of the giver of milk through death. To buy a new milk animal demands an outlay of capital which staggers a thrifty farmer. If his hidden hoard, or his creditor, cannot stand the strain of the investment, he resigns himself to the hope that the calf will survive. Or he buys a calf, and feeds it as little as possible while waiting for the happy days when there will be milk in his house once more.

Some of the most heated quarrels in the village have been precipitated by wayward animals. The sheep and goats which are kept in flocks by the small community of shepherds and goatherds, must be guided past unprotected fields of grain on their way to the uncultivated stretches. If the shepherd or goatherd stops to watch a passing car, or to listen to an argument over field boundaries, his animals may stray into the nearest pulse or corn, and are able to do considerable damage before they can be recalled.

On one such occasion, a farmer happened to arrive just in time to find his field being devastated. Cursing the shepherd, he caught as many of the animals as he could and threatened to keep them. The shepherd's plea was that without his sheep he would be without means of livelihood. He was following the paths and duties of his forefathers and could not turn to any other occupation. When a number of friends had interceded, and a promise had been exacted that the trespassing would not be repeated, the farmer set the sheep free.

In poorer households, the two or three goats which supply the family with milk are taken out to graze by the smaller children. If the children run off to play and forget them, they can do enough damage to upset a section of the village if not discovered. A *sadhu* who settled in the village for several months incurred the displeasure of his supporters by allowing his hobbled pony to wander into their grain fields.

Village boys collect cows and buffaloes from their own and neighboring houses and drive them out to the edge of the village where the herd is formed. Under their youthful drovers, the cattle can do more damage than any of the smaller animals, as they pass tempting, unfenced fields on their way to the grazing areas. Not long ago, a small boy of grain-parcher caste was taken to the hospital to recover from a beating administered by a Brahman. The latter had warned the boy that he must keep the cattle in his charge out of a certain field. When the cows did not move on, the man vented his wrath on their keeper.

Similar complaints of trespassing are frequently heard against the swine. But whenever it is suggested that swine are such a nuisance that they should be banished from the village, the farmers protest—even those who are loudest in their condemnation of the swineherds. Every villager recognizes the services rendered by the swine in cleaning roadways and open spaces on the borders of the village used as latrines. But if on their scavenging trips to and from these spaces, they touch a farmer's grain field or his stacks of fodder, the farmer is overcome with rage. One of the most amusing sights in camp last year was that of a high-caste neighbor, trying to escort a herd of squealing swine from his field, where he caught them trespassing, to the nearest cattle pound three miles away. In one hand he still clutched his small brass water jar, which he had had with him in the field when he discovered the culprits. With the other he wielded a long club, partly to control the swine, and partly to keep them at a safe distance from himself. He shouted and cursed as he careened through the fields behind his grunting victims. He had not gone far when they were scattered through his neighbor's fields, leaving destruction and wrath in their wake. It was hours before the swineherd was able to collect and quiet his animals. They never reached the pound. A similar incident occurred later, when the Sahib was too ill with typhoid fever to intervene. It ended in blows between Christian swineherds and high-caste men, and a lawsuit, with damages to be paid by the swineherds.

The only animals who wander unhindered over fields and threshing floors are the Brahmani bulls—set at large as an act of religious merit, usually at the death of a prominent Hindu. They are the only full-grown bulls available for the service of village cows. One such bull spends a great deal of time in our grove. Sometimes we do not see him for weeks. Then he returns to stay in our neighborhood for a month or two. While here, he wanders off every morning to convenient fields, where he grazes on the best, at leisure. Every evening he returns, following the herds of cows on their way home. Having no fixed abode and belonging to no one in particular, he is in everyone's keeping and entitled to a share of everyone's food supply. A farmer does not try to keep his own bulls after they are three or four years old, because they become unmanageable. He refuses to have an animal castrated while in his possession. Instead he exchanges each of his young bulls for one that has been castrated by wandering drovers. He gets several more years of field labor from the new bullock than he could hope for if he were to keep his own uncastrated animal. For propagation purposes he depends, theoretically, on Brahmani bulls. But as there are only two which visit our village, and one of these comes out rarely, the service to cows is usually rendered by the young bulls which have not yet been exchanged.

The government, knowing the need for good bulls, has made it possible for each district to have a free gift of ninety pure-bred bulls from the Punjab. As villagers come to recognize the value of thse bulls it is hoped that they themselves will purchase them. The idea is that some farmer or a group of farmers will house and care for a bull as a form of community service. With this ideal before us we got one of the young government bulls for Karimpur. We arranged for a farmer to house it and feed it at night; during the day it was taken out grazing with the other animals of the village. All went well until he began to mature and wandered off after some of the cows. In his wanderings, he grazed where he chose like the Brahmani bulls. This was not acceptable to the villagers. Had he been a Brahmani bull, they could say nothing. He would have been no one's responsibility. But this bull belonged to the Sahib. Therefore, the Sahib was responsible for its waywardness. The farmers who complained most loudly did not stop to think that they might be the first to benefit by the service of the bull when it matured. Their eyes were fixed on the present, and the unfenced fields which an unruly bull might sample. If the bull had been old enough to start giving service as soon as he came to the village, they might have accepted him. But to accept the burden of sharing in his feeding with no service in sight was a strain. Matters were complicated by the fact that the farmer whom we had been paying for the grain which the bull was supposed to consume had neglected to mention the fact, and had given the others the impression that no such provision had been made.

One night a delegation of farmers came to the Sahib, complaining of the weakness of his bull for grain fields. When the Sahib explained that he was paying for the feeding and grazing, they turned on the farmer who housed the animal. He said he would have nothing more to do with it. Our beautiful bull was not wanted by any farmer in Karimpur, although everyone recognized his latent advantages. It died shortly afterward.

A year earlier, at the time of a district exhibition, the Sahib had suggested that a government bull in the possession of a big *zamindar* (landlord) of the district be exhibited. One of the exhibition officials sent a request to the *zamindar* for the animal, only to find that no one knew at that time where the bull was. He was serving the countryside according to the traditional custom. It seemed strange to us at the time that a government bull should be treated in the same way as Brahmani bull. But when we began to face the solid opposition of the village, there was only one choice other than that of losing the bull for our village, and that was to do what the big *zamindar* did—and what most other recipients have been obliged to do—release him and treat him as a Brahmani bull. He had been stall-fed in Karimpur long enough to consider this his home and we had every assurance that he would stay in the immediate neighborhood. Accordingly, we announced that henceforth no one was responsible for him and there would be no one to whom disgruntled villagers could complain. We are responsible to the government to notify them if the animal falls ill or meets with any misfortune. The risks are small because of the reverence for cattle and for wandering bulls in particular. Thus has the first step been taken toward a better breed of cattle in the neighborhood of Karimpur, not at all as we thought it would be done, but as custom prescribes.

Animals which share in the family struggle for existence are treated with consideration and kindness. Both milk and work animals fare almost as well as the rest of the household. The baby calves are petted and mauled by the children. When big enough to be taken out grazing, they are pushed and dragged by boisterous youngsters to scattered patches of dusty grass. In our grove they are hauled to some deserted threshing floor where they are made to go through the form of treading out grain while the children drive or push them round and round, imitating the cluckings and scoldings of their elders. In orthodox households, the first unleavened cake of the day is always fed to the cow. The farmer's first duty of the day and last duty at night is the chopping of dry fodder for his animals.

Along with kindness goes the consistent refusal to take ani-

mal life. Rats infest village houses, and yet beyond an occasional flourish, housewives make no move toward extermination. The deer and the peacock destroy the crops in distant
fields. Farmers brandish their staves, and spread thorny
branches along the edges of the most valued plots. But
there is no thought of destroying the invaders. When heads
of grain are ripe and tempting to the birds, the farmers set up
scarecrows, sometimes with an ingenious arrangement for a
clatter when breezes blow. In many fields, platforms about
four feet square are constructed of grass and bamboo and
perched on bamboo poles, high above the heads of grain.
They are just strong enough to hold the children or the old
women who sit on them, clapping their hands and shouting
at the birds. Each child on watch has a long, woven rope
sling with which to hurl stones at the small thieves, but never
with any intention of killing.

Strangely out of harmony with their kindliness, is the irresponsibility of villagers toward unproductive domestic animals. These they casually entrust to Providence. Dogs are
rarely fed. Mangy, and alive with fleas and ticks, they wander about the village lanes, stealing any unguarded food or devouring any waste which their desperate noses scent. Our
suggestion that puppies unprovided for be drowned, is met
with gentle remonstrance. Yet those which do not starve in
infancy are allowed to grow up into an existence of constant
fighting over stray scraps, until they die and are devoured by
vultures and their starving brothers. The dogs haunt our
camp day and night. The rubbish can is upset and emptied
by them after every meal. Some have succeeded in opening
the tin boxes in which our stores of cereals and rice are kept.
Bricks and other boxes piled on top of the flour tin did not
discourage one mother dog. She nosed into it whenever the
tent was deserted in her desperation to get food to care for the
litter of starving pups awaiting her in a deserted house. A
loaf of bread disappeared from the dining table one evening

when the family stepped out of the tent for a moment to welcome guests. Dirty dishes must be washed immediately or there is a crash as some dog tries to carry off a cup partly filled with milk or tea. Even a bowl of paste left on the desk was licked clean and dropped outside the office tent door. Our own dogs have not learned to tear and bite with ferocity of their village neighbors, and offer little resistance. When lured into a fight, they come out battered and bleeding. Dogs which go mad are allowed to wander dangerously until they die, or until untouchables agree to beat them to death. When one of our own dogs contracted rabies, our neighbors sympathized with us in the unpleasant course of injections through which we all went, but they disapproved of the shooting of our dog.

Animals which share in the labors of production sometimes suffer from the same indifference. As the threshing has gone on outside our tent, we have pitied, and eventually championed, the smaller bullocks which, after hours of circling beside larger animals, have stumbled and fallen and are still prodded round and round over the threshing floor. When a bullock collapsed on the incline beside the well just beyond our camp, the owner threw a gunny cloth over it and left it where it lay, much to the dismay of our boys, who were troubled by the possibility of attacks upon it by jackals or other wild creatures which haunt the fields by night. It survived, and the next morning it was helped to a patch of sunshine where gradually it regained its strength. The bullocks on which the oil presser depends for the turning of his press are allowed to work with bodies covered with open, fly-infested sores. Some of our most prosperous farmers have been unwilling to buy disinfectant which they knew would relieve their cattle from a painful and dangerous hoof infection. The washerman and the potter load their small donkeys with clay jars or clothes, or cow-dung cakes, without any apparent thought of the slender legs which bend until they seem about to snap.

Cows and buffaloes too old to furnish milk are not treated cruelly, but simply allowed to starve. The same happens to young male buffaloes. It is the female buffaloes which are in demand. The males are unwanted and little effort is made to keep them alive. The few which survive are sometimes used for field work in emergencies. More often they are sold to wandering buyers or to poorer farmers who have never been able to afford bullocks. By nature and by religious training, the villager is unwilling to inflict pain or to take animal life. But the immemorial grind for existence has hardened him to an acceptance of the survival of the fittest.

A villager's animals could do much better work for him if he were to give them the added care necessary to bring them up to the maximum of utility. Even the dogs now accepted as nuisances, would help in guarding homes and animals, if fed and trained. One dog in the village is cared for, and has rewarded his master by his faithfulness as watchman. No stranger ventures near his door, and the master boasts that he can leave his womenfolk for a month without fear. Farmers have become skillful in reckoning the minimum of food necessary for maintaining animal service. It is difficult for them to improve the quality or add to the quantity until they are assured that the change is warranted by increased service. Cows are fed just enough to assure their calving and giving a little milk. They are grazed during the day on lands which yield little vegetation, and are given a very sparse meal at night. When villagers hear of the milk records of improved breeds of milk animals, they wag their heads and dismiss the marvel as something remote from their problems. They are giving and receiving what their fathers before them gave and received. Visits to the district demonstration farm have convinced them that stronger work animals can be secured by improving the breed. But as long as they sell their young bulls, and buy other castrated animals from outsiders, they realize that there is little advantage in improving the breed of their own stock, except for milk animals. Until they are educated up to the point of undertaking every step in the development and care of better animals, there is small prospect of improvement. They are not lacking in personal interest. There is nothing they appreciate more than help in the preservation of their present inferior stock. They simply accept things as they find them, and go on limiting the efficiency of their animal helpers by fostering a husbandry based on tradition rather than on science.

In Family Courtyards

As we go through the village, we are no longer conscious of mud walls, but of the life going on before and behind them. Before them, in the lanes, children skip and turn somersaults, farmers feed their animals, and craftsmen work at their trades. Behind them, further protected by the cattle rooms, are the women and small children in the family courtyards. Women of families of serving castes are obliged to go out for a part of each day, to the houses of employers, carrying water or grinding grain. But in every home where it is possible, the women and smaller children of the family—be it large or small—spend their lives in the family courtyard. The mud walls which protect the villager's family and possessions are as high at the back of the house as at the front. There are no back doors through which neighbors may slip informally. The family court may be provided with a ladder by way of promoting limited neighborliness among the women. The houses of the most prosperous have narrow, steep mud stairs leading to a small roof room through which they may pass to neighbors' roofs. At the back of the family courtyard or on either side of it are one or more storerooms, used for living purposes only at times when rain deluges the courtyard or cold drives the family behind closed doors.

The men regard this courtyard as the women's realm, and chaff the man who spends much time there. For themselves they have mud platforms at the front of their houses where they do their chores and sit with friends, smoking and talking. Or the men of related households share a *baithak,* or "sitting place" under a big *neem* tree. A man does not go into the family quarters of another unless special business calls him there. Then he usually enters accompanied by a man of the family, coughing loudly to warn the women into seclusion. The Sahib has been in some of these courtyards in times of distress. At such times the daughters have helped with his ministrations; rarely, a wife has appeared. In their own courtyards, the women go about their work scolding, laughing, chaffing, grumbling, without reserve. But the instant a man of the family enters they become self-conscious covering (or making a pretense at covering) their faces, bowing their heads, and in every way emphasizing their sex and their role as subordinates. In families where economic pressure compels a woman to venture beyond her own mud walls, she goes cowering along the lanes, managing to keep her face hidden while balancing the jars of water or baskets of refuse which she must carry. In her own back lane, if she is of humble caste and if the menfolk are away in the fields, she is freer, but still ready to hide herself or her face if outsiders pass by. She is never quite at ease until she gains her own doorway.

Patience and service were required of the Memsahiba before she was freely welcomed behind the mud walls. There was also the period of extensive and intensive questioning through which she had to go. Nothing about her person or her mode of life was overlooked. Questions were not delicately veiled, but came directly and openly to the point.

When she had finally convinced them that in every way she was made like themselves, their curiosity waned and a normal level of companionship was found. Even now when some new relative comes to visit, the Memsahiba is obliged to recount old tales, such as the strange custom of her people which allows a girl to grow up unmarried, to know boys of her own age, and, breathless climax, to decide whom she will marry. But in normal times, there is the mental relaxation of following the topics of interest to women limited in outlook to their own households. Round and round the same circle they move—babies, husbands, food, physical ailments, all interwoven with their simple faith in spiritdom. Affairs of state are unimportant. When newspapers were headlined with the passing of the Sarda Bill, in 1929 (prohibiting marriages of males less than eighteen and females less than fourteen years old), the Memsahiba tried to interest the women in its significance, with indifferent response. On the same day there was a back-page item, reporting a rumor that locusts had devoured a baby in a district some distance from ours. The Memsahiba mentioned this item shortly after the bill had been cursorily dropped. Immediately interest was aroused. The women had heard of it several days before. Again and again they rehearsed the tragedy, expressing their horror and sorrow. A mother losing her baby—this was within their grasp. On other occasions when someone asked about travel, and the Memsahiba was in the midst of a description of Calcutta or Delhi, one of the older women brought the conversation back to the circle of interest by reminding the Memsahiba that her youngest child was four and it was time she had another, or by tapping the abdomen of a young neighbor and wisely suggesting that we ask what she had there.

Babies are longed for, and greatly loved when they arrive. No one considers himself too busy, or too dignified to stop a moment to enjoy the antics of his youngest. The natural kindliness of village folk leads one to expect the same

attitude toward all children. But the spirit of caste has so per-
meated their lives that they are indifferent toward children
outside their own brotherhood, especially toward the children
of untouchables. It still distresses us to see a grandmother of
caste suddenly change from proud smiles to vindictive shouts
because some untouchable toddler has innocently ventured
near her grandchild.

Our village mothers have not had the training which turns
maternal worries to diet and germs. Instead, they think of
evil spirits and jealous deities which threaten their loved ones.
When a baby arrives, there is no more outward preparation
for his coming than there is for the birth of a calf. The village
midwife who officiates is always dirty. She takes less pains
than usual to be clean for this occasion. After the baby's first
cry she gives him a casual bath while one of the women or
children of the household scrambles about in search of some
old, cast-off garment to wrap him in. This, with all the neglect
which follows, is not at all because he is unwanted, but because any fuss over him might attract the notice of some un-
friendly presence. On the rope cot where he lies there is always a sickle or other bladed instrument, or a monkey skull if
it can be secured, to frighten evil spirits away. When the lovable woman doctor was called in to see a new mother, she was
greatly entertained to find a dirty village midwife holding
the wee baby, undressed, in one arm while from the other
dangled a three-foot sword. We support cleanliness and its
allies on every possible occasion, and mothers are eager to
cooperate in the hope of saving their babies. But it is with
fear and trembling that they adopt new methods.

As the baby of the family grows large enough to be
played with, he is the household pet. When a new baby arrives to usurp his place, he sits on the earth floor close beside his mother wailing for the snuggling warmth that has
been his and which is now being enjoyed by the newest
comer. The girls of the family are his willing slaves, often

lugging him about on slender hips when both he and they might be better off if he were on his own feet. There is a three-year-old who spends much time in our grove riding thus on his mother's hip. When we persuade him to try walking, he takes a few straddling steps, then sits down and howls. The mother beams with pride at her importance to him, and lifts him back to her hip, bouncing him from tears to smiles.

Whatever a baby wants he receives, if it is within reach of brothers or sisters or parents or grandparents. If he cries, it is a signal for him to be fed. One of our hardest tasks is to convince a mother that her baby's cries may not always mean hunger, that his dysentery is aggravated by overfeeding. The Memsahiba spent two terrible nights with a mother and baby son when the doctor had warned her that feeding would be fatal. Every time the restless child cried, the mother was frantic in her desire to nurse him. She was too desperate to listen to reason. She hated the Memsahiba that night and the next. But when the siege was over, her gratitude was great.

If a baby's sores must be scraped or if any treatment gives him pain, it is the father or uncle who braves the ordeal. Although a father's tears flow with his child's, he knows enough of medical service to permit the treatment. If the child is in his mother's arms, she refuses to have him hurt, no matter what the ultimate benefit may be. She will endure anything herself. But expose her baby to pain—no. One morning we took the doctor into a home where the women had been worrying the Memsahiba about the slight operation needed for the first born of one of the daughters of the family. When the Memsahiba took the baby in her arms and the doctor began snipping, the baby cried. The mother and grandmother wept, and begged them to stop. The doctor was too busy to listen. They tugged at the Memsahiba's arm, but she warned them that a jerk might cause the baby much harm and pain. They wrung their hands. A sister-in-law dragged herself from the bed where she was lying with her three-day-old son, and came to our feet to add her supplications. One of the women saw a drop of blood, and the demands that we stop grew to cries. Then it was all over. The mother had her baby at her breast again. They have forgotten the torture of the baby's crying now, and take unto themselves great credit for having arranged for the operation.

The humoring of the smaller children goes on until they are old enough to take their places as helpers. Often the Memsahiba has exclaimed, "He shouldn't be eating that sweet cake. He'll have a pain inside." The mother's reply is simple and final, "But he wants it." If a small boy does not get what he desires, he lies on the ground and kicks and cries and refuses to move until he gets it or a satisfactory substitute. Little sisters seldom resort to this. Their training in self-restraint begins early. For them the step from petting and babyhood to a sharing of family burdens is much easier than for the boys.

Like mothers everywhere, those of our village thrill at the dependence of the new little lives on themselves. They prolong the pleasure of this dependence as long as possible, without the knowledge that it might be harmful to the child. A mother is proud of the fact that her baby of two refuses all food but her milk. At the same time she is distraught because the child is languid, emaciated, and steadily losing. Sometimes a child of four comes running in from play, dashes up to his mother as she squats on the ground working or visiting, pushes aside her scarf or short vest, and when satisfied, runs off again. There are other reasons for this prolonged lactation, but when the Memsahiba remonstrates, the explanation invariably given with a sign of content is, "He cries if I refuse it."

As girls grow older, their work and interests draw them more closely to their mothers. As the time of marriage approaches, with the dread of a mother-in-law, a girl clings to her mother as her strongest ally. The boys, as soon as they are able, desert the women's quarters for the fields and the companionship of the men. It is a period when a mother faces the realization that she is no longer needed. Then comes the boy's adolescence with the preparations for marriage. He is drawn again into the family courtyard, sung to, and talked to by the women. The ceremonies through which he must go are in their hands. This is their dramatic outlet, their fun. It satisfies their repressed longing to be of importance to him. During the interim between earlier and final ceremonies, he may return to the men; but the women know that he will come back to them when the bride comes to stay. At this stage, his newly roused passion is fanned by the women. In their restricted lives, they are bound to encourage sexual excitement. They have the bride in their control, and while they have her, they can be sure of the importance of their position in the life of the one-time baby now a young husband. He transfers his interests from the world of men to the women's quarters, and they rejoice.

A short time ago, the Memsahiba was sitting in one of the better courtyards of the village, when she observed the fifteen-year-old son of the household lying on the earth floor, his head and shoulders propped up against a titlted rope cot. His eyes were half closed, and he was obviously dreaming. It was an unusual pose for this particular boy, who has been one of the most promising all around athletes among the youths of the village. When the Memsahiba expressed her surprise that he was not in school, the women nodded and smiled knowingly. His mother explained in a stage whisper that his bride had departed just a few days before, after a visit of two months. She found great satisfaction in the thought that he preferred her courtyard to school, although he spent his time lying about listlessly. School to her was a vague institution somewhere outside, which had taken her son away from her. At last she had him again, and she was proud of her victory. His father scolded and fumed, but he was helpless against the indifference of the boy, supported by mother, aunts, and sister-in-law. An uncle's advice, coming from his own experience and observations, was finally accepted: "Drink plenty of milk, eat rich food, and take life easy. Then after a year go back to school if you so desire." In the early days we were puzzled by the casual dropping of interests among boys who had shown ambition, and by the surprising awakening of youths whom we had accepted as indolent. Also, in the families which we knew best we observed that the older men were more progressive than their sons and younger brothers. We have learned now to read the signs, and know when a youth has emerged from the mud walls only for a respite, and when he has established himself among the men.

No matter how humble a man's position may be in village society, he becomes a personage when he enters his own courtyard. His wife, and any other women who are junior to him, are ready to do his bidding with heads bowed and voices subdued. To the young husband, this authority is most pleasing. He who has always been dependent upon others, suddenly finds a human being under his control. In exercising his newly acquired power he sometimes struts about like a young peacock. The women of the household laugh at him— behind their scarves. But outwardly they approve, and demand submission from his wife. One evening the Memsahiba was sitting with a group of untouchable women, busy making rag dolls. Voices were keyed high. We all raise our voices in the village, and are only aware of it when we suddenly hear ourselves shrilling in some dignified town bungalow or hospital. On this occasion as the women were working and talking, there was a sudden hush. Over their heads came a prolonged scolding in a harsh, youthful voice. In the lantern light the Memsahiba saw Govind, who a year or two ago was a star at turning somersaults and at escaping from irate owners of pillaged sugarcane fields. She was about to ask why the storm of abuse, and to tell him to move on, when she observed a self-conscious smile under the sheltering scarf of the girl at her side, Govind's bride. The older women nudged one another and giggled. The girl rose, head bowed as though she expected a whipping and hurried away, with Govind on her trail. After performing the trifling task to which he had so forcibly called her, she returned, all smiles. Her husband had played his role of master, and she the role of obedient wife, to their own satisfaction.

There is a temptation for these parts to be played indefinitely in the larger joint families where there is always an audience of aunts and sisters-in-law. Husband and wife have little opportunity for a natural relationship, except in their courtyard or roof under cover of darkness. Even this savors of the clandestine, as the husband is expected to sleep among the men at the front of the house. We have known successful joint families in the city who have ensured privacy by providing a separate apartment for each of the smaller groups. But in the village this provision for privacy must be sacrificed to the practical needs of a farm household.

In these larger families it is almost impossible to distinguish real from fictitious fear of husbands, until one knows the individuals and hears the reactions of the women when there are no men about. Whether fear exists or not every woman looks up to her husband as her master. Be he kind or be he cruel, it is her duty to obey him. If he punishes her she accepts it like a naughty child. When the Memsahiba sympathized with a young *dhanukin* who displayed her wrists cut where her husband had broken her glass bangles while beating her, the *dhanukin* showed no resentment toward her husband. The other women teased her, because she had been caught in mischief—talking to her husband's elder brother. While they laughed and teased, the husband appeared and his wife leaned far over her bread board, playing effectively the part of a crushed spirit, while the other women scurried off to suddenly remembered tasks. When the Memsahiba remonstrated with him for his abuse of a faithful wife, he grinned tolerantly and explained that under the circumstances discipline was necessary. His surprise at the Memsahiba's interference reminded her of her own resentment that same morning when a village passer-by objected to her discipline of her small son who had just burned a hole in the office tent.

It would be unfair to the joint family, which has much in its favor economically, to accuse it of disallowing love and companionship between husbands and wives. Such companionship would be possible, if there were less emphasis on sex. As it is, a woman performs her duty to her husband, satisfying his elemental needs, while she lavishes more and more of her love on her children. In the smaller homes, where the walls surround a single family, there is more natural relationship. With no older women present constantly to remind husband and wife of their respective roles, they work together for the good of their little family, without excessive consciousness of sex. In such courtyards, the wife may draw her scarf closely over her face when her husband enters and do his bidding without question, but she is free to talk with him alone. Even while he eats and she stands nearby ready to supply his wants, she may tell him about the baby's latest prank. While he washes and prepares to return to his work or to a visit with his neighbors, he complains to her of the lack of rain or the destruction by the deer in the farthest *arhar* (pulse) field. Some craftsmen work in their own courtyards with their wives, and sometimes their children, as assistants. In these households, we find none of the restrictions of families ruled by conservative mothers and aunts. The tailor and his wife, sitting in their little courtyard which faces Humble Lane without the usual protecting cattle room, are much too busy with their joint labors to think of the minutiae of conventions. Only occasionally does she remember to draw her scarf and assume a cringing attitude—when some older neighbor woman comments on her careless ways.

If a wife resents her husband's abuse of his control, as sometimes happens, she has a means of escape without scandal. As long as her father's house is maintained by one of her male relatives, she is free to return to it for visits of indefinite length. When the Memsahiba asked such a runaway wife what she would do if her husband came and demanded her return, the reply was that her brothers would not let him in. "But," she added, "he won't come—for a long time at least." When quarrels and blows have been forgotten, he may want her and she may be ready to return. They make a fresh start, with father's home in the offing as a final resort. This simple expedient works well, unless the husband's mother interferes and demands the assistance of his wife. Driven by his mother's importunity, he may insist on his wife's return. Or his mother may demand that her grandchild be left with her, and the young wife is torn between her child and escape from her husband's domination. Several years ago we were astonished when a village *panchayat* decreed that a young wife who had gone to her father's house must give up her baby son to her mother-in-law, unless she herself was willing to return to her husband and his mother, whose cruelty was known to the *panchayat* members. Since living in the village we can better appreciate the *panchayat's* point of view. A child belongs to his father's family. The child's mother may leave the household, but she has no right to take away the child.

A wife who is left a widow suffers greatly from her personal loss. But in our village she is not expected to perform the austerities demanded of widows in some communities. Her share of the work in a busy farm household is too great to permit leisure for time-consuming ceremonies. Very few of our widows shave their heads. Most of them wear only silver jewelry, having broken off their colored bangles at the time of mourning. But some have retained these, and bear no outward mark of widowhood. In an ordinary household it is difficult to distinguish widows from their more fortunate sisters-in-law.

After the first year, a widow in a joint family goes on living and working much as she did before her husband's death, with the other men of the family as her protectors. If there are no survivors of her husband's family to shelter her, and she has no sons, she considers herself doubly cursed. A little old lady of tailor caste wrung our hearts when she told us of her homeless state. We pictured her sleeping by the side of the road, until, to our amazement, we found her comfortably housed under the roof of her daughter's husband. This to her was no home, but a makeshift which fate had forced upon her. We have known widows wretched in their proverty, but we know of only one who has been cast off, because she can no longer work. The widow with grown sons retains her position as dictator of the family courtyard. Her sons' wives yield to her authority, though not always without protest. We sometimes hear their voices rising over mud walls, for the benefit of neighboring courtyards. Neighbors shrug and smile. To intrude in affairs between husband and wife is futile, but to interfere in a mother-daughter-in-law quarrel is to invite the verbal obliteration of one's self, one's forebears, and one's descendants.

The influence of the head of the women's quarters must be taken into consideration if the younger women and children are to be helped. Progress, especially in sanitation, can be made much more rapidly and happily if her cooperation is won. In most of our houses the older women are staunch conservatives. At the same time they are lovable and friendly, and willing to listen if they are sure they are not being dictated to. Many a child's eyes have remained swollen and inflamed until the grandmother has been convinced that bathing and medicine will bring relief. When the Memsahiba wants to add milk to the unleavened cakes which constitute the diet of a child, she knows that she must appeal to the grandmother, if there is one.

There are other women whose influence counts in the village, women who circulate through courtyards other than their own. If we are able to help a baby in one family, the news is carried by these women to other mothers in distress. Among them are the *kaharins* who are employed to carry water from wells to the houses where the women observe purdah; the *kachhins* who go into larger farm households to help with the splitting of pulses and grinding of grains; the wife of the washerman who collects and delivers clothes; and the sweeper women who go into most of the high-caste households, to clean privies and drains.

Most influential among them, because of her work and her tongue, is the barber's wife. While she massages a new mother or helps anoint a bridegroom with oil, she chooses appropriate bits from her store of gossip and philosophy. Much of her popularity depends on her questionable jokes and gibes at the recipient of her ministrations. Whenever the Memsahiba encounters her in the intimacy of a courtyard, she prepares for a lively siege of raillery. She retorts—until the barberess's vocabulary becomes too shady to be followed with comfort. The attitude of this worldly-wise lady has weight among her wall-bound clients, and we have found her support exceedingly worthwhile.

When their thoughts and time are not centered on husbands and babies, our village housewives are occupied with food. With no furniture beyond unvarnished, rope-laced cots and a low, rope-laced stool, with their dishes limited to a small collection of beautiful brass utensils, and with most of their sewing done by men of tailor caste, one might conclude that their days are leisurely. But the preparation of food requires much more than goes on in a town courtyard. Their husbands come in loaded with produce from the fields, and the women do the rest. Paddy which is poured out on the floor, must be pounded till the husks are removed before the rice can be prepared for cooking. The making of daily bread means the cleaning and storing of grain, as well as grinding it fresh in the stone mill before it can be kneaded and toasted. The spices which go into the pulse and vegetable dishes, and they are many, are freshly ground each day or two with a stone roller upon a corrugated slab of stone. They churn the milk and later clarify the butter for cooking purposes. Since the Memsahiba undertook the task of preparing all the dishes which appear in the village dietary, her respect for her village neighbors has grown. And her work covered only the final stages of production. The women have enjoyed her efforts and have been eager to share with her their own superior knowledge. The experience has added to their friendliness and understanding. The men may scorn their womenfolk, but they cannot scorn their ability as burden-sharers.

If a woman from the outside world comes into contact with these women of the village who are devoting their lives to their menfolk and children, she is granted a great privilege and responsibility—the privilege of knowing them and of observing their selfless service, and the responsibility of sharing her broader training with them. She is allowed to pass inside the mud walls which bar men. In the family courtyards she can visit and share with women like her nearest neighbor, a young Brahman woman. Her house walls are joined on all three sides by the house walls of other castes. She has never seen the other Brahman women of the village, because she would have to cross a lane to get to them. She sees only those women of lower castes who come into her courtyard as irregular helpers or those who may talk to her when she climbs to the top of her own wall and peers down into their courtyard. Her knowledge of the lanes and houses and families of the village comes to her through her small sons and serving women. Beyond the village she knows only the road to her home village, seen through the holes in a carefully covered bullock cart. Railway trains pass a few miles away, but she has never seen one. She cannot read and does not possess a book or picture. Her husband's younger brother has been married to her younger sister who will come soon to share the courtyard with her. Her only house guests are her husband's two sisters who come to their old home for visits of indefinite duration.

She was terrified of us at first, but like the others, finally called upon us when her troubles were beyond the help of exorcists and prescribers. Her husband and boys constantly brought her reports of our activities in camp, and her fear faded with knowledge. Now she sends one of her sons over when she feels that she is being passed by, to remind the Memsahiba, "You are neglecting your friend." Until she and others like her are free to move beyond their own mud walls, some of us can bring the best of the outside world in to them. They are too intensely personal in their interests to care for any form of impersonal instruction. In some fields their desire to learn is curtailed by superstitious control. But they welcome any knowledge which is not thus banned, and which comes to them through their own happy experiences with their own babies. When once they discover that by adopting a new attitude or method they can serve their loved ones better, they are eager pupils. We cannot expect them to maintain enthusiastic interest in instruction which moves only in one direction—from the visitor to themselves. Like the rest of us, they get more enjoyment and help from knowledge which evolves from an exchange, a sharing of thoughts and experiences. The visitor's contribution may come from extensive study. Theirs comes from intensive experience. If we who come to serve them are prepared to listen as well as to teach, we shall find that in exchange for our contribution from the outside world they have much of value from their own severe schooling to share with us.

CHAPTER VII

The Younger Generation

Cheerfully unmindful of activities connected with the study, our two small sons set about making friends in their own way. As soon as the village children recovered from the shock of our fair skin and hair, they ventured further and further across the road, and into our camp. They were free from misgivings as to our motives—and our play wagon and tricycle were alluring. A slight gesture of welcome brought them crowding about both cycle and wagon. They were soon racing freely between our tents. There was no noticeable difference in the approach of our boys to village children here, and their approach to American children whom they met elsewhere. Each was true to his own form—Arthur, the elder, making his overtures with a shy smile, and Alfred, the younger, advancing with a punch. The difference lay in the response which they received. Warned by fearful parents, our little village friends assume a deference which, had it survived, would have made natural play impossible. It did survive long enough for the punch to run riot, and put the bolder ones on the defensive and the weaker ones to flight. Any other barriers which parents may have introduced were too artificial to hold for children. We still find mothers who try to enforce disclipine with the threat: "The Sahib and Memsahiba will take you away if you do that again." We hear this less and less, however; when it does slip out it has little effect on the child, and is rebuked by friendly parents and children nearby. The children know us and our family life too thoroughly to be impressed by any fabled terrors.

Language was the most lasting handicap. The village boys expressed themselves in a flow of village Hindustani, and were surprised when their new friends could not understand. Our boys tried gestures and a mixture of tongues. The conglomerate effect so delighted the village children that they constantly invited buffoonery on the part of our two. We were not fully conscious of the language handicap until a full-fledged, English-speaking Indian high-school student appeared in the village. A few of our village boys had made a start in English, but only enough to warrant an occasional "good night" and "thank you." This boy spoke it with ease, and always carried a hockey stick as patent of his advanced education. He came to get his wife, whose home is in our village. But he was so delighted at this opportunity for English practice that he stayed on, and came for additional visits to his in-laws, an unconventional proceeding in our village. When he and his hockey stick appeared in the grove, there was a shout from Arthur, "There's my friend," and an echo from Alfred, "My friend," as they rushed from play or meals to greet him. The apparent satisfaction found in a companionship without word constraint was revealing. Now that village-Hindustani flows more easily, the relationship with neighbor boys more nearly approaches that of "my friend." During his school holidays Arthur sits in our night class among village boys of his own age, reading and writing Hindi, a joint struggle which makes their relationship more natural.

The friendship of the children has proved an asset on which we had not counted. The smaller boys and girls of the village wander wild and free, and serve as scouts and messengers from their shut-in mothers and field-bound fathers. From the beginning they have observed and faithfully reported our household, office, and dispensary activities, destroying the last vestiges of suspicion. When talking with men or women in the village, we are still entertained by graphic pictures of ourselves as the children see us, with laughing descriptions of our dish-washing with soap and hot water, our bread, and our cutlery, or imitations of our tone and expression as we drive them from the tent door at rest time, or call out to them to "take turns" on the car-tire swing. Just as they report our doings within the village, they are eager to report to us any interesting village happenings, to which they are more sensitive than their parents. They have urged us to go to every scene of activity, sometimes trifling, but often of value to a study of village life. At other times while they hover about our desks, they are happy to lend their bit toward checking figures and facts. Their information is without prejudice and fairly dependable because of their free share in grown-up activities. Often in their heated arguments over some question we have asked, they rouse in us doubts which might have passed unstirred.

Best of all, through their play in our camp, they have made us aware of certain village attitudes which we would have been slow to recognize in our fragmentary observations of adult village life. Every child imbibes caste prejudice before he takes his first steps. Never does he permit himself to be touched by one of the sweeper children. If in an unguarded moment he runs the risk of pollution, he is snatched to a zone of safety by a big sister or brother. In our grove the *bhangi* children, whom we persistently treat as Christians, enjoy privileges which are granted them nowhere else in the village. Higher caste youngsters resent this. But they have too much fun here to show their resentment by staying away. When a few small Christians get one of the wagons, they can monopolize it as long as they choose. No one dares go near enough to take it away. Once or twice caste children have attempted stone-throwing to exert long-distance pressure, but stone-throwing has been forbidden in our grove.

A few days ago a small girl of "twice-born" heritage came to the Memsahiba with the complaint, "Muni won't give me a turn at the swing." Muni is the son of the Christian teacher-pastor and ranks as an untouchable. At that moment Muni raced off after one of his companions. The little girl saw her chance and snatched the swing. While she swung and sang serenely, Muni returned with a rush. There was a shriek and a swirl of full skirts as she leapt and fled, breathless, but saved from a touch of his untouchable hands or garments. Had he been a higher-caste child she would have clung to the swing and fought for her place.

Untouchable children other than *bhangis* are not treated as untouchables, but are constantly reminded of their station. If a child of higher caste orders one of them to pull him and his baby sister around in a cart, the small untouchable does it without demur. The same attitude exists in lesser degree among those of serving castes. If a high-caste boy comes to the tent door to look in or to talk to our boys, low-caste children give way to him at once. One of our greatest problems with our own children has been the preservation in them of democracy. When they began playing with children of the village, a boy was a boy to them, and not a member of some particular class. They had not learned the first question which comes to a villager's lips on meeting a stranger: "Of what caste are you?" When caste boys came over and found one of our boys busy digging a miniature well with a Christian, they tried to explain that this must not, could not, be done, They turned to us for arbitration. We tried to explain our attitude sympathetically. They had to be satisfied. They were in our camp. Since then, our boys have defended the Christians on occasions when the latter have been driven off, even to the point of teasing the higher-caste children about their snobbishness. But they frequently yield to the call of the larger, more active group and skip gaily away from their loyalty to the oppressed.

It is easy for boys the ages of our two to adopt the ways of the sons of village leaders. When once they experienced the sense of power over others, they found it pleasant enough to use it. To one of Alfred's age, it is particularly satisfying. He knows what game he wants to play, and summons the children of lower castes to follow. Or he wants a ride in a cart, and lets them pull him indefinitely. If one of them resists, he applies his bat or bow, or anything at hand. The unhappy victim flies to us for shelter. Arthur, the elder, with his longer periods in school among equals, prefers to play with the boys of higher caste with whom there is more give and take. We have our bullies, as we would have anywhere in a community of boys. But here power rests not so much with the physically strong, as with the socially high. When the two qualifications are joined in one lad, then do the humble cower.

As we have watched the babies pass from short vests into loin cloths or full skirts, and the older children being fitted into the pattern of grown-up men and women, we have realized the meagerness of their childhood as compared with that of our own or other children protected from the burdens of adult life. Dumbir is slightly older than Arthur. When we first came, he was with us almost daily, delighting in every plaything and every detail of our life which he shared. Last year we missed him until he passed through the grove herding goats. He was old enough to help, and was given almost a man's responsibility. Later his father lost his goats through debt, Dumbir was employed by another goatherd, and his duties increased. One day last year his elder brother came sobbing to our door. Beside him stood Dumbir, silent, scared, propping up his right arm from which blood streamed and a piece of bone protruded. He had fallen from a tree while breaking off dead branches for firewood. We hurried him to the hospital where he was obliged to remain almost a month. We visited him whenever we were in town and found him eager as ever to see and enjoy. We took him with us to the shops and to services in the chapel opposite the hospital, where he sat open-eyed and open-mouthed. His only complaint during the prolonged stay was that he was failing to earn his daily bread. This winter he tried to come to our night school but had to work too late to get here. Whenever he can, he brings his goats our way, and snatches a few moments of play on the swing or tricycle. Meanwhile, Arthur's childhood has changed but little. He has outgrown colored suits and gone into khaki, has passed through several grades at school and become a Cub Scout. The burden of earning daily bread is still far from him.

Lakshmi was as free in our grove as the squirrels. Everyone deferred to her as daughter of the head of the village. When the girls played games by themselves, she was always given first turn and never allowed to lose. She was one of the few girls permitted to attend school, and went racing past with the boys on her way home to a hurried lunch. We found her so lovable that we spoiled her as much as the rest. Last year we saw less and less of her, and this year she comes only for treatments of a troublesome ear. She comes shyly, self-consciously, drawing her scarf over the side of her face toward the Sahib, with whom she has always been on natural, friendly terms. The reason is that Lakshmi is about to be married. She sits demurely among the women, or busies herself with her baby sister and her nephews and nieces, hearing about the search for a suitable husband and the great preparations for her wedding. Her father has told us that he intends to take advantage of the recently enacted Sarda bill in postponing her marriage. Judging from past experiences, his more conservative brother and the women of the household will admit no such unorthodox procedure, and will take advantage of the intervening months before the law comes into effect.

Shanti, living just across the road from our camp, in the untouchable section of the village, is slightly younger than Lakshmi, and was equally attractive until smallpox left her blind. Now one eyeball protrudes from between the lids and the other has almost disappeared. She is a loyal little Christian, joyfully singing the *bhajans* and retelling the stories we have taught her. We arranged for her to attend a school for blind girls. But at the last moment her parents refused to let her go. "Her mother will cry if she has to part with her," was the only excuse her father could offer. As we learned more of the work of the blind school, the more we wanted Shanti to share its advantages. Repeatedly her parents said that they were ready to let her go, and then found some need for her at home. Later it was made known that they were afraid of losing any stray opportunity of marrying her off. Their greatest obligation to her was to find a husband, a difficult undertaking with her disfigurement. All of our plans were unessential compared with this paramount duty.

More than a year ago we were told that a husband had been found. Then the engagement was postponed because the prospective husband was sent to jail for stealing. Again we hoped, and Shanti whispered that now school might be possible. But a prospective son-in-law, even though in jail, was not to be ignored. And Shanti waited. She asked the Memsahiba to teach her a prayer that would help her husband. She is troubled at the prospect of the treatment which she, a bungling wife, will recieve. We have given up hope of working through her parents, who have avoided the teacher-pastor and ourselves except when they need favors. Our hope rests in the desire of her husband to have a wife whose hands are useful though her sight is gone. Shanti, like Lakshmi, has changed from a carefree child to a little woman during the past two years. But the constant reminders of the troubles she is causing her parents, and the insecurity of her future position have brought more seriousness and resignation into her life.

One by one the boys and girls in Arthur's age group have been called to do their share toward family support. We find them at work as we go through the fields, guiding the streams of water that flow in from the irrigation ditches, herding the cattle, driving the bullocks which draw the water bags up from the wells, or working beside their fathers at the craft of their particular caste. Everyone is too busy to teach them anything beyond the labor associated with daily bread. They see no books, and in their leisure evenings during slack seasons, they hear nothing beyond village gossip and occasional singing. They race over to us whenever they are free, to catch a glimpse of the outside world through their tireless questions, or to beg a short ride on the car if they hear it start, or perhaps to play a game of *kabaddi* by moonlight.

When the girls leave our grove, they go to stay—in their own or neighboring courtyards, and later in the homes of their husbands in other villages. When they return for a visit, they send one of the children to call the Memsahiba to come to them. Our grove is too public for them to come.

The changes in Alfred's age group, though not so momentous, are surprising. Once a Mainpuri friend conveyed to us an old saying: "Treat your son as a rajah until he is five, as a slave until he is fifteen, and then as a friend." The change which occurs when a child is about five seems to concur with this. Babies who were riding around on sisters' hips and lying on the ground and screaming for what they wanted, are now faithful nurses of younger sisters and brothers, or nieces and nephews. Boys who had room made for them on one of the wagons by older children, are now themselves fighting for places for someone younger. Little girls who howled if someone did not give them mud carts, are now industriously making them for some smaller person.

Sarmani, who is six, helps her mother every morning before going out to play, and when she goes, it is almost always with her baby brother riding her hip—because he refuses to let mother do her work. When baby brother's eyes are red, she gravely presents him at the dispensary tent for treatment and holds him more courageously than her mother could. When she follows us around, begging for something, it may be a picture or a pencil for herself, but more often stockings or a rattle or an empty ink bottle for her brother. Watching our children has awakened in her a desire for something beyond playthings of paper and clay, the bits of broken clay jars, and grass bracelets and rings which are all that village children have. Whatever she wants is for her small brother, rather than for herself.

The young men of the village, though too grown up to be interested in the activities of our children are not too dignified to take a turn on a slide or a bat at the ball when they are free from the almost constant grind of field work. At Christmas time we have one afternoon of sports for them, and they come hurrying in early from their fields. They go into the races and games with ardor, and are as excited over the prize-giving as the smaller boys. In spite of their regular, heavy toil, they are unused to sports, and go limping about their work for several days afterward. Last year we introduced the high jump. They were unwilling to try it because it was new, until the Sahib went over, followed by Kishore, the grey-haired village clown.

Our sports day in which all share is a new experience for most of them. In their own amusements the performers are few and the audience large. During the hot weather, there are wrestling matches in which the goldsmith brothers star.

On certain rare occasions a group of *kahar* youths appear in a series of short racy dramas. In connection with big weddings there are *nautches* (dances) and perhaps a play enacted by a traveling group. Once a year there is the big fair on the outskirts of Mainpuri which gives them a few days of concentrated excitement. At about the same time comes the *Holi* festival in which they run riot. These and the dramatic ceremonies associated with other scattered religious festivals, are the extent of their recreation. During the rest of the year they are engulfed by work.

The boys of humble caste take up the traditional work of their fathers, without questioning the attractiveness of their work or their own fitness for it. It is theirs to do, and they accept it. The boys of high caste—Brahmans, in our village— have had a little more schooling and are not so content to follow their fathers as slaves of the fields. They are restless until routine finally takes the edge from their desire for change.

One of these is Surgan, who might have gone on to high school had he not spent his time and money gambling. He is married. He and his wife live in his father's house. He is dependent on his father for employment, food, clothing, and housing. His appetite for gambling often leads him to borrow money from his aunts or to steal some of his father's grain. Twice he has run away from home, but not beyond reach. Now when he threatens to leave, the women of the family send for the Memsahiba and beg her, for their sakes, to produce some interest that will hold him in the village. The Memsahiba looks at his young wife, pretty in spite of her pock marks, and wonders why he needs more than her attractions. It is difficult to find work that he, a Brahman, is willing to do. We suddenly remember that we must add to our collection of stories and songs, and employ him during his spare time. He earns enough to pay back his importunate aunts and to buy something for his wife, while enjoying the

importance of being an individual. The crisis passes, temporarily. His father needs his help in his scattered fields,
and is distressed lest his son desert him. Yet, after adminis-
tering a beating, he expresses the desire that the boy go out
and get his fill of the world and return, thankful for the protection and advantages of the paternal home.

Another Brahman youth returned to the village last year
after completing the work of the eighth grade in Mainpuri.
He has gone further in school than anyone else in the village.
He is one of several sons, and it was his father's ambition,
as well as his own, that he find some remunerative office job,
beyond the boundaries of Karimpur. No post has offered itself, and the boy sits in front of his father's storehouse or
passes his time doing odd jobs, disgruntled, dissatisfied. He
will not throw himself into farm work, because he is always
hoping for some opportunity which he has learned to regard
as superior. We have put him in charge of our night school,
and he has enjoyed the experience, although he confessed a
few days ago that it has convinced him that he does not want
to take a teacher's training course.

Another boy of the same caste group attended the Mission
School in Mainpuri for a year after finishing the third grade
in the village school. He did not enjoy school restraints,
and his widowed mother made it possible for him to go to
Calcutta to work. This was a real adventure. Last spring
when the Memsahiba was bound for Calcutta, his mother im-
plored her to bring him back. After a futile search in the
labyrinths of Calcutta lanes, the Memsahiba returned with no
news of him—to find that he had just come home, in time to
take part in the Holi festivities. He remained at home for
some months, unwilling to relieve his mother of her worries
over fields which were almost impossible for her to supervise
as a *purdahnashin*—a woman who does not appear in public.
He finally attached himself to the learned *pundit* of a petty
rajah not far away, and is trying to study Sanskrit. Weekly,

he threatens to leave. But his mother is proud of his association with a learned man, and is counting on her younger son to take charge of her fields. The latter's education is being limited to what our village school has to offer.

In families such as these, our loyalty is divided. We appreciate the feelings of the parents who have always taken for granted that their sons will succeed them, or will restore the family to its old standing, far above manual labor. We sympathize with the sons who do not know what place there is for them in the town, and who hold back from the unrelieved monotony of village life. We once heard a disappointed American mother advise a younger mother of four sons living on a farm: "If you want to keep your boys here, don't send them to a university." The same warning might have been given in our village, with "town school" substituted for university. The boys who know nothing beyond village routine are content. Those who have gone to school are restless. They have disassociated learning from the work which their fathers have to offer them, and they have glimpsed a life full of interesting activity and tempting variety. It is for them that we want schoolmasters who will raise farming from its old standing of drudgery to a position of interest and honor in the curriculum. It is for them and their younger brothers and sisters that we would encourage a new rural life with a share of the recreation, the literature, and the art now limited to the towns.

We acknowledge that such a program demands skillful building. It is remote from that which now holds fast in the village and not at all like that we find in the town. But the possibilities are there. Its attainment calls for rural teachers and other servants of society with training and attitudes far different from that of the two teachers who are now the only link between the world of science and culture, and the village. These two drone faithfully through the alphabet and sums with our boys and girls, and as soon as school is over, lock the iron gate and trudge home to their own village two miles away. It demands men who are statesmen, fortified with all the skill and facts which education can offer. For they will have to deal with parents who are convinced the present regime is the safest for their boys and girls, and who have fixed ideas of what farming, education, and social life should be. They will have to convince leaders that the advantages they want for their own sons are available within the village. They will have to persuade these same leaders that other boys of humble origin should have equal opportunities with their own sons. There are plenty of difficulties—enough to challenge the best which ambitious youth with the advantages of education is willing to share with the equally worthy but less favored youth of the village. They who are ready and equipped to meet the challenge, will be welcomed enthusiastically by our boys, who are restlessly searching for they know not what, and more gradually by the boys who are now content but who rejoice over the advent of anything new and helpful. They will find quiet support among those parents who are ambitious for their sons but restrained by the old order.

Agents of Authority

When a villager approaches our tent looking burdened and distressed, we are fairly sure that either someone is suffering at home—his bullock, his child, or his wife—or some agent of authority is on his trail. If the cause of his trouble is illness, we can express our sympathy in immediate action. If it is an agent, we can only sympathize, since we have learned the difficulty of seeking justice in such cases. We might as well try to help the farmer rescue his field from a storm of hail or a swarm of locusts. When a clever agent makes use of a villager to further his own ends, he takes care to leave no trace of his activity other than the straightened circumstances and bitterness of his victim. It is the story of the unscrupulous strong taking advantage of the ignorant weak, which might be heard anywhere. One would judge from the titles and duties of these agents that they were here simply to serve as links between the village and officials or landowners. But the villager has learned to his sorrow that the chief interest of most of them is their own profit and that of certain men directly above them. Their offices of trust are used to gain a formidable hold over the villagers whom they nominally serve.

The office of village headman is honorary. He is a resident of the village, appointed by the government to represent the village in all matters pertaining to authority. He knows the village and the history of every person in it better than any official could hope to, and is in a position to give useful information regarding offenders against the law. The man usually selected as headman is an outstanding leader. His established leadership added to the weight of his testimony as official spokesman for the village make it possible for him to demand bribes from innocent men who will pay to save themselves the consequences of false charges, and from offenders who will pay to protect themselves against true charges. Also, he has opportunities of winning privileges for himself and his friends through men of low official standing if he is ready to share with them the spoils of his own powers.

Fortunately for Karimpur, our headman has not, to the best of our knowledge, yielded to the tempting proposals made to him. He is interested in his farming, the lending of grain and money, and his religious observances. He regards the office of headman as just one more set of duties to be performed. He gives space on his *baithak*—the broad, unroofed veranda of packed earth before his storehouse—to the government accountant and his assistant. The village watchmen report any possible cases to him. The police constable stops to see him while on his beat, to share the latest bits of police news, and if possible to add something from Karimpur.

If a supervising officer visits the village, he directs the headman to call offenders to his *baithak* for interviews. When some petty officer wants clarified butter, fuel, or labor for wedding festivities, the request is brought to the headman, who is expected to supply whatever is demanded from among his neighbors. Or some other official's servant may tell him to procure a load of fodder for his master's animals from time to time. For fear of displeasing the official who is supposed to have ordered the fodder, the headman takes the required amount from one or two farmers and gives it to the servant. The servant charges his master for the load, and keeps the money. While our headman tries to improve the condition of his people by digging wells and making loans at fair rates, he is called upon to drain the village for the comfort of outsiders. This he has resented to the point of threatening to resign on several occasions.

His unwillingness to take advantage of opportunities for extortion has often irritated those who would profit by his connivance. A year ago a farmer boy fell into the well from which he was drawing the big leather bag of water. He was pulled out at once, while someone came to call us. His skull had been fractured when he struck the stone side of the well. The Sahib took him into the Mainpuri hospital in the hope that he might be saved, but he died that night. His relatives brought him home and came to us early the next morning to ask if it would be all right for them to follow the usual custom of immediate cremation. In their dread of offending the law, that required investigation by a police officer, they wanted us to take the responsibility, which the Sahib unwittingly did. He saw no reason for delaying the cremation as the case had been handled by the Assistant Medical Officer in the district hospital, where all accident cases are immediately reported to the police.

In the afternoon a police officer appeared, irate that the boy had been burned before he was able to make the investigation. He involved the headman in the case by pointing to a section of the government rules for headmen which stated that the body of anyone meeting an unnatural death must be shown to the police before burning. The rules were in Urdu, in Arabic script, which neither the headman nor any other villager could read. The infuriated police officer warned the headman that he would fare better if he would consult the village police watchman in such cases.

Later it evolved that the watchman had worked out a scheme whereby it could be proved, at least sufficiently to terrify the relatives of the boy, that he had been thrown into the well. The watchman took for granted that the relatives would not dare burn the body until they had been granted police permission to do so. He knew that custom forbade them to bathe or eat until after the cremation. He counted on their fasting and waiting beside the unembalmed body all night and through the heat of the day, to reduce them to a state of mental apathy. By the time the police officer arrived late in the afternoon, with word that they had been charged with murder they would have been ready to add or pay whatever he demanded. Anything to save themselves from such a charge, and anything to pacify him so that they might proceed with the cremation.

As it was, they were bathed and fed, and ready to face the obviously invented charge in a normal frame of mind. The headman with our amateur support had frustrated the plan. The villagers conjectured that our "blunder" had saved the kachhi family between seventy-five and a hundred rupees. The murder theory was not suggested to the headman again. He, like ourselves, knew the harmlessness of this particular family in which the accident occurred, a family of simple farmer folk who would not take the life of a rat and certainly not the life of a member of their own family. Moreover, as a farmer, he knew the economic value of a boy of fourteen, entering his most useful years. To associate such a death with deliberate murder was the work of troublemakers with whom he could not fraternize.

The two village watchmen, representatives of the police in the village, receive an honorarium of three rupees a month. This is to reimburse them for their fortnightly trips to headquarters with reports of births and deaths, and any occurrences of interest to the police department. It is taken for granted that they carry on their usual activities as farmers or tradesmen. One of the watchmen, an untouchable, has little

ambition either financial or social, and is content to live on his
honorarium supplemented by trifling donations and the earnings of his wife. The other, an untouchable of slightly
higher standing, first gave us the impression that his police
duties occupied his full time, and that he was poorly paid for
his arduous labors. But as we observed his activities, we found
them to be of his own making and for his own benefit. He
was associated with a small group of men of means and influence in the village, in an alliance which was able to bring
any villager to their terms, or to ruin. A complaint of his
abuse of office was forwarded to one of the landlords, who
recommended that his land agent take steps toward the
watchman's dismissal. The steps were not taken. After an interim of quiet, the watchman renewed his activities, special-
izing on the men who had pressed for his removal. Each
case was so petty that in itself it seemed childish. Yet an
accumulation of such cases was exhausting the savings and
patience of farmers.

The plight of Lakhan, a farmer by caste, is fairly illustrative.
He was cutting grain, and his wife was gleaning. The watchman came to him and announced, "Someone has broken your
lock. Report the theft." Lakhan ran home, found his lock
broken, but nothing touched in his house. He was unwilling
to report a theft for fear of being trapped. Whereupon the
watchman threatened to make a charge against him at police
headquarters for withholding information from the police. The
only thing that could dissuade him from making the report
was fifty rupees. Lakhan raised the fifty rupees—enough to
buy a bullock, or a milk animal. Then the watchman threatened Lakhan's neighbors, saying that they would be accused
of theft if they did not give him something. Six frightened
farmers, never far from starvation, each gave him money ranging from three to eight rupees; and six others gave him head
loads of grain, to induce him not to take them to police headquarters.

Our watchman is a skilled opportunist. One day a Muslim landlord and a friend rode near one of the hamlets within the area of our village. They were hunting, and had no interest whatever in the people. But the watchman hurried importantly to the house of a farmer, reporting that the relative then visiting him had committed some wrong and that two high police officers had come to arrest him. The farmer, peering from his door, saw two imposing individuals sitting in an ekka—a high, two-wheeled cart—not far from his house. The watchman assured him that for one hundred rupees he could persuade the officers to leave the relative alone. The farmer was able to satisfy his demands with seventy rupees, and breathed a sigh of relief when he dared look out again and found the strangers gone.

On another occasion, a Brahman boy struck the washerman's daughter while the two were gathering grain from a field shared by their two families. The girl came home crying, and told her tale to everyone she met, including the headman. When the boy passed on his way home the headman stopped and rebuked him for striking the girl, and the affair was dropped—but not by the watchman. Shortly afterward he appeared at the boy's home with a police constable displaying a supposed warrant. He stated that the boy was reported as having assaulted the girl with evil intent. The father, who with his son was always at work in his fields, was bewildered by this sudden attack. His neighbor, one of the village elders, advised him to quiet the affair by paying the fifty rupees demanded. He paid. But, sure of the falseness of the charge, he said that he would accompany the constable to the head office in Mainpuri and see that the proper officer received the money. When they neared the office, the constable told the old man to wait for him a moment while he stepped into his house to see his wife. He disappeared and did not return. The old farmer, realizing that he had been fooled, went on to the police office. No one there knew what he was talking about, and he was put out as a troublesome old man.

The villagers have accounted for the fifty rupees thus— twenty stayed with the constable, fifteen went to the watchman who utilized the opportunity, and fifteen to the village elder who advised the farmer to pay the amount. Incidentally, the headman was rebuked for settling the case quietly as he did. The police implied that he was trying to hush something which should have been put into their hands. The agents who concoct such schemes are careful to avoid tangible evidence. They know that the word of an agent is accepted in the district court in preference to that of a villager, in case an exposure is attempted. They have no intention of writing such petty but profitable cases up in the report book at police headquarters. Hence higher officials who must depend on records, have no means of investigating them. The watchman continued to apply himself to these and similar questionable activities until a group of farmers asked our help. A statement was prepared for the Superintendent of Police of the district, signed by thirty men who dared face the consequences of the watchman's wrath, showing how threats of charges of rascality, adultery, gambling, disturbance of the peace, dacoity, or sheltering bad characters, had been brought to bear upon them to make them pay varying sums of money. They presented the statement in person, accompanied by the landlord's agent. At this juncture the Superintendent of Police was being transferred and could only arrange for a suspension of the watchman. Shortly afterward the Sahib was taken to the mountains, ill with typhoid fever. The watchman, with tears of self-pity, assurances that the claims against him were false, and the help of the men directly over him, managed to be reinstated by the new Superintendent at the end of his recess. He returned with threats of revenge to be visited upon the men who had exposed him, one of them a member of his alliance. But warnings from higher official headquarters have turned his activities to farming, at least temporarily.

The village *patwari* and his one assistant, are the only full-time agents of government in the village. With the accountant is a record of every plot of land within the revenue area of Karimpur, what is grown on it, the names of its holders, and their individual rights in it. He enters in his volumes any changes brought about by death, with a statement of the rights of each heir. He notes transfers of holdings, and any alterations in legal rights. Also, he keeps a record of all rents paid to each landlord, and arrears. He must appear in court to give evidence in all cases dealing with land rights in his area. If more of our farmers could read, and if each of them would keep his own authorized copy of the record of his holdings made out by the Settlement Officer every thirty years, along with legal records of current transactions, our accountant would serve as an inoffensive employee. But as long as they do not do this and depend entirely on his annual recordings of their rights, they vest him with powers which he, a low-grade agent, could hardly be expected to disregard. Just as they leave their fields unprotected and are perturbed when men and animals trespass, so they expose their treasured land rights to his avarice, and are upset when he takes advantage. The degree to which any village accountant exceeds his duties, depends upon his aspirations. Ours is evidently among the more ambitious.

His opportunities for extortion lie in the juggling of names when each year he rewrites in detail the voluminous land records. A grove is shared by three or four men. The accountant threatens to drop the name of one of them from the list. Rather than risk sacrificing his rights, the unfortunate one agrees to pay whatever the accountant demands. Such an omission of his name may be tragic for a farmer, if repeated over a period of years, because the omission thereby is legalized. The possibilities of its detection amid the masses of records are slim. Once when such a discrepancy was noted by an examining officer, the accountant blamed the carelessness of his assistant.

An old man is anxious that his nephew's name be entered in the records as heir to his fields. The accountant neglects to make the desired entry until the uncle is desperate enough to pay the fifty rupees demanded, or, when the accountant's evidence is required in a case, he finds some excuse for not giving it, until the men who need it come to his terms. One group of men fighting for rights to land which a family division had scattered, have reported paying him two hundred rupees for his evidence. And he is worrying them for one hundred more. If there is a misunderstanding over field boundaries, and the farmers consult the accountant's records, he demands at least one rupee from each questioner for his trouble. This in spite of the fact that his records are supposed to be accessible to those whose land is recorded. Recently, a question arose about some fields which are sometimes fully, and sometimes partially, submerged in rainy seasons, and therefore only occasionally sown. As the village youth who acts as our helper was involved, the Sahib was asked to accompany the accountant and the farmers to the fields in question. With the aid of land maps and the accountant's records, they settled the difficulty easily. But before they were finished, a crowd of farmers had collected, to ask the accountant for information regarding a number of other boundaries. Disputes had gone on for a long time over some of these boundaries, simply because the only accurate records were in the hands of the accountant, and they were unwilling to pay him the irregular fee which he would demand for explaining the records to them. The farmers now took advantage of the Sahib's presence, to secure the facts which were supposed to be at their disposal. The accountant, though obviously annoyed, was obliged to give the information needed to end the disputes.

A widow, in order to pay a debt, made a five-year transfer of her property to a wealthy grain lender. Having no other income in the village, she went away to visit relatives. Before the five years were up, the grain lender paid the accountant fifty rupees, and the land was transferred to his name. When the woman returned at the end of five years and claimed her land, she was informed that it was no longer hers. The accountant justified the transfer on the grounds of rumor that she had remarried, and thus forfeited her rights. With the help of friends she took the case to court. Her land was given back to her, and the accountant was reprimanded. The grain lender shifted all responsibility for the doubtful transaction to the accountant, as the latter could not safely report the fifty rupees which the grain lender had paid him.

When the accountant finds himself thus exposed, he defends his activities by passing the blame on to others. He reminds the villagers that he is obliged to collect enough money to pay the officer immediately over him eighteen rupees a year—the equivalent of a month of his salary. (The scale of pay for a *patwari* is fourteen rupees per month rising to eighteen rupees.) Also, he must support his family in a manner worthy of his post. Both he and his brother are accountants. Frequent appearances before well-dressed officials require a higher standard of dress than that of the average villager. Frequent calls to distant headquarters necessitate the provision of a horse which needs to be fed. Constant association with higher-grade officials creates a desire to give sons better educational opportunities. Daughters must be married into homes with more advanced standards. All of these make financial drains. It is small wonder that they take advantage of their opportunities.

The two brothers who serve consecutively as *patwari* of our village, maintain a joint household which is more like the stronghold of a prosperous money and grain lender than the home of low-paid agents. The stores of grain, the animals, the jewelry of the women, everything betokens wealth far beyond that of the people whom they serve. When there was a wedding in their family, we were entertained lavishly. Among other things, we were struck by the long line of bullock carts which brought the bridegroom's party from the railway station, six miles to the accountant's village home. This was in our early days, and we were impressed by this show of neighborliness. Later we learned that our friends, the farmers, weren't there with their carts voluntarily. Fear of the displeasure of the accountant had led them to carry out his proposal that they make the procession an imposing one.

One agent of authority defending the practices of his fellow officers, said: "Some of our superior officers are very critical of our dress and appearance, and complain that we are not worthy of our office. They offer us no increase of pay. Yet we have to smarten up. We adjust ourselves to the standards of such an officer, when along comes another who objects to our dress, which he knows cannot be maintained on our low pay. What are we to do?"

During our stay in Karimpur we have had opportunity to get acquainted with the *patwari* family. The younger brother who was accountant when we arrived was transferred because he was unwilling to obey the standing order for accountants and make his residence in Karimpur. He insisted upon living in his ancestral home two miles away. However, the brothers were able to keep Karimpur, which is reputed to be a lucrative area, in the family. The elder brother succeeded the younger. He was equally successful in using the villagers to increase the prosperity of his family. But he finally became trapped as a receiver of stolen goods, and was dismissed. Karimpur has offered little sympathy. The elder brother always looked down on simple village folk, and wasted little time in winning their loyalty. He saw greater strength and security in cultivating the favor of men higher up. And he succeeded in making himself useful. With a su-

perior behind him, in a position to sit in judgment on most
complaints registered against him, he could go farther in his
irregular use of office than he would otherwise have done.
But he had not counted on the transfer of officers. A friendly
superior was transferred before he was able to do all the necessary straightening out. And the *patwari* found himself without a job.

Only two landlords, both absentee, control the property of
Karimpur. Each sends his agents—rent collectors and accountants—several times each season to collect rents and settle disputes within their jurisdiction. Because of responsibilities for
wider areas, their interest in Karimpur is not localized as
that of the government accountant. Their visits are too infrequent to enable them to settle many of the disputes that
exist among the tenants; but not too infrequent to enable
them to take advantage of the gullibility of these same tenants
when opportunity offers. On the receipt forms of one landlord
is a printed statement that nothing beyond the actual rent is
to be paid to the rent collector. Nevertheless, the collector
takes one anna for each receipt he gives out. Some farmers
must pay this on seven or eight receipts for different holdings. In addition he exacts one rupee from each tenant. If
a farmer refuses to pay this, his receipt is made out short of
the full payment. A twelve-year-old friend of ours, looking
after the interests of his widowed mother, brought his receipt
to us, distressed because he was too small to oppose the
agent. He could read, and knew what had been done.

Farmers who cannot read treasure such receipts and are
agitated too late—when faced with the penalty of accumulated arrears. Several worried tenants persuaded the Sahib to
send a letter to the landlord on their behalf. In this he
quoted the statement on the receipt. The landlord sent a supervising officer to investigate. He settled the case to his
own satisfaction by reminding the tenants of their benefits re-

ceived, such as wood for implements and grazing facilities. He suggested they give the rent collector a present of something extra as an expression of their gratitude. Since then, further complaints of the demands of this particular collector have come. But knowing the attitude of the men whom he represents, there seems no chance of redress.

The other landlord has recently doubled the pay of all his employees, in the hope of removing the custom of *nazarana* (a fee or present given by tenants). Through this practice the landlord's agent realized from four to five hundred rupees yearly from the tenants, taking one rupee from each tenant. About two years ago this *zamindar* raised his pay from twenty-five rupees plus ten rupees horse allowance, to forty-five rupees plus fifteen rupees horse allowance, and issued instructions to all tenants that the practice of giving *nazarana* should cease. And it has. The *zamindar* has proved his willingness to put a stop to demands made by his agents on tenants. Unfortunately, his residence is two days' cart journey from Karimpur and there is little likelihood of complaints reaching his ears.

Even the *chaprasis*, farmers called upon occasionally to carry out instructions of the rent collectors, utilize their position. A few weeks ago, one of them demanded a large blanket of home-spun wool from a shepherd, as compensation for the grazing privileges granted by his landlord. The blanket was not wanted for the landlord in accordance with the *wajib-ul-arz* (the customs of the village), but to be kept for himself. Another recently brought pressure to bear upon the new washerman who had been called to the village. The new man took for granted that as village washerman he would occupy the washerman's house. But the landlord's *chaprasi* stepped in and announced that he, the *chaprasi*, must be paid something quietly, before he would allow the washerman to occupy the house. The washerman refused, and was temporarily located in a house belonging to the other landlord.

Pressure was brought to bear on the *chaprasi* by the elders of the village, and he reluctantly gave the washerman possession of the desired house.

If one were to accept the complaints of villagers as final, one would conclude that the acting agents were responsible for all abuses of office. If this were so, their removal would be the cure for all irregularities. But it is not as simple as this—while ignorance and superstition remain to encourage misuse of power. A young Indian official who happened to be visiting us when the village watchman was at his worst, expressed his view thus: "If you were to take one of the most harmless men in your village and put him in the watchman's place, he would be a rascal within six months." This may be extreme. But it would be difficult to find men willing to serve in these petty offices who would be above the temptations which now prevail. The sense of power and sudden popularity among leaders which a man experiences on finding himself an agent of some outside authority, is in itself a danger. If he tests the new power, and finds that he does not inspire fear, he may be content to perform his duties without further ventures. But if he finds his neighbors easily intimidated, and if his personal ambition or the subtle suggestions from village leaders or from men higher up urge him on, he repeats his assertions of power until he becomes a hardened tyrant.

Illiterate, ignorant of their rights, dominated by the fear of the known and of the unknown, our more simple minded villagers are an invitation to oppression. They are the ones who suffer most from the tyranny of unscrupulous agents.

On the other hand, there are the men accustomed to lead, fairly well informed as to their rights, and well acquainted with the tactics necessary to increase their own wealth and power. They are too sophisticated to be awed by the underofficers of authority whom they meet in the village. Instead, they use these agents to serve their own ends. With the

simple minded farmer, the accountant is the one who takes
the initiative in threatening to change the records. But often
it is the leaders who make the overtures to the accountant.
They offer to pay him liberally if he will change the records
to their advantage. If the change goes undetected, their gain
is beyond the payment they have given him. If it is detected,
they quietly watch him suffer the blame, knowing that he cannot safely acknowledge the acceptance of bribes. The representatives of the police in the village are still more accessible
as tools of the powerful. Being of untouchable origin, they
take for granted that they are to follow the bidding of the
leaders. The result has been that on several occasions our
original condemnation of agents has had to be transferred to
more clever men behind them. Where clever leaders and
clever agents are combined, they are a menace to simple,
self-respecting all-fearing villagers.

If several villagers agree that they will assert their rights
and expose the wrong-doings of an agent on the next provocation, the agent has little to fear. When the provocation comes
each man suspects the others may be afraid to act and will
leave him standing alone against the agent. Knowing that he
dare not face the consequences of standing alone, he does
what he thinks the others are doing—and suffers in silence.
It was only when a group of men were so pressed that
they must either expose the *chaukidar* (village watchman)
or leave their homes, that they publicly announced their
oppression. After reaching this point it required further time
and courage for them to commit themselves by affixing their
thumb impressions as signatures to a written statement. As
long as an agent can manipulate his activities in such a way
as not quite to drive farmers over the desperation line, he
knows that he is safe from exposure.

Removal of acting agents will not relieve our village friends
from oppression, while existing conditions are maintained.
On the side of the villagers is needed education, not only

cultural and industrial, but in legal rights and still more in community responsibilities. They have not yet learned that as long as each of them works for favors for his own family, regardless of its cost to a fellow villager, they will play into the hands of the unscrupulous. On the side of the agents, a definite understanding as to sources of income is needed. If the authority represented, be it government or landlord, regards the salaries of agents as only partial payment to be supplemented by funds collected from those served, misunderstandings are inevitable. Our *chaukidars* are expected to supplement their pay with their caste trade. This they do to a certain extent. If supplementary support is expected from the villagers, an equally shared tax or a fixed rate for services would be fairer than the present system whereby the clever escape, and the simple pay.

But while the villager's income is such a gamble, he will be shy of any form of fixed payment. In his present state he wants the freedom of informal and irregular methods which leave him the chance of escape. When he is in better control of the vagaries of nature, and thus stabilizes his income, it will be easier for him to accept a regular share of the payment of public servants.

The officers superior to our village agents must likewise cooperate if the standards of service of our local agents are to be raised. To our young Indian friends eager to serve their country, we repeatedly pass on the need as we have observed it: "Take offices of responsibility, and fill them worthily. Make no selfish demands of officers below you, demands which will be passed on down the line until they reach the burden bearers—the villagers. Talking will not help. Villagers have listened long enough. They need men who will give them justice, and who will demand honesty from them in return."

A recent happy experience has shown us what an officer of high standards can do. A young deputy of our area of the district expected no personal gifts from men below him. Instead, he lived within his salary, and ordered them to do the same. He has undertaken a colossal housecleaning. And he is being misunderstood and criticized by upholders of the old regime. But his reward is the growing confidence of the villagers in his area. It has not taken them long to learn that he is honestly trying to mete out justice. Our village friends are too occupied with immediate problems to take much interest in affairs of state. Governors and councils are figures whose activities are remote. Even the heads of departments of their own district do not loom large on their horizon. Villagers judge the government and landlords by the most subordinate representatives—the agents of authority—with whom they have personal contacts in the village world.

CHAPTER IX

"Let All Things Old Abide"

In times of pleasure and of sorrow, under stress of excitement or of fear, and in quiet noonday and evening talks, our village friends have presented to us the Case for the Village. Certain points have been reiterated until we are almost immune to their force, while others have been touched lightly. There are statements which we have been tempted to smooth out for the sake of our own feelings or those of friends, and points at which explanations seem to be called for. But we have tried to set forth the case as the villagers present it, without interfering with their candor. In the process of translation, and for the sake of those who are easily shocked, we have sacrificed some of the zest of village speech, with its rough jokes and picturesque local allusions, but aside from this, we have done our best to follow actual conversations. It is not we, but our village friends who speak.

"To a newcomer we may seem suspicious, obstinate, intolerant, backward—everything that goes with refusal to change. We did not choose these characteristics for ourselves. Exper-

ience forced them upon our fathers. And the warnings of our
fathers, added to our own experiences, have drilled them into
us. Refusal to change is the armor with which we have
learned to protect ourselves. If we and our fathers had accepted the new ideas and customs commended to us, we
might have made greater progress. But greater progress would
have drawn the eyes of a covetous world toward us. And
then our lot would have been worse than before. Where are
the cities that flourished for a time? In ruins. While they
climbed to great heights and fell to the depths of destruction,
we kept to the old reliable level. And we have survived. We
are not blind to the advantages of the new, but unless we
know just where it will lead us, we prefer to let it pass us by.

"At times you cannot hide your impatience with our caution. There was the plow which you urged us to accept.
You saw only the advantages it offered in turning our soil during the months when it has always lain packed and hard.
We saw beyond that. We felt the added perspiration of working in the killing sun of June, and saw the risk of exposing
our bullocks to the cruelty of heat and sun, especially when
they are hardly strong enough to pull such a plow. You know
how we dread the sickness or loss of an animal. We knew the
weight of the plow and foresaw the difficulties of carrying
it on our shoulders from one small plot to another far away.
And we saw the eyes of rent collectors, greedily watching the
results of our added toil. We were sorry to disappoint you,
but we could not risk such an expensive and doubtful experiment, when the benefits would most likely not stay with us.
The plow that Bala's brother won at your exhibition last
spring is better. It is light, like our plows, and good for
ordinary plowing. But Bala's brother has not dared to use it.
He is so prosperous that he is afraid of anything that makes
a show of still greater prosperity. In that he may seem foolish
to you. But we do not blame him for his caution.

"When you insisted upon entering your *bhangi* pastor's boy
in school, we set up all the defenses our intolerance could

supply. All our lives we have watched *bhangis* at their defiling work. No matter how much you clean them up and change their names, they are repulsive to us. From the time when our earliest impressions were formed we have despised them. You can let yourself forget the work which they do, and the flesh of swine which they eat. We cannot. Much more important than this is the change which might come from their new way of living and thinking. *Bhangis* might prove troublesome if not kept *bhangis*. They must stay where they have always been, and remain content with the work which is theirs to do. If they want to rise to something better, who then will keep our village clean? Each of us has been born to his appointed task. Perhaps we are what we are because of former lives. We do not know. Everything is in the hands of the gods. But this we do know: The old order has served us well for centuries. It has provided a task for everyone who is born into it. And it has provided for the carrying out of every task needed for village self-sufficiency, by men trained from childhood. If change once begins, how far will it go? What if *bhangis* should try to be farmers, and farmers try to be carpenters, and carpenters try to be teachers? There would be confusion and wrangling, and work badly done. No, the old order with its unalterable allotments is much more satisfactory.

"If we can assure ourselves that the better implement or the more generous custom will lead to no harmful consequences to ourselves, we may try to make it ours. We have replaced many of our charms with treatments which you or your doctors have advised. We have made changes in our houses, because we have seen that they are good and that they involve no risks. We are sowing new seed because we have been shown the better crops on the demonstration farm. You must be patient with our slowness and caution. An arm that has long been held stiff cannot be bent without effort and complainings. Our sons with their reading and their larger world may insist upon more changes. If so, we pray that

they may have means of self-protection to cover their progress. For us who are not wise in the ways of the new world,
the old, well-measured ways are safest.

"Our walls which conceal all that we treasure, are a necessary part of our defense. Our forefathers hid themselves
from a covetous world behind mud walls. We do the same.
Barriers are no longer needed as protection against cruel raid-
ers., But they are needed against those ruthless ones who
come to extort. For the old purpose, our fathers built their
walls strong enough to shut out the enemy, and made them
of earth so that they might be inconspicuous. For the present
purpose they must remain inconspicuous and yet be high
enough to conceal us and our possessions from the greedy
ones. But now they are better protection if instead of being
kept strong they are allowed to become dilapidated. Dilapi-
dation makes it harder for the covetous visitor to tell who is
actually poor and who simulates proverty. When men become so strong that the agents of authority work with them
for their mutual benefit, they dare to expose their prosperity
in walls of better materials and workmanship. But if the
ordinary man suddenly makes his will conspicuous, the extor-
tioner is on his trail. You remember what a short time it
was after Puri put up his imposing new veranda with a good
grass roof, that the police watchman threatened to bring a
false charge against him. He paid well for his show of progress. Old walls tell no tales.

"Neither do old clothes. When we are to deal with strangers we choose our dress to the occasion, not to our means.
And most occasions call for poor clothes. You have heard
them complain in the hospital that they are at a loss to know
who should be charity patients and who should pay. We
would be foolish to bring upon ourselves big bills, when the
simple matter of dress will give us charity rates. The Memsahiba let appearances influence her that first year when she
picked out what she thought were the ten poorest among our
children. She did the choosing, so we did not interfere. They

had learned the most effective way of appealing to her sympathies, by word and dress. And their reward was a ride in the car and new clothes from the landlords' wives in Mainpuri. What a joke we had on the accountant when the new deputy came on tour. There sits friend accountant, looking very smart, all ready for the deputy's arrival. At the last moment someone breaks the news that the new deputy rebukes well-dressed accountants. Tells them they cannot live within their income honestly and have fine clothes. Off comes the new turban, off comes the yellow silk waistcoat. Friend accountant rushes about and borrows a shirt and loin cloth that look neat but old. In these he bows humbly before the deputy Sahib. And some of us who were absent during the rapid change, did not at first recognize our grand accountant in his shabby clothes. The visiting deputy was properly impressed.

"Some may call our pretense of poverty, deception. Perhaps it is. But there are times when deception, as a means of self-protection, is justifiable. When a small mother bird knows that a hawk is overhead watching, does she fly straight to her nest? No, she pretends to go to another spot, and goes to her nest under cover of leafy branches. Nature has taught her to deceive to protect her young. We are like her. There are always hawks hovering about us. We deliberately mislead the inquirer. We would be fools to give accurate figures, when there is a strong probability that they will be used to our disadvantage. In self-protection we have learned to make it almost impossible for anyone to tell who is prospering among us. You may guess, and we may guess. But who is going to tell us if we are right? The few who have storehouses filled with grain to lend, and better bullocks, and oil lanterns, expose their prosperity. The extent of their business makes concealment impossible; and the hawks are afraid to make enemies of them. But the degree of prosperity remains a mystery. The Memsahiba sees the jewelry our women display on special occasions, and she may thus be able

to compare our investments in silver. But some men are weak
when it comes to ornaments for their women, and spend more
than they can afford. And some prefer keeping their silver
more carefully preserved than on the persons of their wives.
You may know the extent of our fields, and that of our debts,
yet still be uncertain as to our actual assets. A man keeps
his treasure carefully hidden and only in an emergency, or
more likely on his death bed, does he whisper its whereabouts
to his son. He dares not risk sharing the secret with any
other. When he has no son, the contentions begin. You remember how badly some of us behaved when old Jaganath
died. We dug up most of his floor, and quarreled and accused and for almost two years continued fighting in court.
We who considered ourselves entitled to Jaganath's wealth,
felt that we must keep it in the family. We were simply protecting the particular group to which we belong.

"In all of our self-protective activities, each of us is not
thinking of his own self. No villager thinks of himself apart
from his family. He rises or falls with it. In the cities families are scattering. But we need the strength of the family
to support us. We do not trust the outside world, and we are
suspicious of each other. Our lives are oppressed by mean
fears. We fear the rent collector, we fear the police watchman, we fear everyone who looks as though he might claim
some authority over us; we fear our creditors, we fear our
patrons, we fear too much rain, we fear locusts, we fear
thieves, we fear the evil spirits which threaten our children
and our animals, and we fear the strength of our neighbor.
Do you wonder that we unite the strength of brothers and
sons? That man is to be pitied who must stand alone against
the dangers, seen and unseen, which beset him. Our families
are our insurance. When a man falls ill, he knows that his
family will care for him and his children until he is able to earn
again. And he will be cared for without a word of reproach.
If a man dies, his widow and children are sure of the protec-

tion of a home. To make certain of meeting the needs of our families in times of stress, we want hidden silver and we want land. These will preserve us from starvation through all trials. The village has survived the coming and going of many landlords and many rulers by remaining inconspicuous and providing its own sustenance.

"You and others have told us that with newer methods we would be spared much labor. Perhaps, but we do not fear work. You have seen us go out to our irrigation wells at dawn and return at dusk, day after day through chilly winter months. You have watched us driving our bullocks slowly round and round over the threshing floors through the sun and wind of scorching April days. During suffocating June weather you have watched us repairing our roofs and our house walls. Then with the coming of the rains you have seen us back in the fields with our plows. And you know that those of us who care for the crafts, do not idle when trade is slack, but work long hours in the fields. We are well acquainted with toil. It has always been with us. But these new ideas of more results from less labor are untried and confusing. How do we know that they will not leave some of us without employment? You must give us time to weigh them and their consequences.

"You know how little time we spend holidaying. We leave the observances to the women. If they insist upon attending a temple fair, one man can take a whole bullock cartload of them, while the rest of us stay behind to work. We do take time off for lawsuits—much more than we desire. But that is because our courts are lax these days. We go, and go, and go again, put off each time by some slight excuse. Each time we go, we and our animals forfeit a day in the fields. And the attorney demands payment for his time which he says we have wasted. We pay because we think it is wise to pay anyone who knows the way of the courts. If this meant payment for only two or three fruitless times of waiting it would not be bad. But when the trips and the *mukhtar's* bills mount to nine or ten, and we are still waiting for the settlement of our case, we begin to feel burdened. If we want pleasant diversion from our daily grind, we wait until it is too dark to work. You never hear us singing or merrymaking while daylight lasts. Even our Holi fire waits until evening to be lighted. We work. We must work to feed and clothe our families, and to provide for our children's weddings and for those days of adversity which Fate may send us at any time.

"If we do not provide for ourselves completely, who will? Among those who might be expected to take an interest in us, who is there who demonstrates any desire to help? In the cities they devise ways of exploiting us. We know how to drive bargains when we sell our wheat or our sugar cane. We are at home in the wholesale market. But when we get our money and want to take home some cloth, the shopkeepers get out the pieces which they have been unable to dispose of, and persuade us to buy them at exorbitant prices. We know they are laughing at us. But we want cloth, and the next shopkeeper will cheat us as badly as the last. Wherever we go in the town, sharp eyes are watching to tempt our precious rupees from us. There is no one to advise us honestly or to help us escape from fraudulent men. When we go to town to attend the courts, there are men everywhere waiting to take advantage of our ignorance and fear. Our lawyers charge fees which they know are beyond our means to pay. And then if we win a case they think they deserve an extra large gift. Sometimes there is a sincere helper among them, but we are never sure who is what.

"There are the politicians who come to us and declare themselves champions of the village. They must think us very gullible. Do they suppose we are blind to the fact that it is only during the days before election that they take a passionate interest in us? How surprised you were when you found the lane before our headman's veranda crowded with traps and light carts. You were new then. Two cars actually drove into the village before the last election. The voters among us make use of this popularity as far as it goes. Why shouldn't we? It is granted with one hand, while the other waits to get. We might as well get while our other hand waits to give. The results matter little to us. One nominee will ignore us as much as the next. So our votes go to the highest bidder, unless our landlord sends a forceful suggestion that we vote for his particular candidate. That dampens the bidding. But we play up to the pretense to the end, even to the ride in their truck that they gave last time. They took us straight to the polling place and dropped us there while they rushed off to another suddenly popular village. But they forgot the sweets which they had mentioned, and the ride home. And they have forgotten us ever since. Do the men we helped to elect ever come to help us now between elections? All we ever see of them are glimpses of grand turbans as they hurry past in their expensive cars.

"And what of the priests who should be our comforters and guides? Those among us who have priestly duties to perform, go through them punctiliously, just as the ceremonies require. At night our village head sometimes reads aloud from the *Ramayana*. In religion, as in all things, we have learned to depend on whatever we can provide for ourselves, when free from work. The men who devote their lives to priestly duties visit us, to be sure. But they come with a conch or a bell, the sound of which sends our womenfolk scuttling to the grain jar. At our doors they stop just long enough to have the donations poured into their bags. When the bags are full they move on. They tell us that the grain is for the temple on the edge of town, or for one on the Ganges. We do not stop to inquire further. They are priests, and we have always given. Sometimes a priest comes to recite verses. But he does it only in the house where the feast is prepared and his pay is promised; or a wandering priest comes by and stops with us. How long did our *sadhu* stay with us, collecting grain until he had so much he needed a storehouse to keep it in? Was it two years or more? His pony grazed in our fields, and his cart and his family lived under Jonak's big tree. His wife could get our women to give her anything because she was proud and scornful, and they were innocent of pride. He used to read to us occasionally from the sacred books. Then how swiftly he moved on when that youth came from Etah and recognized him and the woman who had been pretending to be his wife. Since that experience we have been more wary. But we have been taught to honor our priests.

"What of the missionaries who come sometimes to camp beside the village? They know a great deal and could help us if they chose. But they are bent on teaching us what they want us to know and are so anxious to go on somewhere to talk to someone else that they do not stop to listen to us. We cannot always understand them; we have found that the pleasantest way is to agree with what they say, and let them go on.

"The agitators who come occasionally to stir us up against someone, usually the government, are much the same. They are excited and speak town Hindustani, so that we are not always sure of what they mean. It is best to let them think they have convinced us, and watch them rush on to some other village. They have no time to stop among us to help.

"And what of the government of which the agitators complain? It goes through the form of helping us without any heart. It sends us officials who try to deal out justice while their servants demand grain and fuel from us behind their backs. The officials go away calling us deceitful, although we could be honest if we were not afraid. That new young Deputy who just made the rounds of the area—he is trying to help. We longed to have him stay and hear our difficulties, but by the time he will have come often enough to be our friend he will be transferred. In the interests of our own safety, we are prepared to treat all as self-seekers. And much time is lost before we can make sure whether a new man is self-seeking or not.

"What of the teachers this government send us? They teach our boys the things which help town boys to succeed. There is nothing in them to make better farmers, or to make our boys honor the work of their fathers on the land. The teaching makes them all want to get sitting-down jobs away from home. Look at Prabhu. When he finished the village school, nothing would do but that he go to school in town. He should have stayed at home to work in his fields, where hired helpers were fooling his widowed mother. And what is the profit from his school-going? He spends his days idly hoping that some rajah will come along and make him his adviser or priest. He could be prosperous without any rajah if he would only look after the land his father left him.

'What of the hospitals the government has established in the towns? You sometimes complain because we seem to lean on you when we go to a hospital for treatments. If we go with you, we know we shall be cared for. They will do what you ask without expecting gifts. It is not of the doctors we complain. But all those men who stand around, and bandage us up afterward, or mix up our medicines—they watch to see how much we are ready to give them before they decide how they will handle us. You cannot know unless you are a villager, how everyone threatens us and takes from us. When you go anywhere, or when a sophisticated town man goes anywhere, he demands service and gets it. We stand dumb and show our fear, and they trample on us.

"What of all these agents whom the government has employed to keep us properly recorded, and in order? Every new office means to us just one more person to be feared and ingratiated. Even the postman who may bring us a money order expects a few annas for his service.

"There are our landlords, to whom we might look for interest and help, if we dared. But we have learned not to dare. One landlord is on a committee which administers the estate on behalf of a trust fund which is used for various charitable purposes. But the charity evidently limits itself to the city. We see no evidences of it in the men who come to collect rents from us. The other landlord has grown rich from his many villages. But we do not begrudge him his riches, because he proclaims his desire to be just toward his tenants. But he is too busy with his many properties to take time for any one village. We have never seen him. All we know about him are the reports which our headman brings from the big *durbars* to which he is invited once a year. The villages around us fare much worse than we. We have the rent agents of only two landlords to watch and please, and they have many. When a man rents his plots from eight or nine landlords, his worries are manifold. This we are spared.

"We were very suspicious of you when you first came. We watched warily to see what it was you were after. Now we let you observe, and we answer your endless questions, because we know that in your heart you mean us no harm. We have had some good laughs over the wrong trails on which we set you, and the puzzling you did trying to figure out some of the wrong facts we gave you. We could not resist, when there was someone in reach who was actually more stupid than ourselves. You have been learning since then. But sometimes still, we must confess you are foolish and rash. And you act stupidly over some of our disputes and lawsuits. You insist that deputies can only pass judgment on evidence presented before them in court, and you say you can give evidence only of what you have seen with your own eyes. So you will not help us when we have most need of it. The deputies are friends of yours. It is hard for us to understand why you refuse to speak to our deputy on behalf of those of us who are your friends. We cannot see why you become agitated, and rebuke us when we let you know how much we have spent in gifts to various officers, to try to help our cause. What else is there for us to do? We are sure our opponents are doing the same, and if we fall short, then what will happen to us? You obstinately refuse to acknowledge the importance of this. When we are sure of justice from others, then we shall be glad to drop the old ways of securing favor. They are a terrible drain on the silver which we have worked so hard to earn. But the change must begin with men more powerful than we. We take our cue from them.

"There is no one outside of our own group whom we dare trust. Everyone who comes to us or to whom we go, thinks of what he can get from us—be it money, or grain, or personal glory. You may call us stubborn and backward and hard. But we have learned bitter lessons, we and our fathers. Those lessons have made us cautious. We know that we cannot make much progress with our limited experience and resources. But we ask just where would progress lead us? We feel safe behind the barriers of our mud walls and our present status. And we are uneasy when you or our sons propose a change."

When we understand why our village friends feel as they do, we cannot pass them by with the light comment that it is futile to try to better their conditions because they do not want anything better. It is up to us to help them overcome the prejudices and fears which make it difficult for them to achieve better things. Theirs is the old story of the weak illiterate and superstitious controlled by the strong and self-centered. And just as the situation has been faced and made happier in other such places, so can it be met here. In encouraging the change, we have not the right to approach them in a spirit of benevolence as from superior to inferior. Rather, we should come to them with respect for their persistent courage and their stability in a regime where everyone has tried to unstabilize them. We can hope for little response from them until they find in us assurance of sympathetic understanding. In the beginning they will want us to limit ourselves to meeting those needs which they themselves present to us. And they will be shy of any move to project something from the outside world into their village life. But if our friendship has gone deep enough and our sincerity is sure enough, their defenses will not be so high as to keep them from peering over the top to take a good look at the new.

Just as education has helped men in similar communities from lives of fear to lives of progress, so it can help here. Whoever comes to educate must be willing to adjust his plans to meet the needs of this particular community. At the same time he must be so sure of the validity of his underlying principles that he is prepared to withstand the discouragements with which the villagers will attempt to overwhelm him. Those who are unwilling to wait for the slower processes of education, can resort to coercion. But our villagers are adroit in their handling of coercion. They do what they think is required to satisfy the coercer and forget his innovations when he has moved on. It is easy for them to drop that which has been forced upon them because in their hearts they have not been convinced of its usefulness. Above all, he who comes to serve the village must not be so intent on his own ideas that he loses sight of the villager. If he gets too far ahead of the thinking and adjustment of the villager, he will find himself outside the mud walls while those we would serve linger within.

We who would work toward a better life within the village, have much to learn from the past. As we set to develop a new order, should we not first ask ourselves what has been the purpose of the institutions and practices that have been established over the years? How can we retain what is of value in their form while changing the spirit where it retards progress? They are part of the old order that has served and maintained the village for many generations. And we cannot dismiss them lightly. No new order can afford to ignore the strong ties which have bound the different castes together into one village body. When the harvest is plentiful, all prosper together. If the harvest is poor, all suffer together. Each man may not consciously recognize himself as a necessary part of the whole. But he knows his livelihood is dependent on that of his neighbors, just as theirs is dependent on him. They cannot count on outside help. This interdependence has developed a sense of unity worth preserving. Likewise, the new order must recognize the part the family has played in providing insurance for every individual. Aside from the few who through misfortune must stand alone, each man has had the security of his family on which he can depend when all other help fails. New insurance may come in some different form. But unless it is as reliable and as readily available as the old, it will not be accepted by those who know well the chances of catastrophe.

In developing the new order, we must be ready to work with the established leaders, if they are willing. They have built up their power through their knowledge of men and their capable use of that knowledge. If they discover that they will be benefited by the progress of the whole group more than by individual progress, they will be able to retain their influence. But if they persist in using their leadership to retard the group for the sake of their own profit, even after their followers have become less ignorant and helpless, the latter will choose new leaders. And they will do it not as they have done in the past, covertly and in fear of reprisal, but with dignity and order. There is at present a personal element in the relationship between the leader and his dependents which should not be lost through changing times. It is this personal element that lends flexibility to the giving and taking between leader and follower which is seldom found where everything is rule-bound. The leader knows the circumstances of the follower who is indebted to him, and the follower knows how far he can count on his leader to help.

Men everywhere, when they are free to think for themselves, express their desire for something more in their lives than the provision for tomorrow's food. And it is this "something more" that we want for our village friends. Before they can obtain it, we must help them to overcome their old fears. First there are the fears roused by the city. The village must no longer be a convenient field for plunder for anyone with an excuse for plundering, but a community of fellow human beings who have suffered much at the hands of unscrupulous city dwellers and who deserve amends. To help them overcome their fears of the city and their suspicion of the world outside their mud walls, we must help them to extend their thinking to larger relationships. Just as each man accepts his place and his duties in the village, so he can learn that he has a place in the nation and in the world. Now the farmer works his land to feed his family, with a little extra to provide for other needs—clothing, a new implement, a bullock or buffalo, medicines, or perhaps a wedding. If he can think of his surplus produce not only as provision for such needs, but as his share in feeding the world, he will begin to regard himself as a part of society and not as someone apart, imposed upon, left out. And he will enjoy the dignity of his essential participation.

In the new order men must be freed from their present fear of creditors by having available a fair means of credit. This may come through credit societies or some other form of organization of which we do not yet know, and which they should work out themselves to meet their own needs. It will release them from the necessity of selling their produce at a loss in order to satisfy threatening creditors. They will be their own creditors. Similarly, when they have overcome their fear of the motives of their neighbors, they will be able to share with each other in the purchase of implements. At present the more efficient farm machinery available is too expensive for the individual villager. Cooperative buying will bring it within reach.

In the same way, cooperative selling will bring advantages, by assuring higher profits than the present individual bargaining. Trust and cooperation among neighbors will make possible the consolidation of holdings, a project necessitating an exchange of cultivated plots in such a way that each man's land is consolidated into one farm. Over generations of inheritors, the holdings of each family, if exceeding a fifth of an acre, have become divided into smaller and smaller plots, scattered on all sides of the village. Everyone acknowledges that consolidation is desirable, but the price in mutual trust is high.

All this, we dare hope, will draw the community together into further efforts to improve life in the village, including education, sanitation and health, recreation and culture—those things which are now regarded as the prerogatives of the city. And if men find it no longer necessary to distrust their neighbors, perhaps they will be less insistent upon the confinement of their wives and daughters-in-law in family courtyards. As now the women share in the labor and fears of their own menfolk, they will then share in the privilege of the new village.

As each old fear is faced and overcome, our village friends will become more self-reliant—their own masters. They will be free to choose what is best for themselves, from the old order and the new. No man will be compelled to follow a specific trade from childhood; nor will it be said of any man, "Unclean." There must be trades and there will be unclean work. But the trades will be in the hands of men who carry them on from choice and not from complusion. And the unclean work will be arranged for in such a way that no one group will be labeled by it from birth to death. There must be leaders. But no man need be bound irrevocably to another. Leaders and the agents of government will use their authority for the benefit of the village as a whole. And those who follow will be prepared to carry a share of responsibility, in contrast to their present tendency, to lean upon patrons. Leaders will be chosen, perhaps from among the sons of those who lead at present, or perhaps from among those of more humble origin, according to their worth.

If the new order were to enter our village tomorrow, we wonder if we should recognize our old friends in the new life. The younger generation might delight in it. But the older men and women would be lost. There would be much creaking of the old, stiff joints of custom, and much quaking because the protection of the old defenses would be gone. And there might be lamenting for the comfortable assurance of the old dictates which spared one the burden of making decisions and facing the consequences. When we try to picture it, we realize the folly of trying to pour new wine into old wineskins. New wineskins must be provided along with the fresh wine. The new order cannot be forced suddenly upon the village. It can only enter gradually, as men are educated to accept each new phase. They may well be on their guard against change in the beginning. But if approached with sympathy and resourcefulness, and given a major share in bringing about each step, they will understand the value of the new order and adopt it as their own, eventually. Surely no one with a desire to combine education and community service could want a task more challenging. It would be easier to forget the village and turn to more accessible fields where there are more congenial spirits. But can we who have been permitted to know the needs of the men and women, the youth and children, and the animals of the village, "pass by on the other side" and forget?

CHAPTER X

Return to the Familiar

We were returning to Karimpur, to the first house that we could consider our own, built for us. It had been designed by a young architect, a member of the Delhi Planning Commission. And his blueprint had been painstakingly followed by Prakash. It was Prakash who had helped us as a young man, both in our dispensary tent doling out simple remedies and in the village, gathering facts. It seemed right that our house should be next to his and that he should be the one to supervise the building. He undertook it gladly, but throughout the process there was much fretting and balking on his part. And he received volumes of advice and criticism from the men of the village. None of them had ever seen a blueprint, and only three had had anything to do with the construction of a new house. The rest lived in mud-walled houses put up by grandfathers or great-grandfathers. The experience of the present generation was limited to that of adding a surface layer of fresh mud plaster each year, extending a storeroom if space permitted, or closing up a door to adjust the old house to the changing needs of the family. But each one regarded himself as an authority. Now, at last, the house was completed, except for doors and windows to be put in later by village carpenters.

I had made a number of trips to the village during the building process. But for Bill (the "Sahib") this was the first visit after ten years. At first he had been too involved in his own experiment in rural development, and later he had been too ill to attempt the journey. Our present visit was not an ordinary one. It was a homecoming, first suggested thirty years before. It was when we had finally folded our tents and sent them on ahead in ox carts to Mainpuri that the village men who were in the grove to bid us farewell told us of their hope. They wanted us to come here to live. It might be soon. Or it might not be until our years of active service were over. But we must come back to stay. As we got into the well-worn car, Bill assured them that we would try. They never forgot. And they reminded us periodically, on visits to us or in letters when we were far away. The village children crowding around our two boys that day exacted the same promise from them as their fathers had from Bill. They could not conceive of anything so final as the very last trip to town. They were dancing with impatience for us to start. And they clambered in after us, squeezing themselves under, over, and around us, with the overflow on the mudguards and running boards and the last few balancing on the rear bumpers. Slowly we drove down the lane and along the road, responding to the many *namaskars* of farewell. Finally, at the milepost, we stopped. There was a rush of small bodies and there they were, a gay, laughing crowd on the roadside shouting to us that they would be waiting there when we drove back from town.

And now on our return thirty years later, it seemed inconceivable but there they were—a crowd of prancing children, looking exactly as they had when we had left them. This time they were not at the milepost, because they knew we would be coming from the opposite direction. They were waiting at the turning from the road into the village lane. These children did not know us. They had never seen Bill. But they knew all about us and had heard of the milepost rides from their fathers or grandfathers. How disappointing was the change in the construction of cars! No mudguards, no running boards, not a thing to cling to. But these children were not disappointed. They had never known the charms of the old car, and they were quite content to come running along beside or behind us, shouting their welcome. We were impressed by the smoothness of the lane. A signboard at the roadside announced that it had been remade by the voluntary labor of the men of the village. But just at the point where the lane enters the village proper, there was a wide, deep mudhole. We learned later that, under the charm of a junior official, the villagers had undertaken the improvement of the lane. They had gone this far when the official departed and the sugarcane harvest demanded the time of every man. And then they had forgotten it. Their ox carts could manipulate it without too much difficulty, and no one had thought in terms of a car. The men who had gathered to welcome us, scattered to collect stalks of grain. They soon filled the hole, while more men and boys gathered around us.

By the time we started moving again, we were surrounded by cheering, gesticulating children and men crowding beside the car trying to shout their greetings above the din. At places, the space between car and mud walls was very narrow and Bill was sure that someone would be hurt. But they were all intact as we bounced around the turn into the broader lane leading to our house. When we stopped at the front door there was a final cheer. Then scores of hands were lifted to carry bedding rolls, bags, and bundles into the house, and many more to help lift Bill to his wheelchair and up the steep incline to the door. We were not sure whether we were the hosts, or they. We were all busy welcoming each other, and repeating over and over how glad we were to be here together. This we could say with sincerity. And we were sure that they were equally sincere. We had known most of the men as young men or small boys. And now with their children and grandchildren crowding close around them, it was uncanny—as though a photographer had cleverly inserted a picture taken thirty years ago into one of today. We alone could see this; the children could not imagine their elders as ever having been young like themselves, and the men were sure that they had been quite different from these noisy, unruly children.

Early the next morning seven village elders, in "town" clothes, came to welcome us back officially. They came on a formal call to recount the benefits which had come to the village during our former years together, and to express appreciation on behalf of all the village of our building a house in Karimpur. We were not strangers whom they were trying to impress with what they or we had done. We were old friends come home.

Under pressure from some of the men who recalled our Christmas festivals in the mango grove, we had agreed, before our return, to a revival this year. They wanted their children to have a taste of the fun they had been recounting these many years. One of them showed us the pocket knife and the small car which he had received as gifts, treasured all this time. The gifts for this year's occasion were ready. We had bought them in Delhi by the dozen, as in the past. From Mainpuri Prakash had brought peanuts, guavas, and *batasas*— sweets as light as air and associated with blessing. We had learned our lesson years before and were careful to touch none of these. Prakash's family and other Brahmans would do the distributing. Because there are more children in Karimpur now, and because our large courtyard would make it possible for the women and older girls to have a share, the men decided that there should be two days of festivities. The first would be for the boys and young men, the second for the girls and women. A crowd of energetic young volunteers offered to take over the games and races. Our role was simply to look on and express approval.

The children who participated in the games of the next two days were so like their fathers and mothers that again it was hard to believe that these were children we had not seen. The seeming bad manners of the youngsters in trying to grab before their turn made us realize that toys and things for games are still rare in the village, apparently as rare as they were thirty years ago.

On the third day after our arrival we were obliged to leave, in response to an urgent message from Bill's surgeon in the Punjab who had just received the report on X-rays of the fractured and mended hip, taken weeks before. He advised immediate surgery. So we bade farewell to our friends and our house, everyone feeling sure that we would be back soon. Bill never returned.

Now I am back in our house, alone—but far from solitary. Anyone who has become part of a joint family is seldom, if ever, alone. And that is my present, happy state. I am part of Prakash's family, one of the most "joint" in the village. Our house meets Prakash's need for more living space; and his loyalty to Bill and to me has been carried over into his whole family. I had known in theory that in the village a house is for use, every part of it. Now I was to learn from personal experience just what this means. Every bit of space is occupied, all of the time, either for labor or for storing the fruits of labor. There can be no room set aside for eating or for sitting or for sleeping. This would be waste. And villagers scorn waste. No one ever says "This is my room, keep out." Every room is everyone's room. A house is ordinarily considered to be the world of women and children. But ours serves both sections of the family. It becomes men's quarters at times, and exclusively for *bahus* at others.

This word, *bahu*, incidentally, is used consistently in our district and neighboring districts. When we were in Karimpur in the thirties, men spoke to us of the women of their families as *mere ghar ki,* meaning "of my house." I do not recall having heard *bahu* then, but perhaps this was so merely because we were not as intimately associated with families then as I am now. As long as a girl or woman is in her father's house, in her home village, she is a *beti,* daughter. In the home of her in-laws, in her husband's village, she becomes a *bahu,* literally "daughter-in-law," although a man may use it when referring to his wife.

My coming this time was far quieter than our heralded arrival of three years ago. Everyone, I have since learned, had heard of Bill's death from the cable I had sent. They knew that I was back in India, but had no idea when I might reach the village. The letter I sent from Delhi arrived the day after I did. Good friends in Delhi had lent me their car and a driver. As we turned from the main highway into the district road, and went rolling and bumping along, smothered in dust whenever we met a bus or truck, I felt at home. And then, as we curved past a mango grove, I saw the *kheru* in the distance, a small man-made hillock, always our landmark. The fields on both sides of the road were similar to those I had watched all along the road from Delhi—odd-shaped, like pieces in a patchwork quilt.

Men coming in from the fields with their oxen, or cutting fodder with their new hand-propelled machines, looked up at the car as we crept past, slowed down by the straggling line of cows and buffaloes being herded home by lively small boys and girls. They were curious. Few cars came this way. We had passed none on the district road, and few on the highway from Delhi. Then came expressions of recognition, followed by broad smiles and the *namaskar,* then each called to others along the road or inside the enclosures, "Our Memsahiba has come." And I felt the warmth of their welcome.

The low sun, shining through the thick dust raised by the animals, cast a lavender haze over the grey mud walls, making them look warm and friendly—quite different from our first impression of them. Children playing in the dust of the lane ran to one side, startled at the sight of a car heading for the village. Then again, the flash of recognition, the gleaming smiles and shouts of delight. "She has come! She has come!" And other children soon gathered. Adults were more sober, admonishing the children. But nothing could dampen their high spirits. There is too little excitement in the village to let any such opportunity pass. We soon reached the house, considerably shaken by the worst stretch of the journey, the lane through the middle of the village and around the turn to our corner. There was the usual contingent of small helpers who grabbed every parcel and bag from the rear of the car and disappeared in the direction of the courtyard. At the courtyard door, we were greeted by furious activity and clouds of dust. Word of my coming had reached the family indirectly, just an hour before. And they were trying desperately to restore the house to its original state. Prakash's eldest daughter and one *bahu* were sweeping piles of scraps, chaff, corncobs, peanut shells, and dust to one corner. They paused to greet us, then went on with their work. Buaji, Prakash's wife, came from the door leading to the back rooms. Buaji—a term of endearment—is what everyone in the family except her husband calls her. She has been one of my closest village friends since she came to the village as Prakash's bride many years ago. Hers was the most intimate welcome, head on one shoulder and then on the other. She led me into one of the back rooms, now swept bare, where we could have a few moments together. She had so counted on being able to make Bill well, with good country food and lots of fresh milk and yoghurt. She and Prakash had come all the way to the hospital in the Punjab, a fearsome journey, to visit us. And they had appeared again in New Delhi with all four of their sons when we were both carried, ill, from car to plane. Now she would do for me what she had hoped to do for Bill.

When the driver had gone with the car and the children

went racing after it, I was left alone at the front door. Our house is at one corner of the village, and from outside the door I looked again over the stretches of green fields and the darker green of fruit groves, to the sky now a pale rose, changing to a limpid blue. Autumn is the most beautiful, promising season of the year in our province. A peacock with long sweeping tail of breathtaking beauty stepped proudly along the top of the low wall bordering a field across the way. Everything was silent, except for the sound of the fodder cutter at the far end of Prakash's house. At such moments God seems very near.

When I returned to the courtyard, Prakash and Buaji and their children were there. As we talked quietly of the past and future, I knew that these were my people, not so close as my own sons and their families, but with ties strong enough to draw me back across the world to be with them.

During my first few days in the village, I was so preoccupied with discovering what had changed that I failed to notice what had not changed. The New is more interesting, more impressive, than the Familiar. But the Familiar, however ordinary, has an important share in the story of a people. It represents what they prefer to retain, perhaps simply because they are accustomed to it and find it comfortable—like a favorite old jacket—or because it has proved useful or, above all, because it has seemed essential to security.

Down the whole length of our lane, every house is occupied by the family that occupied it thirty years ago. Some of the houses are unaltered, some are tumbling down, and some have been divided. There have been violent upheavals behind several of the walls. But the continuity of each family has been preserved.

And so it goes down lane after lane. There are still no plants or flowers along the lanes. How could there be, with cattle and sheep passing by every day? There are beautiful old trees where a junction of lanes offers space or along the lanes that border the village, where there is room for roots and branches to spread, and on each side of the village there are groves of mango and guava trees. The only variation in the irregular lines of gray walls is, as it was thirty years ago, the condition of those walls. Some are well cared for, often with a thatch extending over them to protect them from violent rains. There are a few new fronts of baked bricks on houses belonging to *kachhis* along the district road. But the walls behind them are still of earth. Occasionally, a whitewashed doorway, with two special clay pots above it, indicates a recent wedding. Some roofs have caved in. Balram, the carpenter living nearest to us, neglected the roof of his front room when it collapsed during the rains three years ago. Now, only enough of the back wall of the room remains to serve as a screen for the women working in the courtyard.

The part of the village which we called Humble Lane is as unpretentious, untidy, and friendly as ever. The walls between the houses of the *kahars* have been washed down so low that the several families seem like one. It is almost impossible to tell who belongs where. The *kahars* have little or nothing to store. Theirs is the doubtful privilege of carrying water or preparing food for members of any caste, in return for which they receive enough to keep them alive. Two of the three grain-parcher brothers are trying to supplement their income with shelves full of cheap supplies which they sell to their neighbors or occasionally to others who come with wheat to be roasted or rice to be puffed. The two potters are busy in their front courtyards, shaping the water jars which they will soon bake, ready for the next big festival. They will distribute them then in the hope of receiving grain or special sweets from their *jajmans* (patrons) in return. Walking down this lane, I wonder as I did years ago, how these families survive. They have little, if any, provision for the future; and yet they are the most cheerful of all. I have just discovered one exception—not in cheerfulness but in provision for the future. Ralla

Ram, the second grain-parcher brother, has been lending money to villagers at a reasonable rate of interest for several years, with the result that now he has become prosperous. I had learned that he was elected to the village council, but I did not know of his prosperity until recently. He hardly belongs in Humble Lane now. But he would never presume to move into another section of the village, even if there were space. He is content with his small shop, his roasting furnace, and his small, unpretentious house.

When we refer to the "houses" of the village, we are using the term loosely. Actually they are enclosures, incorporating more than a house. The women of the family live and work within the enclosure, surrounded by the children. The men return to it at night. In the first room inside the door are the cow or buffalo and the oxen. The sheep and goats of the shepherds are within their enclosures, as are the swine of the sweepers. Farmers keep their implements and artisans keep their tools in the stable, the courtyard, or workroom. If the family lives by a craft, the workroom is somewhere within the enclosure. Grain from the family land, or received from *jajmans,* is stored away in a special stone-lined granary or in the large clay jars made by the women and kept in a storeroom. Other food supplies are stored in jars of various sizes made by the potter and suspended from the ceiling. *Ghi* and other treasured luxuries are likewise in baked-clay containers stowed away in large, padlocked chests. Clothes are stored in similar chests. Gold or silver in the form of ornaments or coins, is deposited in a secret place in one of the walls or the floor. There are no windows through which outsiders might peer, and no man enters the enclosure of another unless attended by one of the men of the household. The walls of those who have much to protect are high and thick. Those of families with little are low and often neglected. This is as it has been, as far back as anyone can remember.

Our village houses are exposed to whatever the season brings.

In cold weather we shiver most of the day and are chilled through, morning and evening. It is as cold indoors as out. Everyone complains, but accepts the continual discomfort. The only possible escape from the raw chill is to dance and jump as the children do, bundle up head and ears as the men do, find a patch of sunshine to sit in or work in during the middle of the day, sit close to a short-lived fire of stalks, or wrap up in a heavy cotton quilt at night.

Hot weather is even more relentless. There is no escaping it. Courtyards get the full blaze of the sun. A bit of thatch in a corner slightly modifies the heat. Storerooms are suffocating. Curtains, if we had them, would only shut out the air and make rooms even more stifling. I had intended to have curtains in two doors of our big room. During three years absence, I had forgotten how important any breath of moving air can be. And still further, I had forgotten that children, unused to curtains, push them out of the way with grubby hands or use them for various unintended purposes. A curtain is just another piece of cloth conveniently located. Better an open doorway, to catch any breeze, however dustladen, and keep scraps of old cloth for practical uses. The one place where men find a little relief in May and June is under a large tree out in the open. Here they catch every breeze that stirs and are protected from the sun which seems bent on destroying man, beast, and all growing things.

Inside the houses which I know best, the surroundings are so familiar that I could almost tell blindfolded where certain implements are kept, where the feeding troughs are for the cows, buffaloes, or oxen, where the cooking space is located, where the doors to the different storerooms are, and what will be found in each storeroom. I know where the women sleep, in cold weather and in hot, and where the men and animals sleep. Furnishings still consist of rope-strung cots, and perhaps a low square stool with a seat of woven tape. The cots are light, with legs and frame of light wood, and rope serving as springs. They can be lifted easily and moved from store-room to courtyard or courtyard to stable. Everything in the house is easily moved, except for the grinding stone and the cooking fireplace. If there are not enough cots for all the family, some sleep on the ground in the long hot season or on a thick padding of rice straw in winter weather. Bedding consists of cotton quilts for cold nights or homespun sheets as the weather grows warmer and nothing when it is hot. Life is truly simple. There are no windows to polish, no beds to make, no dishes or glassware or cutlery to wash, no curtains to launder, no rugs to clean, no furniture to dust. There is a table in the postmaster's house, and chairs—regarded as a mark of prestige—in two or three others. But most people say why invest in tables, unless someone in the family is obliged to write. And why use chairs when the ground is perfectly comfortable—much more so than sitting with legs dangling over the edge of a chair.

Throughout the village, families still seem to prefer to live beside others of their own caste, if possible. There are a few exceptions, but where several families belong to one caste, they will ordinarily be found in adjacent houses. The shep-herds are all close neighbors, with the one cotton-carder fam-ily in among them. The *dhanuks* live together at one edge of the village, close to Brahmans, but apart. Goldsmiths, sewing men, *kahars*, grain parchers, oilsmiths, or sweepers—each of these forms a separate unit. There may be bitter quarrels within a family and conflicts within a caste. But just as a man finds security within the walls that enclose all that he possesses, so he finds a wider security within the group to which he knows he belongs.

In addition to this, there is the added security of living snugly together, regardless of caste, within the village. The fear of dacoits—robber gangs—or cattle thieves who might come at night, hangs over every household. And there is certainly a greater feeling of security in knowing that just inside every front door, up and down the lane, there are neighbors within call.

There are other advantages in living close together within the village. Then men can gather easily on their own or a neighbor's stoop or under a tree on the edge of the village where they can talk about their common interests—crops, prices of produce just sold in town, advantages versus disadvantages of the newest fertilizer. Although there are lonely *bahus* in the courtyards, they are not completely isolated. And the older women who move about can always find a few others ready to sit down with them especially in the middle of the day, for a bit of gossip. And even the *bahus* in the house where the older women gather, have the pleasure of listening, though they do not speak. The children, too, benefit from being surrounded by neighbors. In our family there are plenty of children to play with, but where a child happens to be the only one in a household he can step to the door and there find playmates. As far as I know, parents are unaware of the problems of a lonely child.

Like the physical aspects of the village, the lives of those who live up and down its lanes have altered only slightly. The fields have changed, but not the men who cultivate them. Their work and their responsibilities are much the same as they were thirty years ago. And this is equally true of the men who work at a trade or a craft. The women in the courtyards are going through the same daily routine as their mothers-in-law before them. When I step out of my front door in the morning to watch the sun rise, I see the ghostly figures of *bahus* slipping out to the fields, each with her *lota* (the small, pot-bellied brass jar) filled with water. And I think, "But for the junior septic tank, there go I." A friend of mine calls these *bahus* The Dawn Club—they meet at the hour in the day when they are permitted to leave the courtyard and perhaps meet other *bahus*. From then on, there is always work waiting to be done. Flour must be ground between the heavy mill stones for the daily bread. In our family we consume about twenty pounds of flour each day. This may be wheat, corn, or millet. If there is to be rice, it must be pounded in the stone cup set into the courtyard floor by two of the women, each armed with a three-foot club with iron-bound pounding end. They bring their clubs down in rhythm, careful to miss the club of the other and the hand pushing the rice back into the cup. If there is to be a cooked pulse, it must be split between stones lighter than those for flour, and soaked before cooking. The cow or buffalo must be milked, and the milk simmered over a low fire of dung cakes. Dung must be collected, shaped into fuel cakes, and plastered against a sunny wall or smooth piece of ground. The milk of the day before has been clabbered over night and must be churned. The butter is stored until there is enough to clarify for *ghi,* which is then put away in clay jars with great care. The *chula* (small stove) must be freshly mud-plastered each morning and allowed to dry before it may be used. The courtyard must be swept morning and evening. Vegetables in season must be brought from the fields and prepared for cooking. Spices are ground fresh for each meal on a small stone slab with a stone roller. Meals must be cooked and kept ready for the men as they come in, one by one, and the children must be fed. If there is any free time, it is spent in ginning cotton or in spinning. They still seem to do everything the hardest way possible. Manual labor costs nothing. And labor-saving devices are unknown or frowned upon as luxuries.

As for the children, they are still light of heart and fleet of foot, their activities unchecked by parental concern. Those who go to school beyond the third grade have now stepped into the world of the New. Those who are kept at home to work, or just kept at home, are no different from the boys and girls who played with our sons. They devise games that require no equipment or they make whatever they need from clay or sticks or stones. They eat when hungry, and sleep when weary. One mild evening, I sat on a cot in the court-yard of a neighbor. It was late, but the whole courtyard was softly lighted by the moon. We are always aware of moon-light in the village. One of the older children, a boy of ten, came running in, still breathless from some game, and de-manded food. His grandmother brought a beautiful flat brass bowl of vegetables, two flat cakes, and a brass cup of milk. He had barely started eating when his cousin, a boy of eight, followed him. The moment he saw food, he wanted some. His aunt served him. Shortly three others, all small, came in together. And at once, they sat down facing the other two and called for food. All five made a contented, busy circle. Mothers and aunts hovered over them while the grandmother sat by and supervised the serving. When one of the smaller girls was finished, she came and dropped down on the cot beside me, where a two-year-old already slept. Two others curled up close together on the floor where an open door led into a storeroom. Another went to her grand-mother and climbed into her soft lap. The grandmother already had a baby in her arms. The oldest boy took out a school book and began to study aloud by the light of the one tiny oil lamp. But he soon dozed. All slept where they were until the women of the family were free to go to bed. Then each mother picked up one or two of her own, or a niece or nephew, and put them on the cot beside her. I was the only one allowed a cot to myself.

There have been significant changes in personal relation-ships in the village. But the Familiar retains its influence, es-pecially in relationships within the family. Every member of a family knows his or her exact status, and accepts it. There is no doubt as to who directs all family affairs. In our joint family this is Prakash. He plans all field work, and super-intends every detail. He tells each son and each servant, helping on a particular day, just what they are to do. And it is he who calls laborers when there is extra work to be done. He selects the seed and decides what seed is to be planted in which plot. He determines when the fields need cultivating or irrigating, either from their own wells or the tube well. He decides when sugarcane is to be pressed, when other crops are to be cut, when grain is to be threshed, how much is to be sold, and how much is to be stored in his granary. This is a difficult decision to make. He wants to sell as much as possible. Cash is very desirable. But he must make sure that there will be enough stored to carry the family through until the next harvest, otherwise he will need to buy. And the size of his family varies, from sixteen to twenty-one or twenty-two. The serving men are always given a noon-day meal, and extra laborers must be fed as well. There are frequent visits from relatives. And there must be some grain on hand for families which have been attached to his, not only in his generation but in generations past. They come at the time of special festivals, when they receive either grain or unleavened fried cakes made by the *bahus*. Or they may just come for help when out of food. These contributions are in addition to the head loads of grain given to them at harvest time. At each of the two major harvests, Prakash calls to one of his fields the family washerman, the potter, carpenter, barber, and *kahars* who serve him. He gives one head-load of wheat and one of barley, or one head-load of corn and one of millet— about thirty pounds—to each one. They may also get rice, and eight pounds of the particular pulse just harvested. Others, who consider that they have a claim to some of his crop because of services rendered, must come without being called. The sewing man brings a garment for one of the smaller children. The *jadav* (leather worker) brings a leather thong. The grain parcher brings half a pound of a special sweet made from puffed rice. The bangle seller brings as many colored bangles as the daughter next to be married wants. The *mali* (flower grower) brings one or two marigolds. The cotton carder brings bits of twisted cotton, ready to be used as wicks for the small open lamps. The sweeper has nothing tangible to offer, but he comes. Those who appear—and they always do, if possible—receive from twelve to sixteen pounds of grain in a head load, and also rice, and perhaps five pounds of pulse. If they do not come, they get nothing. These same men visit other *jajmans* as well, to accumulate all they can for the lean months ahead.

It is Prakash who supervises the sale of his produce. Others load the ox carts and drive them to town. He goes by cycle and is there when they arrive, ready to carry out the transaction. He looks after all family property rights. He constantly checks the boundaries of his several plots to make sure that no one has encroached on his land. It is Prakash who makes purchases in town. He has begun to give his eldest son money for some particular purchase of which Prakash approves. If a peddler comes to the house, Buaji may make a purchase for herself or for one of the *bahus*. She keeps no cash. She asks Prakash for the money, or if he is away, she may borrow from a male relative who is available. She is free to do this because she has proved herself such a careful spender. Buaji and Prakash have been together so long now that they work as a team, each knowing that the other can be depended upon to keep family interests uppermost.

As each son grows up he learns year by year what is expected of him, so that by the time he is a man, he takes his appointed place without much need for adjustment. Each *bahu* must learn her duties and her status in the courtyard after she comes into the family as a bride. Prakash has delegated very little of his responsibility to his two older sons who are both capable and intelligent. The result is that he is feeling the burden of a constantly increasing family. And with the wedding of a daughter in the offing he is more disturbed than ever. Several times he has brought up the subject of the Hindu concept of the four periods in the life of a man.

He has passed the stage of youth, of learning. And he has accepted the responsibilities imposed by the second stage— that of a householder. He now feels that he has arrived at the third stage, when he is free to leave family affairs in the hands of others. He does not feel ready for the fourth stage when he may retire to the forest where he can meditate in peace. But he longs for release from his obligations as the head of a large household. He threatens to build a small room on the roof of the front part of our house to which he can escape, and let his children and their children fend for themselves. He is worn out by their many demands and their bickerings.

If there must be a choice made by any member of the family, between family duties and those outside, family duties come first. I observed this in the funerals of two relatives, one a cousin of Prakash's and the other Buaji's eldest brother. When Prakash's cousin died, he dropped everything—even the supervision of fields and the sales trips to town—to spend time in the home of the cousin, along with other male relatives. Likewise Buaji was expected to spend hours each day with the weeping women of the family. Prakash's cousin left no wife or children. But the women who had cooked for him and cared for him must be consoled. When the time came to take the body to the Ganges, more than forty-five miles away, Prakash took for granted that he must go, not by bus but by cycle in order to stay behind the ox cart carrying the body. It would have been improper to travel by bus on such an occasion although it would save time and strength. Even cycling through wind and dust threatened to be too speedy. In order not to pass the ox cart, he and two other cousins started late and cycled only half way, where they could spend the night with relatives. From there on, they followed the cart, walking the last part of the journey to the burning *ghat*. He had intended to return by bus, after the cremation ceremony was over. But again, he and the others decided that they must remain behind the cart, and took the home journey in two stages. He was gone for five days. Many things remained undone during his absence. And he would have resented such an imposition for any other reason. According to village standards, he is a man of affairs. But none of these was allowed to interfere with his duties to his kin.

The second funeral surprised me even more. When word came of the death of Buaji's eldest brother, it was taken for granted that some member of our family must be present at his home on the thirteenth day. This is the day set for special religious observances and a feast. In this case, Prakash did not feel it incumbent upon him to attend. Buaji, as a woman, was excluded. It must be one of the sons. It did not occur to me that Bahadur would be sent. For days he had been preparing the agenda for a meeting of the village council of which he is president. He takes his duties seriously and had never missed a meeting since his election a year ago. The funeral ceremonies fell on the day of his meeting. The night before there was a family council; Bahadur was to go. He went to see the vice president of the council and turned the agenda over to him. I knew that this was not easy. The vice president is a powerful man, older and more experienced than Bahadur, and brother of Bahadur's chief rival in the election. And yet there was no sign of resentment, only a rather tired acceptance of his duty. It was the decision of his parents, not to be questioned.

In relationships within the village but outside of the family, there have been striking changes. There are new leaders, younger men, with new outlook and new qualities. But even here the Familiar has carried over. As different men have listed the new leaders, they have added after each name "He is Ganga Ram's son" or "Chitam Lal's nephew." A few of the younger leaders are related to men who were followers in the past. But most are successors of former acknowledged leaders.

In a community like this, men know each other exceedingly well—perhaps too well. They played together as small children. They got into mischief together. Whether they were kept at home to work or sent to school, they had plenty of opportunity to know each other intimately. They knew who played fair and who cheated. They learned from long experience who could be counted on and who was unreliable. The clever ones made decisions and gave orders. The slow ones followed, some from admiration, some from fear. Now as they grow older, existing factions, backed by family pressures, demand adjustments in these youthful alliances. A young man is expected to join the faction of his elders. However, regardless of which faction demands a man's loyalty, he makes his own estimate of the strength and weakness of each ally and each adversary. Arguments and promises do not deceive him. Most of the men are too occupied with making a living to bother with factions. But there always seems to be someone prepared to whip up faction-feeling at a crucial time, often just when village unity is essential to progress. Each man knows that his duty is to support his faction when called upon. But he also knows that he cannot count on help from his faction when his difficulties or needs are personal. The one group to which he can look for unfailing support is his family, and his family in turn relies for its support and its security, on the land and on religion.

The price of land varies greatly, depending on the fertility of the soil. However, farmers estimate roughly that to purchase a piece of land today they would have to pay ten times what they would have paid thirty years ago. In the village, no one speaks of the cost of land. It is beyond price. Everything else is measured in terms of rupees. I can hardly get a new article inside the door before everyone in sight asks how much I spent for it. But land—is land. The man who currently owns it prizes it and guards it, not only for himself and his children, but also for the sake of the ancestors who passed it on to him, and for those who will follow. It is regarded as a disgrace if a man is obliged to sell his land, perhaps to repay a debt. We hear that on the frontier most quarrels and court cases arise from disputes over women. With us, the disputes are over land—perhaps only a few square feet of land. One man who owns a plot of land might shift the small ridge that separates his field from the next one, adding a small strip to his own plot. This can easily be done just after the rains when most ridges have been washed down until scarcely visible. So everyone must be on guard. Even when a man dies, his land is not offered for sale. The chances are that each of his holdings has been held in partnership with two or three relatives who claim it. If it is in his name alone, it goes to his nearest relative. It is still possible for a man to acquire more land, either legally through inheritance from someone in his family, or by bribing the village land recorder to alter a record.

Some poor members of the village have petitioned the council to give them a small amount of undesirable land. One young Christian has just acquired two acres of alkaline land in this way. No one with productive soil would consider it. But by working it carefully, and if the rains are heavy enough, he can get one crop of rice the first year. Best of all, he now owns land. This has altered his attitude toward himself and toward the rest of the village. Those who have no hope of acquiring land put their trust in their *jajmans*, most of whom are landowners. It appears that directly or indirectly, every family of the village looks to the land for support.

Religion still ranks with land in its promise of security. Women are more faithful than men in their observance of the many religious festivals. They make the appropriate designs on walls or floor in order to win the favor of each god or goddess in turn. Also, they make special sweets and other dishes for each particular holiday. Most of the holidays are occasions for religious ceremonies, but even more they are times of gaiety and feasting.

Those who can afford it go to the Ganges by bus or train to bathe. Several months before our house was completed, I took a load of village friends in our pickup to the nearest place of pilgrimage on the Ganges. There were elders like Chitam Lal and Panditain, his wife, and younger people and children. I have never seen a happier crowd. When a group of friends and relatives can combine a picnic and a long exciting drive with the gaining of religious merit by bathing in the waters of a sacred river and visiting temples of favorite gods and goddesses, the experience is most satisfying. They sang all the way home. This past year, a group of men hired a whole bus to take them on the long journey to Hardwar, a place which all Hindus long to visit, at the foot of the Himalayas. It must have been an expensive journey, especially for men who are cautious in their spending. But they were certain that the benefits they received from the pilgrimage warranted the outlay.

We still have the *bhagats* who are called in to treat patients with their incantations and charms. There are *bhagats* belonging to a number of castes. I had a surprise visit from one elderly, gentle *bhagat* one evening, who was a Brahman. I had been having one of my chronic intestinal upsets, perhaps from amoeba or perhaps from the highly spiced food which Buaji was faithfully serving me. She was concerned. Without warning me, she had called her favorite *bhagat*. He came in quietly and unostentatiously and sat on the ground in front of me in the courtyard where I was sitting beside Buaji in a comfortable cane chair. I thought that he had come to ask me for one of my simple home treatments. But instead, he had come to treat me! He had in his hand a bundle of small branches of the *neem* tree—a tree whose leaves and bark are considered of medicinal value. These branches he began to wave in front of me in a wide circle. At the same time he repeated verses, which I learned later were *mantras*. His manner, his quiet words, and the rhythmic motion were most restful and I relaxed. To Buaji's gratification, I was better the next morning. Whether it was abstaining from overspiced food or the medicine I was taking or the *bhagat's* treatment, I shall never know.

Out by the roadside is a circle of stones, brought here long ago from some ancient temple. They have been dedicated to the goddess Maya. We used to watch from our grove when the women went there to worship. The stones have been moved back farther from the road and a small *peepul* tree—of religious significance—now grows within the circle. A ceremony is usually held at this spot in August, attended chiefly by women. This year the ceremony was moved forward seven months, and has been made a special occasion. Four priests officiated, reading from the *Ramayana*, turn by turn, until they had completed the whole story. Everyone in the village contributed money, for new clothes for the chief of the four priests and for *batasas*—the sweets denoting blessing—and for water to be brought from the Ganges. Both men and women came during the reading, whenever free from farm or household duties. There was constant coming and going. There were mats for the men near the priests, who sat beside the circle and the *hawan*, or sacred fire. There were other mats for the women farther back. Children played all around and between the groups. No one could possibly hear the reading. Only the moving of the lips of one priest indicated that it was his turn to read. A line of ardent musicians standing at one side outdid him. Their instruments were varied—a drum, cymbals, a pair of iron tongs with a large ring to jingle, rectangular castinets. And all sang and shouted lustily, *Ram, Ram, Hari Ram, Krishna Hari*. Their contribution being more exhausting, they served in one-hour shifts. Occasionally a group of women would add their songs. The reason for this special occasion is the same as that which prompted similar, much more elaborate and expensive, ceremonies in other parts of India and of the world. Men of the village show so little concern for anything beyond their families and the neighborhood, that it was interesting to find them sharing in this world-wide religious observance. Priests in Mainpuri had warned them of the calamities which would attend the conjunction of eight major planets. And this, they explained, was their effort to avert disaster. They were not particularly concerned with what might happen to the world outside the village, but they feared the possible destruction of their fields or their homes. They were convinced that this emergency called for a special investment in security, and no one hesitated to contribute as much as he could.

Since that day, plans have been made to build a permanent platform of cement beside the circle of stones for the *hawan*. There is a similar platform, square with a circle of earth in the center where the fire is built, beside the Seed Store. Also, one has just been erected beside the entrance to the new cooperative society (the Bank) building. It is ready for the *hawan* and the accompanying ritual which will be conducted by a Hindu priest at the formal opening of the building.

Some of the village men speak of *Parmeshwar*—God. At the same time they, like the others, try to follow the example of their forefathers in honoring the deities who may influence the destinies of their families. The men participate in the more consequential ceremonies. The rest they leave to the women. There are the ceremonies associated with the life of the family—a birth, a marriage, a death. Also in the course of the year there are a good many red-letter days each dedicated to a particular god or goddess. The women welcome every one, even though it may mean added labor in preparing special dishes and cakes. They date events within the family or in families of neighbors or in the village by their association with or proximity to the time of some special religious festival. Some of their ceremonies call for a trip to their special temple in Mainpuri or to the circle of pieces of carved stone by the roadside. Others are performed in the home or nearby where someone has set up a symbol, usually that of Shiva.

Their desire is to appease any deity who might otherwise send disaster to them or to their children, and to please any who have it in their power to grant health and good fortune to the family. They derive a sense of security from their ceremonies and festivals, and also find fun and color in each one. The women and most men of the village would be lost without them.

Has the lot of the untouchables changed during the thirty years? The government has been doing everything legally possible to remove their stigma. In official statements they are now referred to as "the scheduled castes." Measures have been introduced to raise their social and economic position. They are encouraged to make use of government assistance offered in getting an education from primary schools through college. Where the government provides scholarships, first choice is given to members of the scheduled castes. It is possible for them to form a cooperative society subsidized by the government; with its help they may secure loans for productive purposes or buy tools at reduced rates for work other than that which made them untouchables. In a few villages near New Delhi leather workers are now able to make shoes with the aid of such a society; this freed them from their traditional task of skinning dead animals and curing the hides.

However, neither in Karimpur nor in other villages in the district have I seen such a society. There does not seem to be anybody to inform the "scheduled castes" of such a possibility. And there is no indication of a change of attitude toward families of these castes in the village—they still are *dhanuks, chamars,* or *bhangis.*

The New

When life has followed the same pattern for generations, the grooves made by that pattern go deep. To alter the design is difficult. And yet this has happened in Karimpur. The population has grown from 754 in 1931 to 1129 in 1961. Many changes have occurred and there is promise of more to come. Those who have profited from them are satisfied. Those who have suffered from them are dispirited. And all are surprised that so much has been done in so short a time. The changes have not come about easily. Nor have the men of the village rejected the Familiar entirely in adopting the New. They, like their forebears, may have had only a minimum of the necessities for existence or they may have had plenty, but at least they have known what they could count on.

They are now discovering that something better than they have ever known is within their reach. They want it. But experience with its harsh lessons has made them shrewd in their appraisal of anything unfamiliar that is offered to them. It has taught them not to let go easily of the little they have. And the poorer they are the more wary they must be. The result is that while they are reaching out for the new opportunities with one hand, they are keeping a firm grip on the old supports with the other.

Improved crops offer the surest benefits with the least hazards. And they have been accepted with comparatively slight resistance. Better crops bring more money, and more money means more security. Each new kind of seed has had to be tried by one or two farmers with enough land and enough food in the storeroom to risk a field.

One of the first new crops was not food but cotton. About eight years ago, Prakash, head of our household, and one other farmer planted the new seed offered by a government officer. It succeeded. The following year the two pioneers planted more, and others tried a little. Now the new variety, American cotton, is taken for granted. The Mainpuri district offers prizes for producing the most cotton per acre; the first prize is seventy-five rupees (only about fifteen dollars now), and the second is thirty rupees.

Wheat has had a more checkered career. The first seed recommended by government development officers, Kanpur 13, was a disappointment after a brief period of apparent success. The more venturesome farmers switched to Punjab 591, which is now recognized as profitable and is being generally used. A change in the type of corn grown has also occurred. The new variety was enthusiastically welcomed for the first two years. It brought a good price. But the women found the larger kernels hard to grind for the daily cakes and both men and women were sure that the flat cakes of the new corn were not so easily digested as those from the old. Now there is a compromise; a number of farmers raise enough of the old for family use and some of the new for the market, while others have reverted to the old.

As far back as anyone can recall, there have been sugarcane fields. There were three varieties of cane—Java, China, and Machna. Five years ago three farmers decided to plant a new variety—Kalmi Machna. The juice was plentiful and good, but the tender stalks were infested by insects and chewed by mongooses. So a newer variety, Lakra Machna was welcomed. It is tough enough so that no creature seems able to gnaw its way into it, and it provides as much juice as the Kalmi Machna. The *gur* (crude sugar) made from it is considered superior and is lighter in color. This is an advantage when selling it. Farmers raise enough to make *gur* for family use and, if possible, for sale, either to small shops in the village or to larger ones in Mainpuri.

Potatoes have had a varied history. Not content with the small local variety, several farmers went in search of something better. One year they got seed potatoes from Fatehgarh, about forty miles away, well known for its superior potatoes. The next year a farmer hired a truck and went up the mountain to Simla, bringing back potatoes for himself and for sale. But after the hair-raising trip in the loaded truck down the twisting mountain road he abandoned the idea of hill potatoes. Now an outstanding farmer who lives eight miles away, a *kachhi*, brings acceptable potatoes for seed from Dehra Dun, at the foot of the mountains and sells them to our farmers. Some potatoes have come from as far away as Rangoon, brought by sea to Calcutta, where they sell at the rate of fifty rupees a bag. Up-country, where we live, they cost about one hundred twenty-five rupees a bag. Even so, when available, they are considered worth it. Some farmers have been too cautious to take the risk of strange potatoes and continue to raise the old variety. I have watched them digging them up, and they seem hardly worth all the labor that goes into raising them.

Peanuts were not grown here until about eight years ago, when the first came from the Mainpuri Seed Store, a government institution. They proved a great success from the beginning, growing in popularity as the number of mills producing peanut oil in Mainpuri increased.

The newest of new crops are the tomatoes introduced by some of our *kachhis*. They discovered that in Mainpuri tomatoes were bringing a good price, so they got seed, sowed it, and profited. Since then the number of tomato plots has increased. Since *kachhis* are traditionally growers of vegetables by caste, it might not seem surprising for them to introduce new ones. But they are also notably conservative, and it must have taken courage to risk introducing a strange product to the village. As yet no tomatoes appear in the fields of Brahmans, although a few farmers other than *kachhis* have planted them for their own use, in plots located near enough the village so that the fruit can be protected from the ravages of peacocks and crows.

There is no room for kitchen gardens beside village houses. A few farmers used to plant vegetables beside their irrigation wells where water was easily available, but this was not a success. Animals got more than the men who labored with planting and watering. Most families depended on the *kachhis*. Now, more farmers are raising vegetables for family consumption or for sale, planting them in their fields immediately after the spring or summer grain harvest. During the winter months there are not only potatoes, but also sweet potatoes, carrots, peas, spinach, mustard, and other greens. All of these except the carrots are improved varieties. A farmer showed me some of the old variety of peas which he still plants in his barley field. These he held in one hand while in the other he held those he plants in a separate field—the new variety. I had forgotten how small and hard and unappetizing the old ones were, as compared with the large, bright green, succulent peas now grown. As soon as the plots are cleared of winter vegetables, the hot season vegetables are put in. They include several varieties of gourd, cucumbers, and okra. There is also a large plot of muskmelon planted just across the lane from our house. The tube well has made all this possible. The *kachhis* have not suffered from the

change; they still have a profitable market here and in Mainpuri for all the vegetables they can raise.

Government agents have promoted most of the new seed,
but once the farmers have been convinced that the seed offered is better than that which they have been sowing, they go
ahead without need of further persuasion. In the beginning
they had to go to the Seed Store, set up by the government in
Mainpuri. Now there is one here in our village, serving
twenty-five villages in the area, authorized to advance improved seed of all varieites to bona fide farmers. For several
years, farmers had to go to the *patwari* (land recorder),
now known as the *lekhpal,* to beg him to sign a paper en-
titling them to receive seed from the Seed Store. *Lekhpals*
are known for their exploitation of villagers, and ours lived
up to his reputation—making it so difficult for men to get his
signature without a bribe that many gave up. Then a cooperative society, called a "larger cooperative credit society" and
referred to locally as "the Bank," was organized by the government. The Bank secretary now sends the list of members
who require seed to the *lekhpal,* who is expected to sign the
whole list at a fixed rate, eliminating the need for his signature on individual applications. A man cannot get seed unless
he is a member of the Bank.

The Bank does more than this. A man who becomes a
member may pay for one share of ten rupees or he may invest up to one hundred rupees. Then when he is in need of
cash or seed, he is allowed to draw up to five times his investment. He is expected to use this for productive purposes,
but he is also free to use it in other ways, if necessary. In addition he may take an additional "three times" his investment
in kind. This includes implements procured for him by the
Bank, or seed or chemical manure from the Seed Store.
When his grain is harvested he is bound to sell enough to the
cooperative marketing society in Mainpuri to repay his loan
with the interest (9 per cent). The amount of his sale to the

marketing society, a member of which he has automatically become on joining the credit society, is reported back to the Seed Store and Bank here in Karimpur. After this obligation is met, he is free to sell the remainder of his produce whereever he pleases. Loans of up to five times a man's share of money invested may also be given to carpenters, goldsmiths, or potters for materials or equipment. Any artisan who borrows is expected to repay his loan with interest within three months. Failing this, he is given another three months, and after that he is charged overdues in addition to the loan and interest.

My introduction to the Bank came unexpectedly on the day of my return. When I started to go into our large front room to put away some supplies, I found the door of the room bolted, with an oversize padlock hooked through the bolt. On peering through the window in the upper part of the wooden door, I saw an odd assortment of desks, tables, and chairs, strewn with office files; there were more files and loose papers on the floor, and there was a filing cabinet and a large safe. The family explained that "the Bank" had been using the room for the preceding two years while waiting for a new building to be constructed. They had sent word to the secretary, who lives in Mainpuri, to come and clear the room, but his wife had had a baby that morning and he was unable to leave home. He arrived two days later; an attractive, enthusiastic young man. He speedily removed his records to the Seed Store but left the safe with us to be guarded by the men of the family. We became friends, and a few days later he invited me to attend the annual meeting of the shareholders of the "larger cooperative society," which includes forty villages. There were about two hundred and fifty men sitting on the ground beside the Seed Store, all farmers except for a few, obviously townsmen, who were officiating—representatives of the government rural-development program. The secretary was disappointed in the number attending the meeting—there should have been twelve hundred there. After the secretary's long report, the members were free to ask questions. This they did. Their questions were intelligent, much to the point, and sometimes difficult for the development officers or the secretary to answer. Then the officer responsible for cooperatives took over, asking the men who the owner of the cooperative society was. Several answered at once, *Sirkar ka* — the government's. This was formerly what cooperative society members thought, but serious efforts have been made to change their attitude. Simple lessons have been prepared on the purposes and functions of a cooperative credit society and on the responsibilities and privileges of individual members. Apparently our society had been launched without a clear idea on the part of the members of what was expected of them, and at this meeting the officer tried to enlighten them—it was quite sobering. Thinking about the meeting afterward, I understood how natural it was for members to regard the society as belonging to the government. Government representatives had organized it, and the secretary is paid by the government. If farmers want better seed they must join it, and they must sell their grain at the headquarters of the marketing society, also a government-sponsored body.

The next day when I asked the secretary about the condition of the society, he gave me a glowing report of a smoothly functioning organization in which loans were repaid promptly, and there were no arrears. But when I talked with some of the farmers whose money is invested they were more realistic. They are concerned about the members who do not assume responsibility for repaying loans, especially those who spend the borrowed money for weddings. They know that the society is no ordinary money lender, to be put off with promises. It will perhaps be their influence and, if necessary, their pressure, that will keep the society functioning.

Implements have a history similar to that of seed. As soon

as a new implement has been demonstrated and found good someone with enough cash to invest and enough security to run the risk makes the first purchase. Then others able to invest follow cautiously, and gradually still others save enough to buy it. Everyone in the village knows who owns anything as important as a new implement. On lists made for me of the heads of families who own improved implements, especially those that border on the expensive, the same names are repeated again and again—all Brahmans and *kachhis*.

Ploughs have made progress. When we lived here before there were sixty-two ordinary ploughs in use; now there are one hundred and two, and in addition there are twenty-six factory-made ploughs, owned by twenty-two farmers. The old-type ploughs, made by local carpenters, and factory-made ploughs are used side by side. In preparing his fields, Prakash uses the new plough first, because it ploughs deep. This he follows with the old wooden plough with its small iron tip, for shallow ploughing, going over the field with it several times—as often as he thinks is needed. When we lived in the grove, the American who first adapted the steel plough to conditions in Indian villages brought one to Karimpur for demonstration. Farmers were impressed by what it could accomplish, but no one was sufficiently interested to buy one. This plough and a similar plough won by a young farmer from Karimpur at the annual district exhibition lay idle. The men said that they were too heavy to carry from plot to plot and too heavy for their oxen to pull. Now, this same American and others have succeeded in producing steel ploughs that are acceptable. Our farmers carry theirs to the fields by ox cart, and those who own them have oxen strong enough to pull them. The earlier product was good but the villagers knew that it was not practical for them. They did not criticize it—they ignored it. When a plough that met their needs satisfactorily appeared, those who could afford to adopted it. Those who cannot afford to buy, borrow from their more prosperous neighbors. This has its drawbacks. The borrower must wait until the owner has finished his own ploughing. Also, there may be several borrowers lined up and each must wait his turn. This may mean a loss of days when time is important.

A "dibbler"—drill—is used by some farmers for the crops planted after the rains—wheat, barley, gram, peas. No one in the village owns one. The Seed Store keeps three or four at the time of sowing ready to loan, free of charge, for any who ask for it. Some farmers, who have plenty of seed and plenty of land, say that sowing with the "dibbler" is too slow. The quantity of seed saved does not compensate for the extra time spent, especially when the sower is a laborer hired by the day. They prefer to pour the seed through the slender bamboo tube, on the trail of the plough. However, to those who have little land and who must be sparing in the use of seed, the "dibbler" is a saving, and they are enthusiastic about it.

The Seed Store also has two improved cultivators, hoping that they eventually will be accepted. One is reserved for demonstrations conducted by the *gram sevak*, or "village companion," who is employed by the government to assist farmers in Karimpur and seven neighboring villages. The other is lent without charge to those farmers who have watched and understood the demonstration. Thus far the purchase price has been prohibitive, so men continue to borrow from the Seed Store.

Now there are nine sugar presses. There were just two when we were here before. Sugarcane growers had already changed from the wooden press to one of metal with cogs, and this type is still used. Sugarcane juice is very popular; it makes a delicious drink when mixed fresh with curds, and cooked with rice it provides one of the special dishes of the season. Most of the sugarcane is boiled down in a large cauldron, the aroma spreading over the whole village, then is poured out into a shallow container set in the ground, stirred until firm, and pressed into a large conical mold made by the

potter. This is the *gur*, or crude sugar, of this part of the
country. As yet there are no large sugar mills in the area
demanding all the cane. So we have the benefit of home-
pressing every evening during the weeks when *gur* is being
made. The children sit beside the cauldron keeping warm
while they wait, and the moment the *gur* is ready to be pressed
into the mold, they take a sample in a brass bowl and come
running home with it. We feel sorry for those who know only
the taste of refined sugar, or of *gur* that has been standing in
a shop in the bazaar.

The one piece of equipment that has had almost immediate acceptance is the fodder cutter, and there are now forty-
two cutting machines in the village. While we lived here
earlier one familiar evening sound was the steady beat of
hand choppers, as one man of the family sat on the ground
for an hour or two patiently chopping fodder for the animals.
Chitam Lal, the former head of the village, was the first to discover the hand-propelled cutter. He saw it demonstrated at
one of the annual district exhibitions several years ago and
invested in it almost immediately. It was so obviously an improvement over the old chopper that others bought the cutters as soon as they could save or borrow the money. The
new chopper, which is bolted to the ground and cannot be
borrowed, is equipped with a large wheel turned by one or
two men, while another person, often one of the women or
older children, feeds in the stalks of grain. The work is done
much more rapidly and more safely than with the old hand
chopper and block of wood—we have dressed many a hand
badly hurt by the old chopper. Poorer families must continue to chop bit by bit.

Among smaller implements there is a new type of sickle,
resembling the old but with a longer blade and a saw-tooth
edge. This, they say, is excellent for cutting wheat or barley
or rice. They use it as they did the old sickle, squatting and
gradually hitching forward as they cut the grain. The new

model is not too drastic a change from the old and it does bring advantages. Best of all, most farmers can afford to buy it.

A lantern is taken for granted on farms where there is no electricity. For a farmer in our village it is not an absolute necessity. His animals are beside him wherever he sleeps, be it in courtyard or stable, or in the lane outside the door when nights are stifling. While he protects them from cattle thieves they are guarding his household from other kinds of thieves. But when days are short or when he must work in the fields until after dark, he needs some sort of light while he cuts the fodder and settles the animals for the night. Thirty years ago most farmers depended on the small open saucer lamps of clay, containing mustard oil with short wicks of twisted cotton. Now there are two hundred and twenty-seven lanterns, each one a subject of considerable discussion before its purchase. Not all are functioning. Instructions for their care do not come with them. Prakash has two, both giving only half light because the chimneys are blackened by smoke, and one having such large holes in the chimney that only Prakash dares to move it. Even so, they give more light and are safer than the open-saucer lamps. For families with too little money to buy lanterns, there are miniature kerosene oil lamps made of tin, with small wicks and no chimneys to break or to collect smoke. There are more than five hundred and fifty of these now, whereas they did not exist in our earlier day. They are brighter than an ordinary candle and can be safely carried. I have often been guided to the back of a dark storeroom to see some sufferer by the light of one of these.

In addition to improved equipment and new varieties of seed, the farmers have accepted chemical fertilizer as another step toward better crops. Until a few years ago, villagers in this part of the country had never heard of chemical fertilizer. Now, everyone who possibly can purchases it or gets it from the Seed Store as part of his loan in kind from the Bank.

Farmers have learned which fertilizer is best for which crop, and how much of each is required. They are careful not to waste an ounce.

Before chemical fertilizers were known, farmers had begun to use compost. Even before Independence, a few men had changed from the old open piles to the pits. But it was not until the government became actively interested that compost pits were introduced on a large scale. Orders were brought to the village by local government officers that every farmer must dig three pits. This they did. Some neglected theirs after they had been inspected. But wise farmers have discovered that here is an opportunity to turn sweepings with a little dung—all free—into something that makes land more productive. Sweepings include much more than dust. When the women sit on the ground in the courtyard shelling peas, they drop the shells on the ground. The children, when they eat peanuts, scatter the shells wherever they happen to be. In sugarcane season, they come in with long pieces of cane, strip them with teeth or knife and suck the delicious juice. The unwanted pulp is strewn over the courtyard. And when mangoes are plentiful, everyone enjoys them, discarding skins and stones on the ground. Other fruit is treated in the same way. All the possible food value of vegetables is preserved by cooking them unpeeled, except when the peelings are too tough to be edible. Those that must be removed, join other refuse on the ground. Every morning and evening one of the women of the family sweeps the courtyard and leaves the accumulation just outside the door, for one of the men to collect in a basket and carry off to the family compost pit. This is regarded as part of their farm work, in a different class from cleaning the household drain or other dirty jobs still left to the sweepers. I have indulged in a covered container for garbage which I empty into my compost pit. But as yet no one has considered it useful or convenient enough to be copied.

Not only do wise farmers have compost pits, but also some men without land have adopted the idea. They sell their compost to farmers; or, instead of buying, a farmer may make use of the compost and then share his harvest with the man from whom he took it. Din Dayal, a cautious farmer, adds: "I share the produce from a field with a nonfarmer for one year only. If he shares it for more than a year, he might lay claim to part of the field."

Among the most conspicious improvements is the water supply for irrigation. For years the farmers here, as in other villages, sent persistent requests to the government asking for an extension of the nearest irrigation canal, which was the only plentiful water supply known at that time. The wells from which farmers drew water for their fields were inadequate, and there was constant fear of drought. Then, about eight years ago, the government undertook to put in tube wells. Now all through the district we see tube wells along the roads. Karimpur has access to three, although the main water source is the one just beside the village. The apportioning of water was for some time a problem. Farmers were to pay for water at an established rate, but in addition to this the tube-well operator, a government employee, found ways of exacting his own personal rate in return for the favor of granting water. He was able to take advantage of the fact that the demand always exceeded the supply, with the result that those who were in a position to pay the extra amount got the water while others suffered from lack of it. Now a government official appoints six village men, farmers, one of whom is the *pradhan* (the president of the village council), who are responsible for preparing lists of the names of all farmers applying for water so that each applicant receives his rightful share. The tube-well operator follows their instructions, and this safeguards a supply for every farmer. Since there is never enough water for all the crops, farmers use their own wells in addition, during seasons when irrigation is needed. There are now forty-two wells from which they draw water by the traditional method, seven more than there were thirty years ago. A few farmers have installed Persian wheels in their wells, and, although the original expense of such wheels seems high to most farmers, the number of shops in Mainpuri where the equipment is being made and sold indicates that there is an increasing demand in the district.

Within the village, wells supplying water for household use have multiplied more than have those intended for irrigation. There are now forty-five such wells, twice as many as when we lived here before. Most of these are situated along the lanes, and a few are inside courtyards. The Brahman families have private wells either inside the house or just outside the door. Some wells are shared by all members of one caste, or by those belonging to one of the groups below caste lines. Still others are used by several castes. One well, which is down our lane a short distance, is shared by the goldsmiths, a few of the carpenters, the *darzis* (sewing men), and the oilsmiths. All the wells outside the courtyards were freshly repaired about four years ago. A government agent with enthusiasm and with funds from the government for materials initiated the building project. Villagers provided the labor and shared in the pride of achievement. Each well was surrounded by a cement parapet high enough so that children or animals could not tumble in, and around each one was a slightly raised platform of cement where men could bathe or women wash clothes without spilling water back into the well. A few of these wells are still in good condition. But others, which have had hard use, look sadly neglected. No one thus far has considered repairing them. But if another enthusiastic agent, provided with funds for repairs, were to come, the repairing would be carried out with the same pride. Meanwhile, protective walls and platforms around the wells continue to crumble. Building seems to be in one category and maintenance in another. The villagers faithfully replaster and repair their mud-house walls year after year, just before the rains. They do it—or at least the wise ones do—to save the walls from collapsing, and the man who fails to is regarded as a poor householder.

There are two pumps in the village, one of them ours. I arranged to have ours installed in the courtyard as soon as possible after my return. The cost staggered me, but when one considers that it will function for years if cared for, it does not seem extravagant. Moreover, I needed a pump badly. During the first few weeks all my water had to come from Prakash's well some distance away. It is a Brahman well, and my caste is not defined, which made it undesirable for them that I drop my bucket into the well to draw water—with the result that I spent a good deal of time waiting for one of the sons or a *bahu* to come to my rescue.

Several men have said that if our pump proves successful they will consider having pumps in their homes. They are sure that the water is superior because it comes from a greater depth than that of their wells. Everyone, regardless of caste, has come to taste it. And all agree that it is good. The whole family is delighted. The *bahus* come here for water for household purposes rather than to their own well which is out in front of their house, partly because they prefer this water, but also because in our courtyard they are not exposed to the eyes of passers-by.

Almost immediately after the pump began to function, there was an urgent request for a brick-walled bathing cubicle beside it. I had seen such cubicles beside two village wells and thought them an excellent idea, but these have never been used. After all, a woman accustomed to the privacy of her courtyard would find it difficult to walk down the lane obviously to take a bath beside a public well. Even in their own homes, bathing has always seemed to me to be one of their greatest hardships. The only place where they can bathe is the courtyard. Someone stands at the door to give

warning should one of the men of the family approach, or a
cot on end covered with a sheet serves as a screen, while
each woman in turn stands on a stone slab or two bricks and
pours water from a bucket over herself and her *dhoti.* As she
removes the wet garment she puts on a clean, dry one which
also serves as towel. Nothing more than her shoulders is exposed during the exchange. The soiled *dhoti* is washed with
the water left in the bucket and hung up to dry.

Since the advent of our pump and bathing cubicle, our
courtyard is aflutter with drying *dhotis* during the early afternoon respite. Every woman in the family says that there can
be nothing pleasanter than bathing in the sunshine and in
privacy, with plenty of warm water fresh from the pump.
The *bahus* bless our cubicle every day. And so do I.

Over the years, medical care has gradually gained in importance. People used to come to our tent for simple treatments, or, whenever a doctor visited us, for professional help.
But to persuade anyone to go to a doctor or hospital in town
for treatment was almost impossible. Now every family that
can afford it makes use of town medical services, going by
bus or by ox cart. They are familiar with the government
hospital and with several private physicians. They purchase
the medicines prescribed by the doctor and do not quite expect them to have magic charm, as they once did. I can help
them with ordinary ailments, but in serious cases I suggest
going to town. Often they report that they have already
been to at least one doctor in town. Twice I have gone with
patients to the clinics of private physicians, where the doctor,
his assistant, and all patients had to share one room. The
doctor sat at a large desk strewn with prescriptions, notes on
different patients, and bills, and the patients were lined up
on benches facing him. The first doctor took time to listen
briefly to each patient's report, either from the patient himself or from some relative. He also had a table for examinations behind a curtain on one side of his consulting room

and a pharmacist behind a counter on the other. The room
had a wide door opening on a noisy, dusty thoroughfare.
The whole setup made it difficult for both doctor and patients, although the doctor's years of professional experience
under these circumstances must have helped him in his diagnosis and treatment. Obviously, he had a way of inspiring
confidence as he gave instructions. The second doctor, also
surrounded by patients, was without the benefit of an examining table. He discussed symptoms with one patient across his
desk while examining another sitting beside him. Stethoscope
at ear, he shouted questions to someone across the room.
While taking a pulse count he was writing a prescription. His
assistant, standing behind him ready for an injection with a
syringe protected by a bit of cotton in one hand, was kept
busy hunting through papers with the other hand for the
record of someone's past treatment. Through all this turmoil,
added to by the noise from the bazaar outside, the doctor
seemed to be in control, and his advice was accepted with
considerable respect by each patient in turn. Injections are
popular, with both doctors and patients, and perhaps are surer
and safer than medicines taken home to be administered later.
After having visited these two doctors, I am no longer
annoyed by the long recital of ailments or suffering to which
I am asked to listen. What the patient and his relatives
seem to want as much as medical service is a sympathetic
listener, and doctors are much too busy for this.

There are still several *hakims*, untrained practitioners, in the
village. More than one patient has declared that when the
expensive medicine from the town doctor has failed, one of
our *hakims* here or in Mainpuri has cured him. The *hakims*
of our village assume a superprofessional air, perhaps because
they must compensate for their lack of training as compared
with the professional doctors. They are illiterate, but they do
have a knowledge of the virtues of certain roots, bark, leaves,
and herbs, and they have an understanding of village people.

Their mixtures are often effective, but they vary considerably from dose to dose.

Public health has lagged far behind medical treatment. There seems to be little information in the village regarding the prevention of disease and no noticeable attempt at prevention. Schoolbooks contain illustrated lessons on the dangers of flies, but adults do not look at the books, and the flies still abound hovering over open drains and exposed fecal matter and settling on food. With the coming of warm weather the flies increase, until the intense heat of June removes them—temporarily.

Sanitation has not yet entered the scene. Two friends of ours have just completed a diagnostic survey of in-patients, out-patients, and extension patients being treated by a hospital forty miles away. They found that intestinal parasitic diseases topped the list—one fifth of all the cases diagnosed. As long as fields near the village, and the roadsides, are converted into night and early-morning latrines, parasites will flourish. The swine, herded by sweepers, are supposed to clean up the night soil, but the flies are there before and after them. Sanitary engineers are doing their utmost to find some means of disposal that will be an improvement over the swine and at the same time be acceptable. Our hand-flush toilet with its junior septic tank, quite inexpensive, has not yet aroused interest among the adults of the village. It may not be the answer, but something like it, or better, is needed if people are to be free from diseases traceable to a few of their old habits.

Ten years ago the government sent a trained midwife to the village, in the hope of reducing the hazards of childbirth. She was not satisfied with the response the women gave her. They rarely called her, because whether or not she attended them they were obliged to give something to the local untrained midwife (the *dai*) who, like her mother-in-law and grandmother-in-law, had always been associated with their family. The double payment seemed an extravagance. However, the actual help at the time of delivery was only a part of the government midwife's assignment. She was responsible for the distribution of dried milk to children who needed it. (One father told me of his debt of gratitude to her; his wife died when their third son was a baby, and the midwife not only taught him how to prepare the milk, but often came to feed the child herself.) Her chief duty was to train the local midwives, who are women belonging to one of the groups below the caste barrier—*dhanukins*—since birth is regarded as unclean. They had no idea of the need for cleanliness, but evidently she taught them well. A number of women have spoken about the care which these local midwives now take—removing bangles and rings, washing hands, and putting on a clean *dhoti*, boiling the thread and whatever implement is used for cutting the cord. The government midwife was here about five years, and the local midwives complain that although while she was here each of them received a tin box containing soap, disinfectant, thread, and scissors they have never been given refills, nor can they afford to buy them. The materials have been used up or misplaced, so as far as equipment is concerned they are where they were before their training. But the advance in cleanliness has been worth the venture. There is now a partially trained midwife, also sent by the government, who lives beside the district road. People know that she is here, but no one has mentioned calling her. She and her husband supplement her small salary by making saucers and plates of leaves, sold to anyone preparing to have a feast.

The government, assisted by the World Health Organization, has made a major contribution to the health of the public in a nation-wide campaign against malaria. During the rains a team of workers comes to the village and sprays all walls in all the houses with a special insecticide, and every case of malaria is supposed to be reported for immediate treatment.

Thirty years ago malaria was accepted as inevitable; no one thought it possible to free the village of it, and yet this is what is happening. We seldom hear it mentioned, but the success of the effort throughout this area is demonstrated in the hospital survey mentioned earlier. The number of cases of malaria has dropped from six hundred and twenty-one in 1958, to one hundred and nineteen in 1961. The public health authorities are freeing us of malaria by ridding men of the disease and destroying the anopheles which act as carriers, but this does not mean that we are free from mosquitoes. As soon as the flies settle down for the night, the mosquitoes are upon us in swarms. And we have no way of guarding against them. I wear a *sari* every evening, to protect my legs and arms as we sit in the courtyard. These mosquitoes may not be responsible for malaria, but they are most annoying. I sometimes wonder if children whose faces are swollen each morning, from what looks like a rash of mosquito bites, might not be healthier if they were protected. I have three mosquito nets—two available for anyone who thinks it worth the bother of putting up, and one for myself. Thus far, I alone depend on a net. When malaria has been controlled, the other mosquitoes may get attention, and screens may be transferred from the category of luxuries to that of necessities.

The school has had a large part in the changes taking place in the village. We recall it as an ineffective institution, unrelated to the lives of the village children. The masters, with little training, were of necessity more concerned with ways of stretching their meager income than with the teaching of their pupils. Now the picture is different; the school is larger and a well-trained headmaster directs it. He lives at the school six days a week with his one small son and goes to his home on Sundays for home-ground flour and other supplies. He maintains the standards of the physical setup of the school as well as that of the classes. He teaches the fifth and sixth grades. Another master teaches the third and fourth grades, and another teaches first and second. One of these masters boards with a *kachhi* family living near the school, and the other cycles to and from his home, two miles away. There are also two women teachers who teach the girls; one of them has a family in Mainpuri but lives here, and the other belongs to one of the local Brahman families. There are two girls studying in the sixth grade in the room with boys of the fifth and sixth grades. The other girls are all in one room—from the first to the sixth grade—with the two women teachers. One day when I stepped into their room they were all studying aloud, as is customary, with no sign of a teacher to watch them—both women had gone to Mainpuri on an errand. They all stood up at once when I came in—as they do for their teachers. Where could one find better self-discipline?

There are plans for further development of the school. An agricultural master is expected soon, and land has been set aside for his classes. A new building is contemplated on the edge of the village not far from our house, which will accommodate classes through junior high school. The present school is overcrowded, and several classes must be held under a tree beside the school, which is good in fair weather but impossible during the rains. Six boys walk two miles across the fields to attend seventh and eighth grades, and two go to high school in Mainpuri. The new school, like the present one, will serve at least eleven smaller villages and hamlets around Karimpur.

My figures on school attendance for this year are limited to children of Karimpur proper. The council president reports that there are 306 boys and girls in the village between the ages of six and twelve. There are 96 Karimpur boys enrolled in the school and 32 girls. The amount of "wastage," that is the number of drop-outs, is suggested by the fact that in the first and second grades combined there are 44 boys and 14 girls, while in the sixth grade there are four boys and two girls. At least half the members of each class are Brahmans. *Kachhis* are next most numerous. Other castes have one or two in a class—carpenters, water carriers, potters, shepherds, sewing men, goldsmiths, flower growers, and leather workers. There are also a few Muslims. There are no children of the two washerman families in school, and this is easily understood when one watches them at work all day beside the pond.There are no oilsmith children nor *dhanuks*, who belong, like the washerman, to groups below caste lines. And there are no Christians, also classed as below caste lines because all Christians in Karimpur are converts from the sweeper caste. This is disappointing after all the effort on the part of the Christian pastor to make it possible for his son to attend. I thought our Brahman friends responsible for the exclusion of the Christians, but this they denied. Later I talked with Christian parents, who said that no objection has been raised to their children's attending, but that they just do not see enough benefit from school attendance to compensate for the trouble of sending them. They say they cannot afford the fees—which are extremely small. In addition there are books to be purchased, and there is the problem of clothes. School children are dressed simply, like their parents, but they do look neat and their clothes are clean. The *dhobi* will not wash clothes for the Christians as he does for others, because they are the sweepers and he considers them too dirty. The scavenging they do for the village makes it difficult for the mothers to keep their children clean. In addition to their own cooking and household work, they must spend hours every day in other homes, making them clean for other people's children.

The books studied by children going to school now are far different from those which their fathers read. They follow the new pattern of village life. There are the regular subjects—reading, writing, arithmetic, history—all geared to village problems and village interests. In addition, there are textbooks on better ways of farming and on village sanitation, putting farming on a new and higher level. What we lack is a library of books that will interest these boys and girls when they leave school, at the age of nine or of fifteen. There is a tendency to drop reading when there are no lessons to prepare. Both the government and private agencies have published excellent books, short enough to encourage reading, with clear print and attractive illustrations. There are, of course, other more advanced books for those who finish high school.

The village has a night reading class conducted by one of the few young men who have finished high school. This much education has given him prestige, even though because he failed his final examinations he is termed "high-school fail." When one thinks of the handicaps of village boys who cycle to town to school and try to study at night by dim light, surrounded by relatives young and old, one wonders how any of them can pass the final examinations. Few do. This young farmer is sufficiently interested to teach the class after his day's work in the fields. They meet in the stable of a *kachhi* in Humble Lane, with the family buffalo eating or sleeping beside them. It cannot be the pay that attracts the young teacher. All the government gives him is a very small allowance during the five winter months when the school functions, two lanterns, an alphabet chart, small mats for the pupils to sit on, and seven primers. The students write on their black-painted board slates, except for three who own notebooks and pencils. There are twenty-six boys and young men in the class, ranging in age from twelve to twenty and coming from all castes. While some struggle with the alphabet and primer, the more advanced pupils provide their own books, if they can afford them. Two of the young men, Christians, can read well and write letters to their relatives in Calcutta. Neither has ever been to a regular school; all that they have learned has been taught them by the farmer-teacher.

Improved communications have made a great difference in the life of the village. Some say that buses owned by private

companies have been passing by for twenty years, but no one
is quite sure. In the beginning only a few men made use of
them, first traveling to Mainpuri, and then farther afield to
Etah, about thirty miles away. There was the fare to consider—one's own ox cart could carry a number of people at
no extra cost, except perhaps the additional fodder for the
oxen. There was one advantage in travel by bus: it got a man
to his destination much faster than the oxen could, and when
a member of the family was ill the speed of the bus was a
relief. Also, the villagers thought that the bus did not shake
the patient up so badly as the ox cart, although on my several bus trips in to Mainpuri I have been doubtful about this.
Now, there are five private buses going to Mainpuri every
day, and six going in the opposite direction, to Etah. A year
ago, the government opened a bus line on the same route, with
seven buses, labeled "Roadways," going each way daily.
There are rumors that the private buses will have to go out of
circulation shortly and retreat to areas where the Roadways
buses do not go, but for the present we are well provided for.
There is always a small group of people waiting at the bus
stop out on the district road, each laden with bundles of
varied shapes and sizes, or with metal boxes which are hoisted
to the roof. Women are using the buses now, as well as the
men. They are usually accompanied by men, but Buaji, a
confirmed bus traveler, has made trips alone to a doctor in
Mainpuri. The trip each way is a quarter of a rupee, but
even this is too much for the poor. They stay at home or
walk.

An increasing number of men are now going to Mainpuri
on business, either to the district court or to the bazaar—the
marketing section. They have found that much time is lost
in waiting for a bus or getting from the bus stand to their
destination. So they have purchased bicycles. Formerly only
boys going to high school in Mainpuri rode cycles and there
were just two, thirty years ago. Our introduction to the

"cycle age" was during the games at our house-warming festival. Someone suggested that a cycle race would be exciting, and suddenly the lane was awhirl with careening cycles. There are fifty-six in Karimpur now. In families with cycles, the city seems much more accessible than it once did. Before their own vegetables are ready, men can bring them from the bazaar. They can carry cotton for quilts on the carriers of their cycles and bring the finished quilts home the same way. Shepherds carry milk for sale to town. Others go on business, or to visit relatives, or to go to the court. And they all bring home word of what they have seen or heard. This is usually news of the latest railway accident on the local line, or the advertising of some new patent medicine. At the moment, the greatest excitement is over the election of one member of the legislative assembly in Lucknow and one member of the central parliament from this constituency. Villagers are canny, and election promises leave them cold. As they go about their business, they listen to the speeches sent out over loudspeakers in town. But they draw their own conclusions.

As yet there is no radio in the village. And there is little opportunity to see moving pictures. I once asked Subedar, our council president, if young men of the village ever go to the cinemas in Mainpuri. He said that only those go who, like himself, make frequent trips to town by cycle and who have enough money. Those who go by ox cart have no place to park their oxen. Also they must consider the long ride home and the evening chores. No one, either on a cycle or in a cart, chooses to be on the road after dark. This limits the enjoyment of city diversions. During the annual District Exhibition or Fair, however, there are several tent cinemas to which everyone goes.

For the Fair, held just outside Mainpuri, ox carts are still the mode of travel. The whole family—even the *bahus*—can crowd into one or two carts, and the ride is a lark. Some of the men prefer to go their independent way on bicycles, while others walk beside the family cart or perch at front or back. The Fair, which has been held for at least thirty-five years, brings new ideas to the men and women of the village. The men study the improved implements and examine the stock exhibited by the Agricultural Department of the government. The women loiter past stalls of all sorts, seeing many things that they could use and still more that they do not want. For weeks before the Fair, they talk about what is to come, and for weeks after they talk of the wonders they have seen —the perfumes, the scented soaps, the silks, the jewelry, the circus, and the cinema. Like the men, they are cautious buyers and usually come home with a special clay jar, or a few painted clay animals for the children, a sieve, or a few bright-colored glass bangles, or perhaps a *sari* or cotton material for a blouse. Nothing expensive, for costly purchases take more time to think over than is possible in the press of the Fair. But they have had a glimpse of a different world. It is understood that village men and women and their children will attend the Fair by day, and city people by night. But when the roads are alive with carts, villagers dare wait until dark to return home—with someone going on ahead to look after the cow or buffalo. If they delay until the city people appear, the women are provided with many tales to tell. They see *saris* like those displayed in the stalls, on ladies with delicate skins, white, even teeth and glistening hair, some even with their heads uncovered. They see jewelry, more dazzling than any they have treasured as wedding gifts, worn on beautiful, smooth necks and arms. They do not realize that except for a few wives of government officials or lawyers or doctors, these women will return to small quarters in town and spend their days in clothes as simple as their own. They do not envy these women. They accept the fact that town women belong to a different—a magic—world.

The post office has played its part in the development of

communications. It was opened twelve years ago. The post-master serves not only Karimpur but several smaller villages near by. He usually manages to reach these through boys who come here from the other villages to school, turning post-cards over to them to be carried to relatives or neighbors. But anything as important as a registered letter or money order he must deliver in person. Most of his business is in postcards; a few less than one hundred and fifty went out of Karimpur during the first two weeks of last December and a few more than that came in. Letters are not so popular.

A newspaper comes, published by the government, for the headmaster of the school and for the *pradhan* (council pres-ident). No one subscribes to a newspaper. I have seen newspapers in the village just twice—once on the day when India took possession of Goa and once when the *pradhan* brought a copy home because of an article in it of interest to him. The postcards usually concern arrangements for a young woman to be brought to her father's home from her in-laws, or for her to be brought to her in-laws from her father's home. Some have to do with proposed visits from relatives. Sealed letters usually contain marriage feelers or business matters. However, most business transactions are carried on through personal contacts. Farmers say that they know better how to deal with sharp city middlemen if they meet them face to face.

With the greater convenience in visiting the town, men, and sometimes women, are tempted to buy more mill-made goods, especially when these are cheaper or better than similar things made in the village. One of the goldsmith brothers discovered this tendency to buy in town three years ago. He complained to me then, that people would buy in Mainpuri exactly what he was able to make here, simply because they thought that town goldsmiths were more skillful. He hunted until he found a shop and transported his tools and his chil-dren to Mainpuri, where he is doing a thriving business. He called a younger brother here to keep the trade of his *jajmans*. The brother obeyed as a younger brother should, and came, but he is most resentful at being handed the poor end of the business. He gets some orders for silver jewelry and hopes for more as the wedding season approaches.

Like the wise goldsmith, the shepherds have taken advantage of the contacts in town. They had been taking *ghi* to Mainpuri from time to time. Now they have a regular trade with makers of sweets there. Three of them load their bicycles, front and back, with tin containers of various sizes filled with milk. They carry milk from their own buffaloes and milk which they buy from their village neighbors, extended with milk from their own goats. Goats' milk is satisfactory for the boiled-down milk used for making rich sweets, much better than the water proverbially added by milk vendors going to the larger cities. They go early in the morning, so that they are back in time to take their goats or sheep out to graze—unless they are fortunate enough to have small brothers or sisters or their own children to do the herding. They have fewer animals now than formerly; thirty years ago they had more than four hundred goats and more than two hundred sheep, but now they are down to two hundred and sixty-four goats and only eighty-five sheep. This is partly because there is less grazing ground and partly because they have denuded the *neem* trees within walking distance of the village. Goats prefer *neem* leaves to any other, so with sharp sickles fastened to the tips of bamboo poles the shepherds lop off branches and drop them on the ground for the animals to eat.

Two *mahajan* brothers (shopkeepers) living out on the public road have profited not so much from direct contact with the town as by the trade that has come to them from others on their way to or from town. One has a shop, similar to that of his aunt, the *mahajani*, whom we knew in our earlier days here. But he has extended his stock to include oil—both

kerosene oil for lanterns and mustard oil for cooking—*gur,*
ghi, and soap, in addition to the matches, cigarettes and
biris (small home-made cigarettes) sold by his aunt. In front
of his shop, his younger brother has set up a cycle-repair center. He works under a tree, on cycles of those who have had
trouble on the road or others who have discovered his skill.
They come to him rather than pay the higher price for poorer
work in town. He has no rent to pay and his tools are the simplest. Another *mahajan* family of two brothers has benefited
by the increased traffic to the city; each of them has invested
in a pair of oxen and a cart, which they hire out to farmers
who have large supplies of grain they want to dispose of in
town while prices are favorable. And down the road a short
distance from the *mahajan's* shop, a Brahman has opened a
small stand at the bus stop, where he sells home-made sweets
and peanuts raised here and roasted by the local grain parchers. People who must wait for a bus patronize him, and
others who have sampled his wares make a dash from the
bus and return with something to help pass the time on the
tedious journey. He too is thriving.

Others have had reverses rather than benefits from the
closer touch with the town. When I went to see a sick child
in the house of one of the three oilsmiths, I expected to find
the small ox going his steady round. Often I had watched him
turning the heavy wooden pestle pressing oil from mustard
seed, in the mortar made from a large tree trunk. But the
mortar and pestle lay idle. The oilsmith showed me with
pride what good wood there was in each part and talked
of all the oil he could press. But he can no longer compete
with the oil mills of Mainpuri. People find it cheaper to carry
their mustard seed in to town and have the pressing done
there. There is nothing else that he or his two brothers,
whose presses also are idle, are trained to do. So they wait
for jobs as day laborers on the land. When I asked them
why they did not get work in one of the oil mills in the city,

they said they could not manage the six-mile walk before and after a day's work in a mill. And bus fare, though little, would use up most of their earnings. If they had cycles they could manage it.

The cotton carder had a similar story to tell. Villagers say that he keeps more than his share of the cotton which they take to him to card and put into quilts for them. He says that he has to take this much if he and his family are to live. He realizes that the mills do it more cheaply than he can afford to, yet he has found no way of competing with them. Farmers going to town by cycle or with a load of grain or peanuts find it easy to bring back a finished quilt, and they no longer feel the responsibility which their forefathers always accepted for those who have served them. The sewing men likewise complain. Families on whom they could depend for the job of sewing their shirts and shorts, women's blouses, and clothes for the children, now prefer to buy some of their garments ready-made in town. They still have their ordinary clothes, those to be worn in the fields or courtyards, made by the sewing man attached to their family, but the earlier sense of security has been replaced by fear of growing competition. The *jajmans* say that there are too few sewing men left to do the work that needs to be done. Five have died in the past six years, but those who remain insist that they could do all the work required, if given a chance.

The carpenters present the same picture of declining business. When we used to walk, with our two small sons, down the lane where they lived, we always stopped to watch them. Their work area in the shelter of a big tree was full of activity; carts were being built or repaired, large tree trunks were being sawed and planed to make doors and door frames. In sowing season there were farmers waiting while their ploughshares were being sharpened. Now there are just three carpenters at this end of the lane, one of whom is badly crippled. Farther down the lane is Dwarka's son, who served his apprenticeship under Dwarka until he died two years ago; he is young and strong and always extremely busy with his tools or his anvil. The two brothers who moved from the carpenter community here out to the roadside are likewise kept busy. Five carpenters have died within the past four years, and six more died during the previous five. Cholera took most of them, as it did a number of the sewing men. The district medical authorities have taken all possible precautions to prevent such an epidemic, and we hear of cholera much less often. In this case, the doctor came as soon as he was informed and was able to save many from infection, but these two groups, neighbors, had already lost most of their wage earners. Even before these losses some *jajmans* had begun going to better equipped carpenters in Mainpuri when they wanted something with a neater finish or at a lower price, but the bother of hauling the wood to town kept them from transferring all carpentry there. Now they say that all they can count on the local carpenters to do is to sharpen ploughs and trowels, and repair cart wheels. For these jobs the carpenters still receive grain—enough to subsist on. As the younger generation becomes ready for apprenticeship, most of them sons of the men who died, their uncles and elder brothers wonder if there will be enough work available even for subsistence.

One family that has suffered, in part from increased city contacts but more from the breaking down of the established *jajmani* system, is that of the *dhobi*, or washerman. The old *dhobi* and his wife—whose son and daughter-in-law died, leaving them with three small grandchildren—were struggling to keep up with the laundry of their *jajmans*. When things seemed to be at their worst, a younger *dhobi*, remotely related, appeared with his family. The old man and his wife welcomed them and gave them shelter until someone provided them with a small house near the pond. The new *dhobi* soon established himself and his rock for beating the clothes at the

end of the village pond farthest from the beating rock used by
the old *dhobi*. The younger man had a strong-armed wife
and four grown children to help him. With the advantages in
his favor, he has gone into competition with the older man
instead of working with him as they had arranged when he
came. He has taken over more and more *jajmans* until only
a few out of pity for the old man continue to give him some
work. Prakash is one of these. He gives the old *dhobi* just
enough laundry—chiefly work clothes and clothes for the children—to ensure his *jajmani* rights to food at harvest time and
to small gifts of money or clothing on special occasions. The
rest of our family wash now goes to Mainpuri, because clothes
come back cleaner and because the town *dhobi* has a flat iron.
With the menfolk making frequent trips to town, ironed
clothes seem a necessity. The old *dhobi* and his wife cannot
understand what has happened. To have *jajmans* ignoring
their needs, distresses them. Their grandchildren go underfed
and underclad; they try to help with the washing, attempting
work far beyond their years. They wear cast-off clothes too
small and torn, and their hair, stiff with dust, is a dull brown,
not like the sleek black heads of the children in our family.
This pre-emption of patronage could not have happened while
the *jajmani* system was actively functioning. If changes had
to be made it was the *jajmans* who made them, and if a
change necessitated dismissing someone who had served them,
they replaced him with one of their choosing and made themselves responsible for him.

Some men who have found it impossible to make a living
in the village have gone in search of work elsewhere, but
considering the size of the village their number is not large.
During the past ten years, eight *kahars* have gone, five of
them with their families; they can serve any caste from Brahmans down, even to the preparing of food. The Christians,
still called sweepers, form the next largest group to go; seven
of them have gone—four to Calcutta, one of whom took his

wife along, and three, two with their wives, to Kanpur, which is much nearer. Those who have left their families behind have done so in part because there is no room for families in the slums where they live, and in part to retain their *jajmani* rights to food, housing, and clothing. Others who have left have been *dhanuks* (also below the caste line), two men, one with his wife; a *mali*, who provides marigolds for all ceremonial occasions, and his wife; and one shepherd and his wife. One *mahajan* and his wife have moved to Mainpuri. Two *kachhi* families have left, one going to another village and one to Delhi. Three sewing men left with their families before the cholera epidemic, two to other villages and one to Delhi. Two bangle sellers moved to Ferozabad, a center of the bangle industry. The goldsmith with his family and youngest brother shifted to Mainpuri. And two Brahmans moved to other villages to take charge of property of their in-laws who had no sons. They left brothers to look after their land here. Contrary to the general impression that it is the "smart villagers" who move to the city, it is chiefly menials who have gone from Karimpur. The so-called smart ones are those with property, who have much to gain by remaining. The two owners of land who left did so in order to acquire still more property, not because they were out of work. Occasionally a younger son in a family owning land has left the field work to his father and elder brothers and gone to a city in search of a job. There is little opportunity in the city for such boys except work in factories as unskilled laborers. They seldom stay long.

During these same years a different group has come into the village. Nine Brahmans have come, seven bringing their families. Just as our two Brahmans went to hold the land of their in-laws, so a few of these have come on behalf of their in-laws. Others came to claim land belonging to someone in the family who has died, or to help a relative unable to look after the family interests. A younger goldsmith brother came during this period; his was actually a return after many years spent in his wife's village. The new *dhobi* arrived with his family. And a Muslim came to carry on the business of one of the Muslim bangle sellers who left. This shifting of men and families to and from the village has been important to the individual households concerned. But it has had no apparent effect on the life of the village as a whole, nor has it had much effect on the size of the village population. Actually, more people left than came in. What population growth there has been (an increase of 375 since 1931) is chiefly in the size of families which have remained here. In Prakash's family, for instance, there were seven in 1931—five adults and two children. Now, in 1961, there are sixteen—nine adults and seven children. Also, the married daughter has spent most of her time here during the past four years with her two children.

There are few changes to report in the lives of the women of the village. The one radical change is in their style of dress. The women who must go out to work, either in their fields or in the households of others, still wear the traditional long, very full, colored skirts, with head scarves of a different color, and short blouses with sleeves. Those who remain in their own courtyards, or step out briefly to visit neighbors, have changed to what are known as *dhotis*. The men have always worn *dhotis*, some short, some well below the knees. Town women have worn, and still wear, *saris*, the draped gowns noted for their graceful lines. The *dhotis* now adopted by the village women are a cross between the two, longer and wider than those worn by the men and plainer and scantier than *saris*. They are usually white with colored borders and with just enough cloth to allow for a few folds in front to make movement easier, and enough to cover the head if drawn straight up the back—not over the shoulder. Ordinarily our women wear nothing under the lower portion of the *dhoti*. It is only when a woman leaves the village for a visit to her parents' home or to go to a fair that she wears either a *sari* and petticoat or *dhoti* and petticoat. If a woman, like Buaji for example, is free to go visiting within the village, she throws a heavy cotton mantle over her *dhoti* while walking down the lane. Most *dhotis* are of fairly thin material, or are worn thin by the washerman, and the warmer the weather, the thinner the *dhotis*. Younger women make a charming silhouette, not so the older ones. The effect might not be strange in some places, but in our village, where the women are extremely modest and take pains to keep their heads covered at all times, it is startling. They usually wear a short, tight blouse under the upper *dhoti*—but not always in hot weather. The women say that their *dhotis* are much more comfortable than the full skirts that weighed them down, and the initial cost is less. *Dhotis* wear out faster than skirts, but what woman objects to buying a new garment? The *dhotis* can be washed at home frequently, to save the wear of being beaten on a rock, whereas skirts are too heavy and voluminous for this. It is still customary for a girl to be given a beautiful *sari*, complete with blouse and petticoat at the time of her wedding. These she keeps carefully in a box, to be taken out only on special occasions.

Aside from this innovation, the women's world—the courtyard—is unchanged. For women, living and working are still synonymous. The older ones are weatherbeaten; their eyes are dim from years of leaning over smoky fires and their teeth are discolored and worn down or falling out. The younger ones retain the beautiful smooth skin, bright eyes, and shining white teeth of childhood. Their hours of work are as long as they ever were, with little change in the simple equipment which is theirs to use. A few now carry zinc buckets in place of the large clay jars, to the nearest well for water. This reduces the number of trips each day. In cities women are using aluminum or stainless steel utensils in addition to, or instead of, brass. The women in our houses use clay jars for water and milk and for curds and *ghi*. But for cooking and serving they continue to use brass exclusively, except for the one iron griddle for toasting the flat unleavened cakes and the iron basin-shaped kettle for deep frying. All the brass is used daily and scoured every morning—the saucepans, the *lotas*, the bowls, and the trays. When spread out to dry in the sun, they are a beautiful shining array against the drab background of gray walls and floor. The women of our village seem more at home in the setting of the Familiar than in the New.

To the government must go a great deal of the credit for initiating the New in the village. We, personally, have been impressed by the progress of rural development as sponsored by the government throughout India. We now see what for many years we have hoped for. There had been efforts at what was called rural "uplift," later rural "welfare," then rural "reconstruction," made by the government and by private individuals and institutions. But city people had all the advantages and expected to keep them. They had the schools and colleges, and communications, police protection, medical services (both Ayruvedic and modern), the hospitals, libraries, entertainment, the bazaars where their needs were met, and the comforts of daily living. The city people and most minor officials, regarded villagers as country bumpkins, incapable of adopting new ideas. The role of the villages was to provide the cities with food and materials for clothing. City buyers took advantage of villagers who brought their grain or fruit or vegetables to the market. There were senior officials who were concerned with the betterment of village life, and a few of them succeeded in setting up programs, usually for some specific purpose—health centers, child welfare, rural schools, improved agriculture, rural cooperatives. But most of these efforts depended on the interest of some individual and became ineffective when he was transferred. Not much that was done for villagers "took." When we set up our own experiment in rural development—India Village Service—in 1946, we were considered pioneers and like most pioneers were faced with obstacles, chiefly the doubt, if not the suspicion, of the villagers themselves. Everyone who had come from outside to them had come with the intention of getting something from them. Bill had made an exhaustive study of rural work in countries where programs had recently been set up to improve rural living, and we made use of their successes and failures, plus our own experiences in villages over the years, to formulate some basic principles which we were prepared to test in a small group of villages. Eight young Indians joined us, four men and four women, all city-bred and college-trained, one with a degree in agriculture. For all of them it was to be in-service training. Most of them had visited villages in connection with some kind of welfare program, but none of them approached the villagers as we expected them to.

In the beginning they had to unlearn the assumption that they were superior. It did not take them long to discover that they had little or nothing to feel superior about. They became convinced that village people, given the opportunity, can do what anyone else can do. They began to work *with* the people rather than *for* them. The principles which we asked them to test are now so commonly accepted throughout the country that it is hard to realize how radical they seemed then.

We were well along with our experiment when the government undertook rural development seriously, beginning with the Pilot Project in Etawah, a neighboring district. In their early days the project builders worked closely with us, making use of our experience as we had made use of the experience of others before us. Because of this and because of our faith in village people we have attached considerable importance to the government program. And now, after several months in Karimpur I am greatly encouraged not only by what government representatives are accomplishing, but even

more by their methods. At every turn, in studying the progress of the village, I am reminded that some government
agency has provided the initial idea or program.

In addition to the projects described earlier, there are the
larger, more costly and far-reaching measures which only a
government can undertake. One of the most revolutionary of
these was the bill to abolish the rights of landlords to hold
large tracts of land. These *zamindars*, or honorary rajahs, had
owned whole villages, collecting rent from the farmers and in
turn paying the taxes to the government, a system that sim-
plified tax-collecting for the government. Shortly after Independence, the government decided, in effect, to take from the
landlords any land which they or their families could not cultivate and to transfer it to the men who had held the right to
rent it. It was not as simple as this of course; the details
of the Zamindari Act filled volumes. The local farmers have
given me their interpretation of it, as it has affected them.
Orchards, land on which there was a well, and plots which
certain men held as a favor from the landlord could not be
redistributed, but all other fields were allotted to the men
who, like their forefathers, had cultivated them under legal
rights as long as they could pay the rent. Since the passing of
the act, these men have paid taxes directly to the government.

The farmers receiving the land were to pay as the purchase
price an amount equal to ten years taxes in advance, in order
that the government might have funds with which to compensate the landlords. This was such a strain on their slim
resources that ownership of the land seemed beyond their
reach. Also, past experience led them to doubt the promises
of full ownership made by the petty officers who came to collect the money. When the officers demanded the "ten times"
tax in Karimpur, the men did not oppose them—they simply
stated that they could not pay such an amount. They knew
that if the few who could afford to pay, did so, the pressure
upon the rest would be very great. Although the scheme was

officially voluntary, considerable pressure was exerted, which
increased at the lower levels of officialdom; eventually the
police actually threatened the resisters with jail sentences,
whereupon they replied that they would all go to jail together.
Finally a way out was discovered. Officials agreed that the
men should just continue paying their annual taxes as assessed,
but with this understanding: if a farmer could somehow
manage to raise the full amount asked by the government—
the equivalent of ten years taxes—at any time before the
ten years terminated, he would be given full ownership of
the land. Until then he could cultivate the land as he had
been doing, but it was not entirely his and he could not sell
any part of it.

In fact, during the ten years allowed, all of our farmers
were able to pay in full. They were surprised when the land
really became theirs—it seemed too good to be true. Every
farmer with whom I have talked said how much more the land
means to him now that it is his. If in the beginning they had
clearly understood (if anyone, in fact, had taken enough pains
to explain things properly) and if they had been able to trust
the government officials who presented the plan, much resistance and misunderstanding could have been avoided.

They have told me, for the first time, of some of their former
troubles caused by the men who collected the rent for their
two landlords. The man who represented the nearby rajah
was brutal. Some of the methods he used in forcing men to
pay rent were almost unbelievably cruel. Fortunately, that is
now in the past. There appears to be one drawback in the
stronger feeling of attachment to the land; it has led to more
serious quarrels and court cases. Even with the special council or local court set up to decide land disputes, there is an
increase in the number of cases carried to the court at district headquarters. This always has caused, and still causes,
heavy expense.

The transfer of land ownership was essential as a first step toward rural development. Without it, the efforts which have followed would have had little hope of success. Before the reforms were executed, we heard repeatedly from farmers: "What good will it do us to produce more? As soon as the landlord discovers that our crops are better, he will claim more rent." Now, with their fields in their own possession, they are prepared to invest in any extra labor or materials that will improve their crops, for they know that the benefits will come to them and to their families.

A later major undertaking on the part of the government, even more far-reaching, has been the establishment of the "block." Blocks have gone through various phases, but as they have now emerged they form the base of a carefully designed framework which will eventually cover all rural India. The purpose is to provide every village with an opportunity to produce more, to learn more, to earn more, to consume more, and—as a result—to enjoy better living. The average number of villages in a block is one hundred. Karimpur is within the Mainpuri block. The word "block" is now a part of the village vocabulary, heard chiefly among members of the village council. It is the service arm of the government and the officers within it are to render whatever advice or help is needed.

When the villagers first heard of the advent of this new set of officers, they were apprehensive. Their chief contacts with officialdom had been with petty officers, who have a reputatation for making their low salaries more than ample at the expense of the villagers. What would these new men expect of them? It took them some time to comprehend that block officers are trained to help them. The old officers are still needed as the new ones do not keep records, nor collect taxes, nor keep law and order. They are here for constructive work that will better the conditions of the villages—an entirely different purpose.

From the point of view of the government, we should start

listing the block officers from the chief administrator down, but the villagers start from the ground up. The man whom they meet in their fields or in the lanes, is the *gram sathi* or "village companion." Our village companion serves eight villages and any hamlets recorded as attached to them. His chief job is to discover the farmers' special problems and to teach and to demonstrate better methods. He would describe his duties in more impressive terms—to carry the problems of the village to research stations and to bring the results of research to the village with a view to increasing production and raising the standard of living. Village companions are given two years of training, during which time they receive an allowance. They are required to have a high-school education. (Our village companion has completed two years of college.) In the beginning, the post of village companion was not popular, but now, with the lively interest in rural development and the larger opportunities, there is strong competition for it. At the Mainpuri training center for village companions, sixteen hundred young men from the district applied for admission to the most recent course.

They were high-school graduates "pass" between the ages of twenty-one and twenty-five. There are three divisions in the final high-school examinations, and they had to be in the first or second. However, those belonging to so-called scheduled castes (below the registered castes) could be in the third or lowest division and eighteen years of age or older. Of all these, eight hundred were selected to take the written examination, which one hundred and eighteen passed. After other tests and a study of merits, the number was reduced first to forty and finally to sixteen. The Mainpuri center trains men for four districts, with a total admission of fifty each year, selected from all four districts.

The first Karimpur village companion whom we met was brought to visit us in our India Village Service center several years ago, under the wing of a group of Karimpur farmers.

He was young and inexperienced, with little special training, and our impression was that he was overawed by these experienced farmers, successful by village standards, while they were apparently exploiting any knowledge he might have for their personal benefit. The present village companions have had longer training, are more self-assured, and are less influenced by the influential.

When the village companion is faced with some particular problem which his training has not covered, he consults one of the Assistant Development Officers, known among villagers as A.D.O.'s, each of whom has had training in one special field. There are seven in our block. One has specialized in agriculture, one in animal husbandry, one in cooperatives, and one in rural industries; another, the "overseer," examines wells for household use and for the cleanliness of the village; still another is sanitary inspector. There was a separate officer to advise the village councils, the *panchayats*. But last year this was combined with the office of social education. In addition to these there is the A.D.O.W., or woman Assistant Development Officer, who gives help in matters concerning women. There are other members of the block staff —a district medical officer, a compounder, a health visitor, two women village companions, and four midwives, as well as office workers. The B.D.O.—Block Development Officer—is responsible for all work conducted by the block, and, in turn, looks for instructions to the D.P.O., or District Planning Officer, who is in charge of the fifteen blocks within the district. Over him is the District Magistrate who has authority over all government services in the district. Because of his many duties, he delegates most of the block supervision to a deputy, known as A.D.M.P.—Assistant District Magistrate for Planning. This is the structure as far as villagers care to reach, and in fact most of them do not go beyond the village companion and the specialists who appear from time to time to help them. It is the members of the village council, particularly the president, who must be somewhat familiar with the work of the senior officers.

Of chief concern to the village farmers are the services of the block which are recognized as directly affecting them. Now that I am closer to them than ever before, I have concluded that the heads of families of our village are among the most materialistic of human beings. They are not so from choice. Circumstances have forced upon them a stark materialism—food, or money for food, money for clothing, money to cover wedding expenses, money for emergencies. This has gone on for so long that even those who are now prospering, with a safe margin between them and poverty, cannot seem to break away. Their children may dip into their hoardings for a few comforts and perhaps a touch of man-made beauty in their surroundings. But the present generation wants only that which meets an urgent need or promises greater security. When this much has been acquired, they cling tenaciously to it, unwilling to move further ahead. This limits the possibilities of what block officers can accomplish. One young B.D.O., after three years experience in a comparatively progressive district, exclaimed to me: "This rural development is the damned hardest work in the world!" Perhaps it is. But it need not be discouraging. Rather, it is the most challenging. Certainly, it demands qualities in its officers not called for in the more conventional government services.

There have been two situations here in which a block officer either lacked the necessary qualities or failed to exercise them. On one of my "house-building" trips to the village I stayed with a friend who showed me a new, screened food cupboard, which most of us accept as an essential piece of kitchen equipment but which village housewives have not yet considered using. It had been brought to the house by a block officer, with the idea that it would serve as a demonstration. This cupboard had two shelves. On the top shelf was a bundle of raw cotton which was waiting to be ginned;

this was a convenient place for setting it aside. On the lower shelf was a bowl of milk intended for one of the babies of the family who was ill; the doctor had advised protecting it from flies. The family liked the appearance of the cupboard and appreciated having it for the milk in this emergency, but when I came a few weeks later, it was carefully put away in a storeroom, where the children could not damage the screen. It was empty, ready for the block officer to call for it.

In another house where I was staying I found to my delight what we call a "smokeless *chula.*" The familiar *chula* is the low, horseshoe-shaped cooking fireplace, just large enough to support a griddle or sauce-pan. In our village every *chula* is kept ceremonially clean, with a fresh coating of clay paste each morning. Its chief drawback is that it lacks a chimney and the smoke pours out into the face of the woman doing the cooking. Rural workers have been trying for some time to devise a *chula* which will remove the smoke and still be acceptable. There are several designs now available, all of which have two advantages over the old *chula.* In addition to sending the smoke up the chimney rather than into smarting eyes, they make it possible for one kettle of food to cook slowly or be kept warm at the back of the stove while other food is being cooked over the flame at the front. On the ordinary *chula* only one thing can be cooked at a time. A block officer had constructed this particular *chula* himself and left it ready for use in the home of my friend. But it had not been used. At first the women said that they were waiting until work was less heavy to try it. Later they said that the chimney, which, unfortunately, had been made of tin, had rusted during the rains, so the new *chula* had been rendered useless. They had been told of its advantages, but they expressed no regret at its loss. We had discovered earlier from our own experience and the experience of others that in areas where orthodoxy is strong the women cling to the old smoky *chula* in spite of its disadvantages. They are sure that they can keep it ceremonially clean, but they are doubtful about this aspect of the new one.

The young officers, city-bred, were baffled by their failures— that of the food cupboard and that of the *chula*. The importance of the cupboard screening had been explained by both the block officer and the doctor, but the lesson seemed to have been forgotten after the child's recovery; flies are regarded as a nuisance but not as dangerous, and although the school children bring home books from which they read aloud regarding the diseases carried by flies, the women are too occupied with household chores to listen. Actually, most of the food in the kitchen is either being cooked or kept hot for late eaters, and there is little left over to be stored, except after the evening meal. So flies are less a hazard in the storing of food than in some other ways, such as the flies that sit on the food while it is being eaten, and those that crawl over the baby's eyes and mouth while he tries to sleep. Given repeated opportunities to learn, from many angles, mothers will grasp the relation between flies and their children's suffering and accept their responsibility in the sequence.

As for the *chula*, the women are willing to go on sacrificing their eyes if this is necessary to safeguard the purity of the food which they prepare for their families. When this problem of ceremonial cleanliness is solved to their satisfaction, the new *chula* will have a better chance of being accepted. In villages near Delhi, where city contacts are frequent and where orthodoxy is more relaxed, I have seen a goodly number of smokeless *chulas* obviously being used. Out here in the country we do not move quite so fast. It was not from lack of intelligence that our women rejected the innovation; they were not ready for it. For them there are other improvements that might be suggested which are innocuous and which might help them discover the possibility of change. The idea of change in household equipment is still unfamiliar to them.

On the edge of the village is a farm demonstration, as satisfying in its results as the other attempted innovations were disappointing. A young farmer recently took me to see his field near our house, where he and the village companion are testing a new commercial fertilizer. He explained carefully how he had divided the field into four plots. In three of the plots he had applied the new fertilizer, by itself, or combined in different ways with the one he had been using. The fourth plot was left without benefit of fertilizer. The contrast between the fourth plot and the others was most striking, and the gradations of growth in the other three were also impressive. The farmers going to their fields and the men passing by on the way to their own villages have begun to stop to discuss the experiment with their friends. The village companion and the young demonstrator are gratified.

This particular farmer had plodded along cultivating the family fields under his father's supervision. He must have been outstanding in his interest in agriculture because two years ago he was chosen with another farmer in this block and others from neighboring blocks to go on a conducted tour of North India. He described vividly the places they had visited, including centers where rural development had made exceptional progress and famous places of pilgrimage. He came back eager to move ahead. All that he needed was the encouragement and advice of someone with the training which he lacked. When the village companion outlined the project to him, he undertook it with enthusiasm and is seeing it through. And now, with hot-weather crops being sown, he is asking for a new demonstration.

One of the most important contributions of the government to the life of the village is the development of new leadership. Greater power has been given to the village council, and the members of the council are elected by their fellow villagers. Thirty years ago there was no such election; the elders who made up the council then were men acknowledged by every one as leaders, who settled disputes and gave advice informally. Their power lay in their personal wisdom and influence; no one was bound to abide by their decisions. They have now willingly stepped aside in favor of younger men. The most outstanding new leaders are sons or nephews of former elders, which is taken for granted in the village as being in accordance with tradition. But they have earned their positions on their own merits as well; and not all have had birth in their favor. Several young leaders are sons of men who were formerly followers, and they too have had to earn their present status.

The twenty-three members of the *gram panchayat*, or village council, are elected every five years. The most recent election was held a year ago and was the third time that the men and women of the village gathered together to vote. After ten years of experience with a council, they realized that it had much greater power than they had supposed at the time of the first election. When the first elections took place, our Indian colleagues in the India Village Service (our experiment in rural development) tried to explain to people the gravity of their choice of council members, but it was too new an idea. Since voting was by show of hands, voters knew that the men elected would be able to make it difficult for those who voted against them. So it was politic to vote for the most aggressive men who kept assuring others that they would be chosen. The voting is still by show of hands, which is simpler and much less expensive than voting by secret ballot. But now most men and some of the women who go to the voting spot, usually under a large tree, have talked over the candidates and what they might or might not do for the village. The members of our present council are predominantly young men or men in their forties. As I watch them and listen to them, I wonder if we should not speak of this as a time of Enlightenment rather than of the New. They may not know much of the ways of the central government or even of

our province, but through the block officers they are learning
about proposals and legislation which concern rural development. They are prepared to cooperate with the block officers
in their efforts to introduce improvements, and, best of all,
they know the men of their village and what they will or will
not adopt.

A village court has also been introduced, known as the
adalati panchayat. It is composed of men selected from among
members of several *gram panchayats.* They are nominated
by the district magistrate, with the help of the *gram panchayats* from which they come. There are eight of these courts
in the Mainpuri block. Karimpur has three representatives on
the court for our area. Smaller villages have two. Members
must be able to read and write Hindi and must be more than
thirty years of age. The convener is the *sarpanch,* elected
from the membership in the presence of the district magistrate
or his official representative. This court can decide both civil
and criminal cases and can fine defaulters. The civil cases in
which it may make decisions are limited to five hundred rupees. And fines may not exceed fifty rupees. Most cases
brought before the court have to do with land boundaries.
The purpose of the village court is to save farmers money by
enabling them to bring their disputes before this local court
rather than going into the district court where lawyers must
be paid and much time lost. However, members of the local
court apparently find it possible to get money from both plain-
tiffs and defendants, and this has discounted its influence.

To the villagers, the *gram panchayat,* which they themselves elect, is more important than the court. The court covers
an area beyond the limits of the village and therefore seems
less concerned with them individually. The council is their
own, most of the members being from Karimpur proper, with
a few from adjoining hamlets. It is the villagers' working
committee, available when they need help with their problems,
and it is also their spokesman in any dealings with block de-

velopment officers. The most important post in the village is
that of *pradhan*, president of the village council. Thirty years
ago, it was the *mukhiya*, the man chosen by the government
as head of the village, who was most influential and respected.
Now the title of *mukhiya* is in name only, with little power
attached to it. The *pradhan* is elected by secret ballot one
week before the open election of council members. His election has become the most bitterly contested election in the
village.

People were casual in the beginning, as they were in voting
for council members, but after suffering from the financial demands made by an early *pradhan* who abused his office, they
have become more cautious. A year ago there were eight candidates, each of whom used a different symbol on the ballot
for the benefit of illiterate voters: a lotus blossom, an um-
brella, a lamp, a kite, a grain basket, a mortar and pestle, a
drum, and a lion. Subedar, Prakash's eldest son, was elected,
and since then he has devoted his time and his strength to
the office. I know of other *pradhans* who are less conscien-
tious, who meet with the council once a month and do the
minimum between meetings. The post is honorary, and after
observing Subedar's activities these past months, I have concluded that a *pradhan* who is as active as he is needs not only
a family able to support him and his wife and children, but
also willing to take over his load of work in the fields. At a
meeting of all sixty-one *pradhans* in the Mainpuri block, Subedar was elected to represent them. As their representative,
he receives special training which he passes on to the others,
and also, he may speak on their behalf when attending meetings with block officers.

The *pradhan* presides at the monthly meetings of the council
and may call additional meetings. Nine members are needed
for a quorum. The council members discuss the collecting
and the use of taxes, prepare the budget, check regularly to
make sure that they are not exceeding it, and take up any

welfare matters which the *pradhan* presents. At the time they are working on plans for fifty new cement-sided compost pits. The council members are trying to keep people from throwing rubbish into the village pond. They are concerned about the wells that are in need of repair, but they have not yet been able to tackle them.

They have talked about the bad state of the lanes and are working on them. Day laborers are hauling in cartloads of *kankar* (earth which has become hard but not to the stage of rock); it is being brought from poor land, under the control of the council, so only the digging and hauling must be paid for. The spreading and pounding down will be done by the men of the village as voluntary labor. This has been the council's biggest undertaking so far.

Almost equal to this task has been the securing of small fish from the Fisheries Department for the village pond. This was proposed years ago, but formerly the pond dried up each year during the hot season. Now the council has the right to use water from the tube well to maintain the water level. The council hopes to earn enough money from the sale of the fish at the end of one year to cover additional or desired improvements.

The council has also put in a request, which has apparently been granted by the District Board, for a new school building. The government will pay half the cost and the village council will be responsible for raising the other half, over a period of several years. The new school will relieve the strain on the old building and make it possible for children to attend school near home through junior high school.

The *pradhan* presents such cases to the council as the request of a poor Christian for a two-acre piece of land on which the soil is so alkaline that no one has tried to cultivate it, and the council votes on these. One of the dreams of council members is street lamps; they are aiming at seven, chiefly to discourage thieves but also to light men on their way home after dark. The council counts on donations for the kerosene oil which will be necessary.

Besides, the *pradhan* carries a good deal of responsibility alone. He appoints the village watchman who goes the rounds of the village each night and reports any "bad characters" to the *pradhan*, who decides whether to report them to the police. The watchman also summons all members to council meetings and on occasion acts as errand bearer for the *pradhan*. In an emergency when all village men may be needed, it is the watchman's duty to call them to an appointed spot.

The *pradhan* is responsible for collecting taxes due to the council and keeps a record of all money spent by him or the council.

It is the *pradhan*'s duty to report immediately to the B.D.O. if any epidemic such as plague, cholera, or smallpox strikes the village. The B.D.O.'s duty is to send a doctor, and if he does not act quickly the *pradhan* is to inform the District Magistrate, who is ultimately responsible. The *pradhan* is also supposed to inspect the village school periodically. In addition, he checks the services of the tube well, together with five farmers appointed especially to assist him in controlling the distribution of water.

When a dacoity or a theft in the village comes before the *adalati panchayat* (court), the *pradhan* is supposed to present whatever evidence is available, and usually on the basis of this evidence punishment is determined. When there is a quarrel over land boundaries, he is expected to attempt to solve it on the spot. He is free to call the village land recorder, the man most inaccessible to the ordinary farmer without a generous fee, and the disputants and half the village look on while the land recorder spreads out his map of the fields and measures the two plots. Then they wait while the *pradhan* makes the final decision. He has had some success in such cases, but more often the quarrel has gone too far to be so simply settled. When such a case becomes serious enough to go before the nearest minor judiciary official or to the district court, the *pradhan* is usually called upon to go with the party. If the men are illiterate they look to him for help, and even those who are literate know that they have a better chance of an early hearing if he is with them. All this was once the *mukhiya's* duty.

The *pradhan* is expected to attend any block meeting to which *pradhans* are called, and is usually given an opportunity to present the needs of his village. Not long ago, the District Magistrate summoned all *pradhans* of the district to two days of meetings in Mainpuri. With the help of block officers, he built up their self-confidence, emphasizing the importance of their position as *pradhans*, their responsibilities, and their powers. The Magistrate told them how much the government depends on them. He assured them of his desire to support them in their endeavors, and reported that he was leaving immediately after the meetings for the capital of the province to present the requests which had come from them. At the meeting special projects were urged. They were: giving land to the poor and making sure that it is properly registered, increasing grain production, growing more vegetables, keeping better breeds of cows and buffaloes, and working toward better opportunities for children of all groups to attend at least a primary school.

In most efforts to increase production, the *pradhan* works with the village companion, and when necessary they call on the block agricultural inspector. Together they promote the use of tested chemical fertilizers. With help from the animal husbandry specialists, the two young men—*pradhan* and village companion—urge farmers to feed and treat their animals better. It is the village companion who must see most of their projects through, but he reports to the *pradhan* daily when some special project is under way.

In other words, the *pradhan* is an extremely busy man if he does all that is expected of him. Once, when Subedar was looking more exhausted than usual, I asked why he does not delegate some of his duties to members of the council, as he is allowed to do in some instances. His reply made me realize how alone he is: "There is not one member of the *panchayat* whom I can trust to carry through a job. And where money is involved a man buys inferior material or underpays workmen and puts into his pocket whatever he has not spent. The money entrusted to the *panchayat* belongs to the government or to the people of the village. I will not let it be misused." Council members have yet to learn that there are times when the welfare of the community must be given priority over family demands.

During the past year, they have learned much about the services of the block officers, of the Seed Store, and the larger cooperative society. They know why better composting is needed, and they know more about the construction of roads. Not all of them are literate, but they realize the advantages of education and desire it for their children. They understand why there must be new village taxes, to which they, like others, have strongly objected in the past. They want the village to make progress. The next step is to accept their share in bringing progress about, even though it may mean the sacrifice of some family interests. As compared with the members of the first elected council eleven years ago, they are decidedly enlightened.

The Young Men Speak

I have had opportunity to talk with most of the men of the village. They sometimes come with an ailment of their own or bring a sick child, and linger to talk. Or they may drop in during the afternoon, when field work is not demanding. But evening is the most popular time for visiting. I have the advantage of a Petromax lantern which we light nightly. Instead of a wick it has a mantle, lighted by gas formed from ordinary kereosene oil by air pressure, and it is dazzling as compared with an ordinary lantern. There are a few others in the village, but they are kept for special occasions. When evenings are long and chilly, the bright light and our large room are an attraction. And when nights bring relief from the heat of the day, our courtyard proves inviting, with its comparative freedom from clutter and confusion, and the bright light in a far corner to keep insects at a distance. Villagers like to talk—talking is our favorite diversion when work is done. There may be only one or two who drop in of an evening, or several may come to join the men of our family.

The older men talk of the problems they must meet in keeping their families fed and clothed. They are in the "house-holder" period of life, when a Hindu man is supposed to devote himself to family duties. The few who have passed beyond this stage prefer to talk about the *Ramayana* or to discuss their religion and mine. They are all eager to talk of the good old days when we lived here, when they enjoyed the security of the Familiar.

The young men talk of the present and the future. It was the older men who served as spokesmen when we wrote "Let All Things Old Abide." Now it is the young men's turn to speak. One evening eight young men, friends of Subedar's, came in, all set to talk. They said that there were others who might have come, but they were foolish fellows who cared about nothing beyond "filling their stomachs." Those who did come were alert and as full of questions as of answers. Their ages ranged from sixteen to thirty. All but one were married, and all of them except this one have children.

Before relating what they had to say, I should like to picture briefly the background of each one. Together they present a fair cross-section of the forward-looking youth of the village. Four were farmers, two of whom expressed dissatisfaction—one because his father gives him orders like a servant, and, although well off financially, refuses to buy any improved implements, and the other because he had hoped for an office job. The first young man, a Brahman, is "eighth-class fail," having failed in his examinations at the end of the eighth grade. This much education is of little help in securing a post. However, he has qualifications which may prove useful in realizing his ambition to get into the Police Department, being broad-shouldered and strong, a wrestler who has brought the village a series of victories. He is seventeen now and must wait until he is eighteen before applying. The other has all that a farmer could want—plenty of good land, four healthy oxen for field work and two buffaloes for milk, and a roomy house. His father has invested in two improved ploughs and other new implements. But having gone through high school—he is "high-school fail"—he feels he should get a job as clerk in some district office, and this has been his father's plan for him. An older brother and a hired man can do the work of the farm. He is like many young men we have known in other villages.

There was a time when ambitious parents could send one son to high school with the expectation that some sort of government post would follow. Competition has altered this, but farmers in villages like Karimpur are not yet aware of it. A boy who passes high-school examinations in the first division has only a slim chance of an office job, and anyone who is in third division or who fails has no chance at all. Such boys see the many offices at the district headquarters and are sure that there must be a place for them. But B.A.'s and M.A.'s are now competing for clerkships which high-school graduates could once hope for. Subedar's young friend, a *kachhi* whose people have always been farmers, keeps thinking of the effort that has gone into his daily trips to Mainpuri to high school and into his years of studying and of what this should bring him. Recently, he went to a recruiting office to offer his services to the Army. He passed the physical test and could read and write. But then came the fatal question, "Do you have any *bhaibandi*—any relative or good friend already in the Army to put in a good word for you?" *He had no one.* So he has resigned himself to farm work, for the present at least. He goes in to Mainpuri occasionally by bicycle to see school friends, but is usually too tired to "go wandering." Both these young men regard employment elsewhere as the means of acquiring a regular income, some of which they can put into their land to improve it. They look forward to the time when they can take over the management of their fields.

The two other farmers, whose families own land, are content with what they have. One of them, very young, enjoys farming. His father owns just one field of four acres, but from it, by careful planning and much labor, they get three crops a year. Two of these are vegetable crops which have a good market both in the village and in the city. He finished fourth grade in the village school before giving his full time to farming.

The other, several years older, has plenty of land, plenty of everything that he wants or needs. He too enjoys farm work. When not needed on his father's fields, he goes to help an uncle who lives twelve miles away. When evening comes, he enjoys his friends. He is more excited than any of the others over the "consolidation of holdings" which will soon take place in our village. This is a land reform which has been discussed for forty years, and is now being carried out by the government. This young man's father owns land in a number of widely separated plots on all four sides of the village which range in size from one-fifth to four-fifths of an acre. When the consolidation is completed, their land will be in one piece. This is the purpose of the reform, to enable farmers to have their fields adjoining so they will be spared the time and labor now spent in carrying their ploughs and other implements and driving their oxen from one plot to another on the far side of the village. Each farmer will have a compact farm on which to concentrate planning and effort, and fewer boundaries to build up and to guard against covetous neighbors. Good land and poor land are to be redistributed in such a way that larger landholders will get some of each, and those with only two or three acres will be given good land. Each farmer is supposed to be granted as much total land as he now owns, minus a small amount which will be turned over to the village council for community purposes. Where several relatives own one plot they decide whether they should hold the land together or separately. The consolidation procedure demands painstaking scrutiny of existing records and accurate calculations in redistributing the land, meter by meter. It takes at least a year to be carried out in one village area. The older men of Karimpur are worried. From friends in villages where consolidation has taken place, they have heard that the success of the project depends on the particular consolidation officer assigned to the village. If he is intent on filling his own pocket, he gives the most desirable land to those who give him the most money; those who cannot give much get inferior land; and the poorest of all suffer most. But if the officer is honest and refuses bribes, the land is distributed fairly. Like most of the younger men, Subedar's young farmer friend is sure that the officer and his assistants who will be sent to our village will be just. He is enthusiastic about what he will be able to do with one large farm now impossible on small, scattered plots. From the way he spoke I assumed that his will be one of the largest farms in the village, but I learned later that his father owns just eight acres. This is plenty, he says, and his uncle owns more.

After the consolidation, the size of the farms of the village will range from the smallest of one or two acres to the four largest which will be from eighty to one hundred acres.

Just one in the group, a boy who has had one year of schooling, works as a day laborer in the fields, like his father. They have saved enough money to buy two oxen, making it possible for his father to farm on shares with a landowner unable to do his own cultivating. Now they are saving all they can in the hope of purchasing two more oxen, so the son can do as his father is doing instead of depending on work at sowing time and harvest. They do not always have enough food and their clothing is barely sufficient, but where could they hope to find anything better?

There was a carpenter in the group, a young man who has never thought of doing anything other than carpentry. He has a pleasant hut with a veranda that serves as workshop just across the lane from his house with its small courtyard and one storeroom. Since his father's death, two years ago, he has been his own boss. He has plenty of work in which his small son helps after school hours. His friends stop by to visit and he gets one of them to work the hand bellows for his iron work while they talk. He attended the village school for a short time, but has not tried to read or write since he left school in order to help his father in this same shop.

The shepherd boy who came looks about twelve years old but is sixteen. He has two older brothers, one of whom herds the sheep and goats and their one buffalo while the other goes to town with milk to sell. This boy, not being needed, found work with the Public Works Department as one of a road gang on the district road between here and Mainpuri. He fills holes with *kankar* and pounds it down by hand, or helps prepare a stretch of road for the big roller. He walks to and from his work if his job happens to be near the village, or eats and sleeps with other workmen under improvised shelters beside the road. The only thing he likes about it is the regular pay which he brings home to his father to help with the family expenses. He and his brothers want land above all else. Sheep and goats are not as secure an investment as they were formerly; there is increasing difficulty in finding pasture for grazing, and *neem* leaves for fodder are becoming scarce.

The student has gone further in school than anyone in the village. He is now preparing for the intermediate college examinations—two years beyond high school. He lives in a hostel in town, but comes home week ends, when he is constantly at my side with his English textbooks. He reviews and reviews the difficult passages which may appear in his examination—extremely difficult ones for anyone not familiar with English. None of his schoolmasters speaks English, and all subjects are in Hindi. His father, after being told by the principal that he was a particularly good student and should continue, has agreed to send him through college and law school. He himself likes the idea of becoming a lawyer. Village people need a good lawyer who will not cheat them. His only fear

is that people from Karimpur who go to court will expect
him to present their cases without paying him fees! His father
has shown no interest in arranging his marriage and so the
women of the family threaten to send someone out in search
of a wife. A boy of seventeen, unmarried, is a disgrace to
the family.

I was familiar with the problems of several of these young
men, but new insights came from hearing them discussed with
each other. They were not close neighbors, nor were their
castes such that they would ordinarily spend an evening talking together. Not one of them spoke of his wife, and their
children came into the picture only in connection with opportunities for schooling or for employment. Families were
mentioned, but seemed less important at the moment than
their own interests as individuals. They were more frank
with each other than their fathers would have been. I have
tried to combine the ideas they expressed, and in doing so
have been struck by the difference between their statements
and those of their elders in "Let All Things Old Abide."
They are not afraid to acknowledge their faults. And they
are concerned with what they can do to make life in the village better.

My eight guests and Subedar sat on the floor in an un-
even circle, as other groups were no doubt sitting in other
parts of the village, talking, talking. They began almost at
once, asking me questions about America. Then the student
and the "high-school fail, " having spent many evenings here
and feeling most at home, were the first to express themselves on their own interests. But quickly all plunged into the
discussion.

"We who are farmers or artisans have to work hard and have
little time or energy to think, or to plan how we can make
things better. We have always found something or someone
other than ourselves to blame for our lack of progress. We
complain that storms or pests have ruined our crops. We

have found fault with rent collectors and government officials because of their greed. We are free of the rent collectors now, but we still have the land recorder, the police, and other minor officers of the government to blame.

"Sometimes we cannot escape their avarice. When we see a police constable or deputy's assistant in the village we know that someone is going to be threatened and will have to part with some of his money. Who are the men who own watches and live in brick houses? Not one of us here thinks that he can afford a watch, it is in the luxury class. But the minor officers all own watches. Our land recorder has one and so has his brother who lives here with him and has a similar job in another village. They do not need watches any more than we do, and they cannot afford to buy them on their pay. The other government men, who come from their brick houses in town, wear good clothes and flaunt their watches. Who pays for all this? We do! And we shall go on paying until we know more about our rights according to the law, and until we ourselves are more trustworthy.

"We are not entirely ignorant, nor are we free from blame. We sometimes take the initiative in offering a bribe to a government man to further our own ends. All of us here know the saying that is popular these days about our government officers. [And one of the boys took the pad and pencil from Subedar and wrote five words in Hindi. Translated freely they mean, "If you offer me a bribe, I overlook your misdeeds."] If we could resist the temptation to bribe, we might have fewer misdeeds to be overlooked, but while greed is there we continue to take advantage of it. If my uncle thinks that the plot of Gopi's father is larger than it should be and his own plot next to it is smaller than it should be, he takes a thin slice from Gopi's father's field and shifts the barrier between the two in his own favor. Then he goes to the *lekhpal* with a bag of money, perhaps more than the slice of land is worth. And with the money transferred to his own pocket, the *lekhpal* changes boundary lines. If Gopi's father suspects my uncle and calls the land recorder to bring the map to the field, the recorder can slyly include an extra foot or two of Gopi's father's land in the measurement of my uncle's land. Of course, if Gopi's father is smart he will pay the *lekhpal* a little more than my uncle did and get the slice of land back and perhaps an extra sliver. My uncle cannot object for to acknowledge publicly that he had already bribed the *lekhpal* would be a disgrace. Now that the *pradhan* is also present when such land quarrels are under discussion, the bribery does not work as well, at least not with this *pradhan*. [Subedar, who looks stern and tense most of the time these days, suddenly grinned, "And you know it," said he.]

"Here is another loss we suffer because of the combination of our folly and the cupidity of some of the men in government service. We do not like to see someone better off than we are. If my father has just one thousand rupees, and knows that Shankar's uncle has twenty thousand rupees, he will make a false charge against Shankar's uncle or find some other way to force him into court. His uncle may try to bribe his way out or pay lawyers excessive fees to get him safely through the trial. In either case, he loses most of his money. My father cannot benefit from this, but he has the satisfaction of pulling Shankar's uncle down nearer to his own level. There seem to be more court cases now than ever. Our fathers choose to go on wasting money on these cases, perhaps just to work off their anger against someone or to safeguard their property or their position, and we could make good use of that money in improving our land or buying better animals. We do not need to stay so poor. We who are sons do not like these practices especially when our parents' conflicts hurt our own friendships. Every time one of my relatives makes a false report against a relative of my friend or one of his relatives cheats a relative of mine, our families become more antagonistic and more suspicious of each other, and that includes us. We often wonder if we can keep from falling into these traps when we are heads of our families.

"We know that we lavish far too much money on the weddings of the girls in our families, because everyone is afraid to be the first to spend less. Here we are at the mercy of families outside our village, the families into which our girls will go as brides. We are afraid that if we offend them by giving a modest dowry they will be hard on our sisters or daughters who are to become their daughters-in-law. What we can do is demand less when a girl from another village is married into one of our families. Uma Datt is doing this in the wedding of his eldest son, but everyone laughs about it and says that it is because it is hard for him to find anyone willing to send a daughter into his household where she will be the only woman to cook for him and for her husband and her husband's two younger brothers. Most of us want to get all that we can when we bring home a bride. We not only want her help in the work of the courtyard, but also we want all the money we can get out of her parents in expensive dowry gifts, in cash, and in elaborate feasts and entertainment. If each caste would come to some agreement among themselves, we could all be sensible together. For the present we try to make enough on the sons of the family to repay us for the money spent on the daughters. We like the feasts, but they help to keep us poor.

"There are two other weaknesses of ours that hold us back. One is suspicion. We must stop suspecting one another of hidden motives. How can we make progress when we habitually reject an improvement simply because we are afraid that the person who proposes it is planning to get some personal benefit from it, at our expense? The other is the abuse of leadership. We know men who misuse their position as leaders and we are disgusted with them. Because of jealousy or ignorance or both, they are constantly blocking those who are trying to make our village better. When these men are with some block officer or in a meeting of the council, they agree that some measure is good and that we should be willing to pay the tax to carry it out. Then they leave the officer or the meeting and go back to their friends and followers and speak against it. They say, 'Why should we be taxed again, and for such a useless thing?' What we ask is, why do they not speak up and say what they think when the measure is being discussed instead of waiting and talking behind the backs of those who are working hard to bring about the improvement? How can we make progress as a village as long as this goes on?

"If we get fed up with the demands of our families and the carryings on of the leaders and want to get away from the village for a few years, where can we hope to find jobs? We have no relatives already in government service to pull us in. And we do not know whom to bribe, nor for how much, to buy our way in. Besides, there are too many young city men going around hunting jobs. They are getting in each other's way and would surely push us out. We have no training in special skills, and the only jobs open to us are in factories in some large city. From the sweepers when they come home from Kanpur or Calcutta we have heard about those jobs and the way the laborers live. It sounds much worse than living at home and working on our own land. After all, we are fortunate if we have land to work on.

"But there are good things in our village as well as bad. We have a good deal of fertile land and we are learning how to keep it fertile, not wear it out. We have some poor land too, and this we are trying to improve. We are even learning ways of cultivating some of the land that we once considered useless. We have better seed than we used to have, different kinds of fertilizer, and more water for irrigating our fields. We have better animals than formerly because we are learning about better breeds, and we feed them better. Our fathers tell us that our oxen are worth twenty times as much now as they were when you lived here, and our cows and buffaloes would sell for ten times as much as they did then. We have heard about the good breed of bull you brought to the village. Proper care was not taken of it after you left, and it died. Then our fathers began to see how they had benefited from it, and they asked for another, which they got, but after it died no one bothered to get a third. We have put in a request for a new one.

"If we are prepared to invest the money we can get more improved implements. And if we do not have enough money for some implement, we can borrow what we need from our Bank, providing we are sure that we can repay the loan with interest. We have more orchards now and are enjoying the extra fruit. Our pond is stocked with big fish, not for us to eat but to sell for improvements in our village.

"We have the help of our village companion and of the block officers. Now, instead of coming around occasionally and lecturing us on what we are doing wrong, they demonstrate before us how we can do it right. It is they who are responsible for our getting such good crops. Just looking at our fields you can see the difference. We have more to eat and more to sell. Town people groan when food prices go up, as they have been doing. We are the fortunate ones now, with bigger harvests, our own food, and higher prices on all we sell.

"We even have our own shops. They may be small, but they are no smaller than most of those in the Mainpuri bazaar. We can buy right here most of the spices and extras for cooking, and oil and peanuts and sweets, and the small articles we need. There is an ordinary cloth shop, and a new 'Gandhi Ashram Bandar' where we can get good materials that are hand-spun and hand-woven at a reasonable price. People from other villages often come here to buy, instead of going to Mainpuri. Long ago, Karimpur was a thriving market town. Perhaps it will be again.

"Our lanes have been hard on our carts and our oxen. But now we are going to have smoother ones. The *kankar* is already in piles along the sides or down the middle of several lanes. And we ourselves are going to do the pounding down, to have everything finished before the rainy season.

"We have a good school, much better than when we were studying in it. After not too long a time we expect to have a new building, with higher grades so that our children will not have to walk so far or cycle into Mainpuri when they finish the sixth grade.

"There are fewer caste restrictions than there used to be. Now we young men can do most things together, without considering our caste—like sitting here and talking with each other. Being in classes together in school is one of the biggest helps. Just two caste conventions remain which separate us. We do not yet feel free to accept food from someone belonging to a caste lower than our own, and we do not consider marrying anyone outside our own caste—a boy may marry a girl of a lower division of his caste, but not one of a lower caste. These two rules regarding food and marriage have not interfered with our personal relationships with each other. Each one of us here has friends of other castes and we think nothing of it. Friendship is more important than caste, anyhow.

"Some have decided on their own that they should have a higher position than their forefathers. Most of us are satisfied with what our birth has made us. If we want something better or if we see that we need some reform, we do it together—the whole caste. When we meet as a brotherhood, we take courage. No one of us alone would try to introduce a reform.

"The *chamars* have tried to raise themselves higher by changing their name to *'jadav'!* As long as they were *chamars* everyone associated them with *chamre*—hides. Their special duty in the village remains the skinning of dead animals, and because of this defiling work, we keep them down below caste lines. By calling themselves *jadavs*, they feel that they have better standing. A few of them have land, and others work on our farms as day laborers, but when an animal dies, we call on them to remove the hide. Even as *jadavs*, we exclude them. Some day this may change, but not yet." (*Jadavs* are those who claim membership in the *yadu* clan to which Krishna belonged.)

This gave me an opportunity to ask: "What about the two Christian brothers who are sweepers? They are thinking seriously about the future. Why could they not be here with us to express their ideas? I know their bitterness over the lives they must lead because of the stigma attached to their birth as sweepers and their own unpleasant assignment—herding the swine along lanes and fields to clean up the night soil. They see no future for themselves or their children in the village as long as caste retains its power. They should like to venture to some city, but someone in the family must stay on here, to claim their *jajmani* rights to food and shelter." The young men agreed that although caste restrictions are relaxing, the barriers between those within the caste fold and those outside, like sweepers, washermen, leather workers, and *dhanuks*, still exist. However, even these are weakening. "After all, Din Dayal, a Brahman, is teaching both of these sweeper boys in his night class. This could not have happened a few years ago, and if one of the brothers gets a piece of land that will help. But as long as they are connected with the village sewage system—the swine—they cannot become friends with any of us." This is where sanitation and social relations meet. Their conclusion was: "Let the old men herd the swine. They do not care about being excluded. They are used to it after so many years. This might give the younger men a chance—in the city, if not here."

Then their discussion turned to other things of greater interest to them: "There are some things that we should like to have that we do not have yet. We should like more games. When field work is heavy, we are too tired to play. But there are times when we are not tired, and then we enjoy a game. Volley ball is good, but we need more sets to put up in other parts of the village so that more can share. If we had a newspaper we would read it ourselves and read it aloud to others. Few of us go to town where we might hear the news. Even better than a newspaper, we would like books. Otherwise we shall forget how to read. We would enjoy books about other people, about heroes of our country and of other countries, about religion, or about good argiculture, and we like stories, also. We see books in shops in town, but to us they seem to cost too much.

"We are trying to get permission for enough electricity to have a mill for grinding flour, husking rice, and pressing oil. Why should all the mills be in Mainpuri? We are as clever as the people there. Jagat had one here out by the district road for a few years, but he had to run it with a motor, and the fuel oil was expensive; and when it broke down he gave it up. Electricity is best. And now we can get mechanics from town to do the repairing.

"Most of all we want walls of baked brick for our houses and sound roofs. We are tired of mud-plastering our walls year after year, and we do not like it when our roofs cave in in a storm. If wood or coal were not so hard to get and so expensive, we would have a brick kiln near our village. We see them along the roads that lead out of Mainpuri, and we wonder how those villages manage to run kilns. If we had one of our own, we could all have brick houses, like those they tell us they have in the Punjab.

"We depend less on our elders than young men used to. And if we can share our ideas with each other like this, giving and taking, we shall begin to do more of our own thinking. If I keep learning from you and do not teach you something, then I am not really learning but becoming dependent on you.

"As long as our *pradhan* is friendly and talks with people and listens, we can all cooperate with him to improve our village. We want to work together, all of us, in a friendly way and not oppose each other or be afraid of one another.

"If we do this and if the block officers will spend more time showing us ways of doing our work better, our village will be as good as any place in which to live. People in cities have little that we do not already have. They may have better and more schools, through college. They keep their lanes cleaner than we do and some of them have cleaner habits. They have more convenient medical services. Some day we shall have all that they have. In addition, we have plenty of fresh air, which they lack, and plenty of sunshine. Our children have more than enough room to run and play in safety. We do not have to go to a crowded, dirty bazaar to buy our grain or vegetables or our fruit or milk or *ghi*. In the city, vegetables and fruit are half wilted; the milk is half water and the *ghi* is seldom pure. We have our own food, fresh from our fields and groves or from our animals.

"We are not driven, the way men in the city seem to be. We take time to enjoy our families before we go out to work in our fields. And after work we sit with our friends. We enjoy telling about jokes on ourselves and on others. There is much to laugh over. Perhaps we are just as well off without watches; actually we want them more for show than for use. Those who live by them become servants, not their own masters. We know the time by the sun and the stars, and we know how much work must be done. If our fathers plan everything for us, we do not care whether the day's work is finished. If we plan our own tasks, we get them done. We who are farmers have to work hard at the time of planting and while irrigating and during the harvest season when we must cut and thresh the grain. But we are not afraid of work. Perhaps you hear one or another of us singing as we pass your house on the way to our fields.

"We are no colder in winter than they are in the city where they do not even have the comfort of a little fire of sticks and stalks. And in hot weather they are shut in with the heat, whereas we can find a shady tree—all day long if there is no field work or for a long while at midday if there is work enough for morning and evening. We do not have the cinemas and loudspeakers that make city life exciting, but we have our own good times. We enjoy every special festival, and there are plenty of them during the year. Or someone who has reason to be thankful invites a priest to come and read the *Ramayana* to us and gives us a feast. There are the wrestling matches with other villages, and once a year, usually at the time of Holi in the spring, we have a drama. Then there are the weddings; we go in ox carts with a wedding party from here if we can claim an invitation from the bridegroom. We go for the fun and the good food. And we make the most of weddings at the homes of brides here. Sometimes there is a dancing girl for entertainment, and fireworks, and always a feast.

"Of course some city men have easy jobs, sitting at desks in offices or sitting on the floor of small stores. A few of us, like Barkat, want office jobs. But even Barkat is thinking of the regular pay rather than all the hours bending over a desk full time, with someone watching to see that he copies figures or words. Most men in cities work in mills. That is not for us. We want to be free. The time is sure to come when some of our children will be obliged to get jobs in the city. Our fields are being divided and redivided with each generation until they already seem too small. The land can no longer support us all. But even those who must go out to work can live at home and cycle to and from Mainpuri. We shall not send them as far away as Kanpur or Calcutta. We have our worries, but they are not as bad as those of city people. When we stop to think about it, we have a good deal in our favor. It is time we took advantage of it."

These statements did not come out as smoothly as reported here. One would bring out something that was on his mind. Before he had finished, one or more of the others pounced on it. And suddenly everyone would be talking, each hoping that by raising his voice, at least one person would listen. As abruptly as each outburst began, so it ended, apparently when arguments and oratory were exhausted. Two might agree, not always the same two. One by one, others stopped to listen to them and usually ended by tilting their heads in accord. Agreement was not unanimous. Neither was there strong opposition. In village groups it seems easier to give final verbal consent to the statements of those who have taken the lead, or at least to compromise. It hardly seems worth the effort to press one's own point.

If these young men can stimulate the others who "think only of filling their stomachs" to share in their enthusiasm, the changes will come. There is one possible hazard. In a recent election for a member of the state legislature and a member of the central parliament, a surprising number of young men swung to an extremely orthodox Hindu party in their voting, a party that stands for a revival of the historic Hindu control of the country. However, Indian friends in Delhi, who know more of political trends than I do, say that this particular party has a doubtful future because of lack of a strong, united leadership. Its popularity is temporary, a reaction against the corruption of the representatives of the present governing party. It may serve as a warning that reforms in some of the current practices are badly needed. So this may be just one more symptom of the refusal of younger men to follow the dictates of those senior to them, even though they come under reactionary influences in doing so. It is one of the risks of growth.

There will always be need for government aid in projects requiring greater expense than the village can bear. And there will be a place for advice from men like the block officers with their special training and wider experience. However, after listening to the eight young enthusiasts, one dares to hope that more changes will originate within the village. At least some of the men, now the young men, will be prepared to pay the price of progress. They are sure to meet obstacles, inside and outside. But they are on the move and intend to keep moving. They are already talking about new, electrically driven fodder cutters; the hand-turned cutters, which most of us still consider new, are being criticized as old-fashioned, for they require the labor of at least two persons, and the fine particles of dry stalks and dust irritate the eyes and nostrils of those turning the wheel. Electricity will do a better job and will not cause discomfort from dust and chaff. Electricity will make a number of other new machines possible, they are sure, and work will become more interesting. The few who will have enough land in adjoining fields after the consolidation to make a tractor practical are discussing the prices of different makes, and the advantages of cooperating in the first purchase. They have heard rumors of a threshing machine that can relieve them of the seemingly endless task of driving the oxen round and round over the grain on the threshing floor. The use of four or six oxen in a line instead of two reduces the hours of walking but a machine would be easier and faster.

Things are moving too fast for recording these days. The young farmers have not merely heard about a threshing machine, they have one! As I was preparing this manuscript for mailing, I heard shouting at the courtyard door. And there, just outside, were the three elder sons of our family with several of their friends pulling a small thresher, lent to them by the Seed Store as a demonstration. It is fitted with twenty upright discs with saw-tooth edge. They were on their way to the family's two threshing floors, a short distance outside the village. I followed later, to find a number of men watching and giving conflicting advice to the driver. The ma-

chine is drawn by two oxen, which must still make the old
round over the circle of stacked wheat, but the driver sits in
state on a wide seat. Today there are half a dozen youngsters sitting and wriggling beside and behind him, hanging
over the side to watch the discs turn, but when the excitement
dies down they will find other pleasures and there will be less
strain on the oxen. Beside us, on the adjoining threshing
floor, a hired man was trudging around on his circle of grain
behind three oxen. The men standing by agreed that the machine is more efficient than the oxen alone. While watching I
learned that three families have just now invested in similar
machines for this year's harvest. Then came the inevitable
question: Is it worth the cost? Close by two men were tilting and shaking their baskets of threshed grain in the breeze.
They winnowed each small pile twice over, to rid it of the
chaff. A tedious job. Several onlookers remarked that the
next mechanical device should be for the winnowing. How
can anyone keep up with them?

For those who like ourselves have had first-hand experience in rural development in India, or who have made intensive observations, an apology for Karimpur may be due—
not because it lags behind, but because it is making more
progress than we would expect in a conservative community.
A year ago I would have been skeptical. I knew only too well
how difficult it is to introduce change for the better, where,
for generations, change has not occurred. The obstacles that
we encountered and studied led us to expect little and to be
doubtful when there appears to be more than that little.

Karimpur is far from ideal. But it is changing. We are distant from any large center. And we have no visitors to
impress. With the exception of the District Magistrate, few
people in the nearest small city or the district headquarters
adjoining it are interested in what goes on. I have not seen a
"white collar" since I returned, now almost a year ago. The
men who do come from outside are the rural development

officers. They travel by jeep, in dusty clothes. They come to advise and assist, not to be charmed. Without newspapers or radio, we know little of what communities are accomplishing in other parts of the country.

Then how explain the present readiness to move ahead? It cannot be entirely due to the development officers. They are going through the same routine in other villages. All signs seem to point to the holder of the key office—that of *pradhan*, village council president. He is in a position to accelerate change or to discourage it. Subedar, our present *pradhan*, is old enough to be realistic and yet not so old that he has lost his earlier ideals. In his efforts to stimulate progress he is supported by a small group of forward-looking friends. In 1951, his father sent him for three years training in tractor driving and repair. This took him first to a training school near Delhi, then to several centers in the Punjab. He lived and worked in an atmosphere of new machines and new developments. Since then he has been a farmer here, without benefit of tractor.

Most of his ideas originate in the regular meetings of block officers and presidents of the sixty-one village councils in our block. He returns from such meetings resolved to carry out the suggestions for improvement made there. He calls the local council together, presents his recommendations, and is ready with plans for carrying them out. He is a determined young man. As long as he is prepared to shoulder the load, the council usually agrees with him. After all, they will share in the credit. Other *pradhans* return to their villages from the same meetings, raising their hands in the familiar gesture of, "What can I do about it?" Before the election of Subedar, two *pradhans* had been elected here, each serving a term of five years. While they were in office, improvements depended almost entirely on the efforts of the development officers. The people had resigned themselves to expect little or nothing from their council or its president. Now the attitude has changed. Things are moving. Subedar and his cycle are out from early morning until dusk, perhaps at court supporting fellow villagers, or at the block headquarters collecting materials or information, or in the lanes or fields of the village. After dark he circulates on foot. And wherever he goes, something constructive is happening.

At a recent meeting of the officers of our block, they voted to arrange a bus tour of the most progressive villages in the area. All sixty-one council presidents are to be invited, the intention being to spur the inactive ones to action. Five villages were chosen. Karimpur is one of them. If I were to draw a less optimistic picture of a village in the present early stage of rural development, it might be more generally true. But—this is Karimpur, for better or worse.

On the evening when Subedar came in with figures on the children of the village, I had just turned out the Petromax and was standing at a window opening into the courtyard, where we keep a miniature oil lamp burning all night. Apparently while going from house to house, he had been thinking about the past and future of the village. After handing me the list of names, he expressed his thoughts, his eyes shining with excitement. "There was a time—long ago—when there were no lights at all in the village, except the glow from cooking fires. On grand occasions men soaked rags in some kind of oil and bound them on the ends of long sticks to carry as torches. Then we had *diwas*, the tiny clay saucers filled with mustard oil and with a cotton dip, which burn for about an hour at a time. Next we had little tin oil lamps like this one of yours, with or without a chimney, which many still use and which last for hours. And we also have lanterns; they are better. Now we have a few Petromax lanterns that give very bright light for meetings and feasts. And many of us use flashlights; it was mine that started me thinking about this tonight as I was walking in the dark. Next we shall have electric lights in the lanes and in our houses. Then we need not stay all night at the Exhibition, just to enjoy the rows of bright lights. We shall have our own." If an outsider had said this, I might not have accepted the idea that changes in lighting are indicative of real progress. But coming from Subedar who is giving all he has to the welfare of the village, it was symbolic. With leadership like his, more than lights will change. Change, they say, is in the *biyari*, the breeze.

At the same time, there is much in the Familiar that is worth retaining, and which will be retained, I hope. It has stood many tests, and has proved its soundness in certain areas of life. And it has its own special values to offer.

I should like to be the fortunate one to return to the village ten years from now to write the story of the newer New. But I shall leave that to our one college student who is almost as interested as Subedar in improving conditions. Or there may be others who will have achieved a "B.A. Pass" before then. If the men of the village continue to move forward at the present pace, while preserving the best in the Familiar, college graduates will find this a good place to live—good enough for them to take pride in telling others of its progress, not the outstanding prosperity of any one family or caste, but of the village community as a whole.

The Village in 1970

Charlotte and the women and children of Prakash's
household in 1968. After the Wisers returned to the
US in 1960 and their old home collapsed in the rains,
this family moved into the then empty Wiser house.
Upon Charlotte's return some years later,
they shared it with her on visits to Karimpur. (1968)

CHAPTER XIII

The Village in 1970

Now it is "ten years hence," and here am I in my own home watching change after change occurring around me. Karimpur has made more progress during those ten years than it had in the thirty years before, but we who have lived here have failed to recognize this, chiefly because we did not expect it. Like my neighbors, I assumed that those communities which had advanced rapidly either were near large cities from which new ideas radiated, or were fortunate in having the aid of highly trained community development officers. Neither advantage was ours. Nor were we in a position to get information directly from a state agricultural college or government experimental farm. New ideas reached us circuitously and unofficially, introduced by local farmers or by visiting relatives, and acceptance of each one was delayed so long by misgivings and discussion that by the time it appeared in practice it had lost its identity as new. As a result, we had underestimated our progress until this spring, when six young outsiders visited us. Three of them were Indian, three American. None of them had been inside an Indian village, but all of them had read *Behind Mud Walls, 1930-1960* more than once, and were bent on learning as much as possible. They arrived at the time of the wheat harvest and were amazed to find the newest variety standing in the fields, and were excited as they watched stacks of it accumulating day by day beside the different threshing floors.

Inside the village, they were enchanted. Here were the people about whom they had read, coming alive at every turn, people who were civilized without dependence on the amenities offered by city life. They found themselves watching and listening to women and men who were not strangers. They wandered down lanes and discovered landmarks that were familiar. They felt at home in the walled enclosures, where the women worked and the children played, where grain was stored and cattle spent the night.

At the same time, they looked about for signs of change, or what they with their urban background were prone to call "progress." Could a community so far removed from progressive influences undergo change? What changes could I show them that had been introduced since 1960? As we sat together discussing obvious changes, and later when we went in search of others, I discovered that Karimpur had accomplished more than my neighbors and I had recognized. Our changes have been fewer and less spectacular than those in the Punjab or parts of the South, but they are indicative of willingness to change when opportunity is offered.

As my visitors and I wandered through the village, we were constantly surrounded by the children. Wherever we went, they went. They have always been curious about visitors, but now there is a difference. For every question we asked them, they promptly asked one or more of us. Often the youngsters tried their newly acquired English on the visitors. In earlier days, English would not have been taught in our schools, nor would children have been as reponsive as they are now. There is no trace of fear or suspicion. These changes have been fostered by a better quality of education. When we visited the elementary schools, we found a far different institution from that of 1930 or even of 1960. The teachers are better prepared; the four men who teach in the elementary school have completed high school and hold a Basic Teacher's Training Certificate. The three women teachers in the girls' school have the same qualifications. And the three masters in the junior high school have had two years of college and in addition have a Junior Training Certificate. There are one hundred and forty boys attending the elementary school; in the junior high school there are one hundred and fifteen boys and ten girls, all from Karimpur and outlying hamlets. In addition, a number of our boys have chosen to go to a better-equipped junior high in a town three miles away, and a few attend school in Mainpuri. There are eighty-seven girls and three small boys in the girls' school, also from Karimpur and nearby hamlets. There are audio-visual aids available now in the schools. Some children have replaced the wooden slates and bamboo quills of their fathers with ruled notebooks and pencils. A few displayed new ball-point pens, an innovation associated with prestige.

Twelve boys from Karimpur are attending high school in the district headquarters. From their classes and from the books they read, they are gaining a broader view of India and of the world than was possible in the local school. Incidentally, they have acquired new ideas regarding appearance and are copying the town boys with whom they associate. Although parents criticize this as inappropriate, most of them accept it as an accessory to higher education.

The first young man to leave Karimpur after completing high school was a *kachhi*, a farmer. After failing to get an office job in Mainpuri, he enlisted in the Army. Being literate, he was assigned to the post of storekeeper in the medical corps. When he returns on annual leave, he wears his uniform for a day or two and is a hero. His prestige is now above that of *kachhis* who have remained in the village, and his peers of all castes have envied him his equipment and his military air. But only three, a carpenter, a shepherd, and a Brahman, have enlisted. For only two years he was stationed at the famous Red Fort in Delhi and caused a stir in his caste community when he secured quarters for his wife and took her there. Neither his own family nor his neighbors had ever heard of a daughter-in-law going away to live with her husband without her mother-in-law or an older sister-in-law. She was there a year and is proud of the fact that her second child was born in the Fort. Later, his mother and elder sister joined them for a week of sightseeing. This visit has made a subtle difference in relationships within the family. The young wife is freer to talk with her mother-in-law, although she still does not speak in the presence of men of the family, nor does she uncover her face while one of them is in the courtyard.

This year there are fifteen young men attending college in Mainpuri. Most of them are freshmen from several castes. Three others had gone earlier, all Brahmans. Two of the three now have B.A. degrees and the third expects to receive his B.Sc. next year. The first one to achieve a bachelor's degree has never abandoned the village. While living in town during his college course, he retained his place among his peers and continued to devote as much time as possible to working on his father's land. The other B.A. continued his studies and has qualified for the degree of M.A. this year, a further step toward the government appointment which he covets. If this ambition is not realized, he is confident that he will be commissioned a second lieutenant in the Army. Although he lives in his house in Karimpur while cramming for examinations, he evinces no interest in his former friends. Apparently his assignment, whatever it is to be, will carry him far from the village and from the village girl to whom he is married.

Two younger boys from Karimpur who completed high school have gone to a training school not far from Delhi in order to learn machine-shop techniques. They had discovered that there are thousands of B.A.'s in the state competing for the few opportunities offered, whereas there are openings in industry for trained personnel, and candidates are few. Both now have jobs. Away from the village they are able to work and to live together. One is a Brahman and the other a shepherd. The shepherd, much lower in caste than the Brahman, cooks for them both. Although they have broken caste rules, in this and in other ways, their relationship still reflects an unconscious inferior-superior status. Each of them has been called home for marriage this year, that of the Brahman arranged by his grandparents and that of the shepherd by his mother. The shepherd was kept at home so long by preliminaries and ceremonies that he lost his job and had to find another. Village customs and the demands of city employment clashed, leaving his mother puzzled at the lack of consideration for tradition. Both boys enjoy brief home visits, but the village has nothing to offer them by way of support. They like their work, even though their wages are small—barely enough to cover the cost of food and the room they share. It will be several years before either of them will be able to support a wife. Until then, the young wives must wait in their own homes or live with their in-laws. A third boy, from an extremely poor Muslim family, passed the high school examinations with higher grades than Karimpur has ever known and was awarded a scholarship for two years of technical training. He has completed his first year in a technical school of high standing, where he has been learning to construct and repair radios.

Others of this generation, who have not studied beyond the local school and who have emigrated, have gone in search of work not requiring skill—with one exception. The younger brother of the *kachhi* who is now a soldier had left school in the seventh class. When his brother joined the Army, he decided that he would excel in a different role. In Delhi he learned to drive motor vehicles and now ranks high, both in driving and in repairing heavy machinery, on a large government experimental farm. A few have gone to large cities where relatives were already employed, and where they have remained as peons, watchmen, or unskilled laborers.

Our sweeper colony is small, consisting of seven families. Eight of the men have gone to Calcutta or Kanpur to work. Some are young, others middle-aged. All but one have left their families behind and return to visit once or twice a year, sending money home between visits. In many ways, because of their urban experience, these men are more sophisticated than others above them socially. Sweepers at one extreme have good reason to leave. Landowners at the opposite extreme have good reason to stay.

Of the young men whose discussion is quoted in the last chapter of *Behind Mud Walls, 1930-1960,* none has emigrated. Only one left while a college student, and he has returned. The others, including the young carpenter, now a landowner, are among our more progressive farmers. To them, ownership of land is of primary importance. Now that their land is yielding increased profits, they have even less desire to leave it. They belong to the large majority of men of all castes who have stayed on in the village, particularly for security as they know it, whether based on land or on services. Their families are here, their homes and their hearth fires are here. Here they know their neighbors well, those whom they can trust and others on whom they cannot rely. Such understanding would not be possible among strangers. Some who are most content to stay have tried working elsewhere, but because of illness or loneliness or higher living costs they have returned. They provide an additional channel for the flow of information and ideas. Each one who returns brings in new impressions, either positive or negative, from the world outside and, without deliberate intention, contributes to the New.

Those who have traveled beyond the village more briefly have been responsible for adding new ideas or methods. A farmer from our village, while awaiting his turn to have grain weighed in the wholesale market in a nearby town, began discussing crops and farming with men from other villages in our district. He discovered from several that the new seeds which they had begun using were producing yields far greater than he had thought possible.

He came home and requested the manager of the village Seed Store to apply for these miracle seeds from district headquarters.

Everyone who has been influenced in any way by the outside world has had a part in breaking down our isolation. It was the boys attending high school in town who startled the village with word of President Kennedy's assassination. To them he had been a hero. John Kennedy had lived on the other side of the world. Neither the boys nor their parents had seen him or heard him speak. But most of them had seen his picture and had heard men in town talking about his service. They felt that in his death they had lost a friend. Their awareness was even more impressive, since a daily newspaper had not yet come to Karimpur and radios were rare.

Another method of informal spreading of information is provided by visits to the doctor's office in town. Here rumor and gossip beyond the village limits, as well as news, are distributed. Villagers when away from home—whether in a bus, in a third-class compartment on a train, in the grain market, or in the doctor's office—waste no time in silence. If the nearest neighbor does not open the conversation, the villager will. There is always an exchange of questions, at first general and then more personal, including caste, business or trade, financial status, the number of sons, and the purpose of the present trip or visit. Buaji, mother of the family sharing my house, is expert at this. Having made frequent visits to the office of her particular doctor, either with her own grandchildren or with some uninitiated friend, she is completely at ease. She begins with inquiries regarding the ailments of the women near her and in exchange relates her own or that of the patient she has brought. This leads to probing into the more personal affairs of each one. What does her husband do? To what caste does he belong? How many children has she produced and how many are still alive? How much has her family spent on dowries for her daughters? How many *bahus* does she have and what are their dispositions? If there is time, Buaji goes on to the financial standing of her neighbor's husband. She has already surmised this from the woman's attire and the jewelry she wears. Most of the women she meets in the doctor's office are from town. Their buying and selling is in cash, not in grain or services; and they are prepared to spend more than farmers on such luxuries as medical treatment. She returns from each visit with a store of miscellaneous information, none of it very enlightening, though of great interest to her cronies who gather in the afternoon and to her *bahus* when they are free to relax after the evening meal. With an air of importance, she gives them glimpses of another, novel way of life. She has learned how most town families live, not in a house with plenty of courtyard space and storerooms like hers but in flats above small stores along the roads and bylanes of the bazaar. If there is a courtyard, it is on the ground level behind the store. A family living on one of the upper floors may have a balcony around the sides of the opening that gives them light and air but provides no extra space. Our *bahus* are envious when she elaborates on the leisure of town women. They are not obliged to shape fuel cakes or collect twigs to keep the cooking fire burning. Instead they have plenty of matches and a supply of kerosene oil for their small stoves. There is no grain for them to grind, no rice to husk, no *dal* (legume) to split. This has been done for them and they have cash with which to buy the finished products. However, the *bahus* are sorry for their sisters who live in town when they learn that the milk they buy is diluted with water, so there is no whole milk to churn and no butter from which to make the precious *ghi*. How can they possibly fry *puris* or special dishes with a commercial substitute? Buaji is nauseated at the thought. She saves the most shocking bit of information for the last, and announces it in the same hushed voice that she uses in passing on the latest village scandal. Because there is no cattleyard or separate front room where village men sleep to guard the animals, the men in town must sleep in the narrow balcony just outside the room in which their wives sleep or right in the same room! This brings a gasp of surprise and excitement.

News that the men bring home from town is chiefly of market prices and perhaps of local politics. Ten or more years ago they looked up to townsmen as having advantages over them financially.

Now farmers are overtaking the townsmen and, in some cases, sur-passing them. Food prices are soaring while most incomes are static and others move up at a slower rate than expenses, except for that of the grain merchants, who grow richer each year by fleecing farmers. Those in the most difficult position are the clerks in gov-ernment offices. These are the men once envied by young villagers who completed high school and were refused clerkships. The tables are now reversed, and it is the clerks who envy farmers with plenty to eat from their own fields. Most of our men return from town with an air of satisfaction, especially if they own land.

Weddings are another source of information. Anyone with any reason for being included in a wedding party goes in a spirit of adventure, and is ready for new experiences and ideas. When a group of men joined a bridegroom's party from Karimpur, travel-ing in bullock carts to the bride's village several miles away, they found the bride's father to be a "progressive farmer." He had tried a different fertilizer applied in a new way and exhibited the results. Our farmers were duly impressed, and several of them on their return to Karimpur implemented the new method.

One reason why ideas now flow into Karimpur more readily is the improved transportation between village and town. Bicycles first came to Karimpur about 1930. For the next ten or fifteen years, there were few. Now most boys who go into town to school ride cycles, as do the men who go there on business. They still use their ox carts for heavy loads, but often the head of the family goes by cycle, sending the cart ahead in charge of a hired man. With cycles, men are able to go greater distances from the village with-out having to pay bus fare. The cycle rickshaw is new since 1960 and has increased contact between Karimpur and the outside world. We have had bus service for a number of years but can-not depend on the timings, which are erratic. When the goldsmith discovered that cycle rickshaws were bringing large profits in Mainpuri, he purchased one. Its immediate popularity tempted others to invest, until now there are at least ten in the village.

They are in demand by women old enough to go to town without a male escort. Two or three friends crowd into one, with several children, and off they go, ostensibly to visit a doctor, but with a shopping excursion in mind. Men use them for loads too heavy to carry on their own cycles and too light to require a bullock cart. Still others ride into town by rickshaw to the bus depot, where they can get regular bus service to other towns and to cities.

Bicycle transport has stimulated the shepherds' milk trade. Where two and sometimes three shepherds loaded their cycles with cans of milk to be sold in town, there are now six, and their cans are larger. Each man carries from twenty to thirty quarts of milk. Members of higher castes have always been reluctant to sell milk, particularly cow's milk, which was too highly valued to be treated as merchandise. Now, early each morning, members of any caste may be found waiting on the edge of the village near the shepherd community, each with a brass *lota* of milk to be sold to one of the cyclists. The milk is measured and the amount recorded, for payments at the end of the week. Buyer and seller may be illiterate, but both are apt at mental accounting. The milk may come from a cow, a buffalo or goats. The rate is the same.

One shepherd has moved a step ahead and is operating a unique dairy of his own. He began by selling his goats in order to purchase two healthy buffaloes. Then he gradually acquired twelve under-fed, unproductive cows, each one purchased for a few rupees from a family glad to be relieved of the burden of an unremunerative animal. These, along with his buffaloes, he takes out to graze each day, rather than entrust them to the small boys and girls who serve as herders. If one of his animals strays into a field for a short meal, he does not interfere. And farmers who would beat a small herder for such negligence hesitate to tackle Banki with his heavy staff and huge frame. He is one of the two village wrestlers. His cows are giving more milk than their former owners thought possible. And he sells their milk through his own agent, his younger brother whom he has provided with a cycle.

Even the children enjoy their share in the New. One enterprising *kahar*, of serving caste, goes into Mainpuri on his cycle each morning during the hot weather and brings back popsicles packed in a box of ice along with bottles of colored water, on the carrier of his cycle. They are extremely popular with the children. A popsicle costs five *paise*, or it can be exchanged for grain tied in the tail of a shirt.

Around us there are still other changes. Perhaps the most dramatic is in the construction of houses, with many now made of baked brick instead of mud. In 1930 we found that villagers preferred to conceal their possessions behind unimposing mud walls. Now, there are over forty *pakka* homes in Karimpur, and in every lane I notice piles of bricks purchased from the proceeds of one good harvest waiting for a second such harvest to provide enough to build a whole house. *Pakka* houses are no longer restricted to the Brahmans. They are to be found in the *kachhi* community as well. Three *mahajan* (shopkeeper) brothers share a brick house. Two shepherds have built themselves *pakka* houses; so has the bangle seller and a grain parcher in Humble Lane, also a carpenter and an oilsmith. One sweeper has built a *pakka* house. He would not have dreamed of doing this twenty years ago, and members of the caste communities would not have permitted it. Now they pass by with a shrug. Building a *pakka* home indicates that there has been a surplus of grain sold for cash, or that a new business venture has been profitable. Unlike mud, which is free for the collecting, bricks sell at the rate of fifty rupees or more per thousand.

Villagers are spending their surplus on other symbols of status as well. Gifts now demanded as part of the dowry are increasingly expensive, beginning with a cycle, then a watch, a ball-point pen and perhaps a transistor radio.

There is more concern over medical care, and going to a doctor in town is much more common than it was ten years ago. A compounder, often referred to as "doctor," has been resident in Karimpur for more than a year, and has won the confidence of an increasing number of families. He also has authority from the government to vaccinate against smallpox, a greatly needed service. The limiting factor in consulting a physician is the fee, which seems exorbitant to frugal heads of families. It is because of this that they tend to delay going to a doctor until illness becomes serious. There is always the hope that the patient will recover without medical care and without a medical bill. When someone finally goes, he or she hurries home to report to the waiting family. A visit to the doctor is considered a success if the patient has been given an injection. Without it, little benefit is expected and objection to the fee is stronger. If the doctor's prescribed treatment is not visibly effective within a few days, the family turns to a local *hakim*, a self-trained practitioner. He himself is a villager—skilled in the use of roots and herbs—and his fees are comparatively low. More often, both doctor and *hakim* are consulted simultaneously. Both are made aware of this by relatives, and they accept it, knowing that it conforms to village ethics. If the patient recovers, the doctor is seldom informed and the *hakim* takes the credit.

There is no doubt of the confidence of the younger generation in trained medical personnel. It is often they who convince their elders that a doctor's care is needed. The doctors in Mainpuri are all men except for the one woman in charge of the government hospital for women. More women might be expected to go to her in preference to a man, but they regard her as a stranger and unsympathetic.

A cash economy now exists side by side with the bartering of goods and exchange of services that characterize the traditional *jajmani* system. Some farmers prefer to pay their laborers in rupees rather than in grain. For a day's field work, a laborer receives ten to fifteen kilograms of grain or three rupees and one meal, or two and a half rupees and two meals. Until recently the *jajmani* system controlled the exchange of goods and services within the caste framework. There are now examples both of the system's being maintained and of its breaking down. In the case of the oilsmiths, however, the *jajmans* have accepted none of their traditional responsibilities and take their oil to a mill to be pressed at a lower rate. The cotton carder is a similar casualty.

In 1960 the carpenters' trade had been reduced to the point where they feared they would lose their *jajmans* as the oilsmiths had. But a new generation has stepped in, and the small carpenter community near my house has made a valiant recovery. The carpenter who was incapacitated by stiffened arms and burdened with the weddings of five daughters has been rescued by his one son, now tall, hard working, and skillful. And simultaneously the father has recovered the use of his arms. The son, with no encouragement and without instruction, now makes miniature ox carts and ploughs. Villagers are not interested, and as yet his market is limited to visitors from Delhi. The second carpenter, who was suffering from cataract, has died. He has been succeeded by his son, a good workman, who is now busy serving his father's original *jajmans*. He has excelled his father in skill, producing ox-cart wheels, regarded as an achievement in village carpentry. The third carpenter, Balram, now has three grown sons assisting him, all stronger than he. They not only have expanded his trade, but also have joined him in his farming ventures. There is a revival of activity in his workshop; and in the dilapidated courtyard behind it and in his new, partially built house across the lane, there is an air of freshly acquired prosperity.

There are now two mills in the village. I reported in 1960 on the *mahajan*, a shopkeeper, who had a small general shop by the district road. When electricity became available, he installed a flour mill, then a rice husker, and later an oil press and a cotton carding machine. Knowing that villagers object to the taste of flour ground with metal, he uses stones similar to those turned by the women in their homes. Villages on all sides of Karimpur are taking advantage of his services. Smaller families in our village send no grain to be ground. A few larger families now depend on him for all of their flour, while others refuse to give up the traditional hand-grinding as long as there are daughters-in-law to do it without charge. In our family, after the harvest, when the hot season comes, Prakash allows the women to send 180 pounds of grain at a time to the mill, enough for *chapattis* for a fortnight or perhaps three weeks.

Our village council has not been as persistent as the *mahajan* in procuring electric current. Although wires and poles were installed in 1966, current has been withheld until this summer. Other than power for the two mills and the tube wells, electricity is more a potential than a reality. Villagers are prepared to wait until current becomes inexpensive before they will consider using it for light or heat. Meanwhile they are content with their hand-made *chulhas* for cooking, and with kerosene lanterns or small lamps burning mustard oil for lights.

The greatest and most significant changes in Karimpur in the last ten years have been in agriculture. As yet, whatever has come from official sources has been in agricultural technology, the one point at which new ideas and practices have penetrated to the core of the Familiar. Our farmers were doing their best with what they had. Their fields were so much more productive than those of their fathers that they were satisfied, until word of better results filtered through to them and they realized that they had still more to learn. If better results were possible, they wanted them. But for better results, what did they need and how were they to get it? To begin with, three needs were clear. First, they needed better seed. If they could procure an allotment of the improved varieties, they would be one step ahead. Second, they needed more fertilizer. Next, they needed more irrigation. The government tube-well served them, but they required more water for wheat.

One by one, these three needs have been met. With the appearance of the first improved variety of wheat in the Seed Store, everyone was interested, but the supply was small and only three young farmers offered to purchase it. The Seed Store's manager could not guarantee its success. They were informed that it was hardier and supposed to be higher yielding than the old seed. Each of the three sowed his share in one plot, following the instructions of the Village Level Worker. The operator of the government tube well, himself a farmer, was impressed by the venture and assured them of his cooperation. Under the eyes of skeptical elders their wheat matured and flourished. When harvested, it far surpassed any of the familiar varieties. It was a dramatic success. From that first harvest the young farmers were obliged to return as much seed as they had drawn plus one-fourth more as interest. This still left them with enough for the next sowing and some left over to sell. A report of the Rockefeller Foundation in India has a striking picture of one farmer pouring twelve precious wheat seeds from his own hand into the hand of another. This was all that he could spare and enough to give the other man a start. So it has been in our village. When the time came for sowing the second year, farmers who were members of the cooperative society affiliated with the Seed Store claimed as much seed as they could get. And apparently when harvest time came, they shared some of their grain with non-members. As still better appeared they were immediately adopted, until now the very latest and best available are to be found in all of our fields. Being shorter, they are less vulnerable to wind and storm, and they produce a great deal more grain. Meanwhile, our own State Agricultural University at Pantnagar was producing seed for distribution from its own research projects. Our farmers, who had heard only of seed from Ludhiana in the Punjab, began praising Pantnagar for the excellent seed coming from there. Later the supply of fertilizer was increased, with enough for every farmer who was willing to purchase it. And with ten private tube wells the need for better irrigation has been met.

Formerly, crops had been intended for family use, and as farmers increased their production they were able to eat better. Now with a larger surplus of grain, they are planting with the intention of selling more. Wheat is a profitable cash crop. If a farmer uses the seed most recently provided and follows the instructions of the Village Level Worker regarding fertilizer and care, if he makes use of the irrigation available, and if Nature does not visit him with some catastrophe, he can get nine times as much wheat per acre as he did before the changes began.

Crops other than grain are now being produced and marketed with success. Peanuts are becoming popular as a cash crop. One young farmer has netted a thousand rupees from one acre of peanuts this year. Last year, Prakash, head of the family sharing my house, found onions and garlic profitable. As the garlic brought a better price than the onions, he has devoted three and one-half acres to it this year. Neither he nor any member of his family would touch food seasoned with garlic, so the whole crop will go to the market. And he is assured of several thousand rupees from its sale. Soya beans have recently been introduced in our state. As a result of research in Pantnagar, the growing season has been shortened to four or even to two months, making it possible to sow soya beans at the same time as the two main crops. One of our farmers has just now secured a small amount for planting, from Pantnagar. The tradition that *kachhis* are the vegetable growers for the village is no longer relevant. Each year more farmers of all castes are planting vegetables for sale as well as for their own use. Peas are increasingly popular. Some were grown in small plots earlier. Now one sees whole fields of them, intended primarily for sale. More farmers now raise large potatoes for the market as well as the very small ones which they prefer for themselves.

To encourage the production of grain for sale, the government is constructing a warehouse in Mainpuri where a farmer may store his grain at the rate of ten *paise* per month per gunny bag containing a quintal. This is far better than the customary storing of grain

within the household enclosure where it is exposed to rats and
weevils. About two years ago a private cold storage plant was
opened in Mainpuri, offering storage space for potatoes under
conditions not possible in homes. There they can be held for the
next planting or until market prices become reasonable.

Consolidation of land is the most striking innovation we have
experienced in Karimpur for many years. In government circles
involved in rural development, it had long been regarded as a
necessary step toward increased production; but the implementing
of the idea was postponed until 1966. The farmers who heard
rumors of it dismissed it as ridiculous. From the youngest to the
oldest, they had cultivated land inherited from their forefathers.
The fact that their holdings were in small scattered plots had not
disturbed them. Each plot was treasured by the owner and his
family. There may have been larger fields in the distant past, but
when there were two or more sons, the original field had been
divided among them and divided again with each generation. No
one seems able to account for the wide distribution of any one
family's plots. Instead of being contiguous, they are more often
scattered on two or more sides of the village and separated by
plots belonging to other families. To an outsider concerned with
progress in agriculture, this was shocking inefficiency. But neither
our farmers nor those in villages around us had heard of any different system. To be sure, a son might grumble at having to carry a
plough from plot to plot, or at being obliged to hurry from one
plot to another while water from the government tube well was
theirs to use. Disputes over the low, earth boundaries separating
one man's plot from those of his neighbors on all four sides were
continually being brought before the land recorder or even to the
court. But all of this had been accepted as inevitable.

When word finally came from district headquarters that the government was definitely preparing to send officers to Karimpur to
evaluate each man's scattered plots and later to exchange them

for one or two larger fields, they were alarmed. How could they entrust their land, their inheritance, to unscrupulous officers like those they had known? They were told that the plan would save a farmer time and labor and would result in greater efficiency. Besides, they were given no choice. It came as an order from the government hierarchy in Lucknow, the State capital, or possibly from Delhi, and no alternative was offered.

In their evening circles, the discussion of consolidation went on into the night. They reached the point where they could accept the advantages in theory but saw the dangers in practice. Their fears were not allayed when the village was invaded by officials from several ranks, among them the men whose tactics they had learned to fear, like the land recorder. The officer in charge was known as the A.C.O.—the Assistant Consolidation Officer. His superior, the C.O., was located at district headquarters. Housing was demanded for the A.C.O. and any others who choose to live in Karimpur rather than in town. Ten or more clerks had to be given space for their desks and, in some cases, living quarters.

The A.C.O. was supposed to evaluate the plots belonging to each man, along with a committee of four or five farmers, so that the farmers might have a voice. But when the A.C.O. found that time was lost waiting for farmers to join him, he worked on it with members of his official staff. This left him with a great deal of power. Decisions were virtually his alone.

Every landowner realized that what he was granted now would be his and his descendants forever. And because land was his paramount security, he was prepared to pay heavily for land he considered good. It soon became evident that the A.C.O.'s mind could be changed as to the evaluation of plots and later in the allocation of a particular field, by a small payment from the villager. I did not suspect what was happening until there was unprecedented agitation over the sudden transfer of the first A.C.O. Farmers were upset because he went off richer, while they were poorer. No one would acknowledge what he had given, and the A.C.O. had no intention of reporting what he had received. When the second A.C.O. came, the farmers knew what was expected of them. No man divulged to his neighbor or to his brother what he was offering. As a result, suspicion between neighbors and even between relatives grew until long-standing relationships were disrupted.

When the third and last A.C.O. announced the final settlement, there was an outburst from those who felt cheated, followed by quarrels throughout the village. Again, when the Consolidation Officer, the A.C.O.'s superior, came from Mainpuri, his visit resembled an auction. Later, a still higher Consolidation Officer came to make the final pronouncement, and again claims and counterclaims were rife. When he left, there was satisfaction among some and distress among others. As happens anywhere in the world, those who already had plenty and were clever, were the gainers. Those who had little and did not know how to maneuver were the losers. Appeals and court cases are still going on. However, one can hope that in a few years men will have accepted their allotments, and life will become normal once more.

There is no doubt of the ultimate advantages of consolidation, at least for those with large fields. It makes radical improvements possible in agriculture, it is ushering in fundamental changes, and it encourages new investments. I recall the time when a farmer considered long and seriously before investing in a fodder cutter to replace the old, cumbersome chopper. Now it is regarded as an essential piece of equipment. Ten years ago there was the same reluctance to spend cash on a simple thresher. Now nine families own them and others are prepared to buy when a more efficient machine becomes available. All farmers agree that consolidation has saved them time and labor. And it has helped in irrigation. A man with a large field can afford to install a tube well of his own. He can irrigate his own field without waiting his turn for water from the government tube well and can charge others for water from his. Ten privately owned tube wells have appeared in the past six months, where there was only the one government tube well in 1960. Farmers who now own large fields are beginning to think seriously of tractors. One young man has already invested. He startled the village a few weeks ago when he drove down the lane in a bright new tractor. Another was torn between buying a tractor and installing a tube well. He finally decided in favor of the tube well because the benefits would be immediate. However, he has taken the first steps toward the purchase of a tractor, knowing that he may have to wait as long as two years before he can get one of the particular brand he wants, because of the heavy demand.

New crops, new fertilizers, electrically powered mills, *pakka* homes, cycle rickshaws, radios—all announce the newer New. But to be complete, the picture must include those characteristics which have not changed. In many ways life in the village continues to move as it has for hundreds of years. In spite of trips to town and occasional salesmen coming from town, such as the cloth merchant, the village remains aloof and prefers to be self-sufficient. The farmers are frugal and aim to raise whatever they need, except for white sugar used on special festival days, spices, salt, and matches. Everyone is obliged to purchase cloth at some time, and oil may be wanted for lamps. Soap for washing clothes and bathing is becoming more common. Only those who have lived in a city indulge in tea.

Villagers, those who have lived and worked elsewhere and those who have stayed at home, still question the motives of strangers. This wariness seems as strong as it was in 1960. The local representatives of the government use their power for personal gain, and are distrusted above all others. Higher ranking officials live in the civil lines in Mainpuri and seldom if ever visit the village. Before the advent of motor cars in Mainpuri, they came on annual tour and pitched their tents here for several days. Now they pass us by

on their way to the subdistrict headquarters farther on. In their
offices they are inaccessible to ordinary men, guarded by peons
who know which callers to admit and which to bar. A villager,
highly respected in his own community, makes no further attempt
to enter an office if once rebuffed by a peon.

Politicians are expected in the village only before elections. My
neighbors remark, "We are very popular around election time and
then they forget us and forget the promises they have made to us."
However, men and women of Karimpur are making use of the
right to vote. Seventy per cent of them voted in the last election.
They still tend to vote by caste rather than by party or qualifications of candidates. Brahmans vote for Brahmans, *kyasths* for
kyasths, kachhis for *kachhis.*

They avoid the police as much as possible. When anyone from
the police department appears in the village, people remain indoors. When a crime has been committed, they go to extremes to
conceal whatever has happened, in order to prevent the police from
laying brutal hands on the persons implicated. This has not changed
since we first came to Karimpur, because the police have not
changed.

Our farmers have a penchant for court cases. Those who part
reluctantly with a single rupee for any other purpose are prepared
to spend thousands to contest a small piece of land. In the courts
lawyers abound, ready to offer legal advice in return for a large
fee. The affluence of lawyers in district headquarters like Mainpuri
is proverbial. Money is lavished not only on lawyers but on count-
less visits to court. Men go on the date scheduled, only to be told
that the case has been postponed for two weeks or a month. They
dare not risk the consequences of absence, so they go again and
again. In spite of their aversion to dealing with strangers, they
yield to the will of strange lawyers and officials.

Religious beliefs and practices of Hinduism, which undergird the life of the village, remain strong. I have been made acutely aware of this since my neighbors, Prakash and Buaji, brought their joint family to my courtyard for shelter, five years ago. They were driven from their large century-old home by the crashing down of walls around them during two consecutive seasons of torrential rains. Their sojourn was to be brief, but they are still with me and there are no signs of rebuilding. I have appreciated living with them and especially the grandchildren, now numbering thirteen, for the sheer enjoyment of watching and listening to them. Buaji and her four *bahus* have patiently taught me the significance of each duty and its associated ritual as performed once or more each day or week, each month or year. And they have explained the purpose of their fasting, and of the individual *puja* performed by one of them before the sacred *tulsi* plant in the courtyard or at Prakash's center for Shivaji worship in front of the old house. These are intended to win favors for the family or for a particular member, from the deity or deities to whom homage is given.

Karimpur has acquired three temples during the past three years, all gifts of widows, all small, and all dedicated to Shivaji. Two are exclusive, intended for the worship of the donor, alone, or for her near relatives. One of these was built by a *dhanuk,* of scheduled caste, and the other by a Brahman. The third, slightly larger, is the only one that has made an impact on the life of the village. Like the others, it is designed for individual worship, but it is open to any member of the village community. It came as an unexpected gift from an unexpected source. Many years ago, a *kahar,* as poor as his neighbors, gathered up his few belongings and, with his family, made his way to Calcutta. There they were lost sight of. In the city he shed his menial status and eventually became a prosperous business man, aided by his two sons. And two years ago, his widow returned, to erect a temple in his memory. She brought with her enough money for an unostentatious temple, furnished only with the altar to Shiva in the center and a doll-like figure of

Parbati, his consort, at one side. She herself superintended the building of the temple and the restoration of the *dharmshala* beside it. The *dharmshala*, once constructed as a rest house for mendicants on pilgrimage, had long been neglected. Its courtyard has ample space for a large crowd, seated on the ground. And now, refurbished, it has replaced the informal worship center beside the district road, with its circle of stones under a peepul tree. For almost a week ceremonies were held in the courtyard as part of the inauguration of the temple. At the end came a great feast to which all were welcome. The widow returned to Calcutta, and the village adopted the temple. It is seldom visited, and no priest is needed to preside over it. There is a priest who lives in the village and officiates at weddings, *kathas,* and other ceremonies in village homes.

On a number of occasions, Prakash has said to me, "You and the Sahib, and Buaji and I, have been together in this life. We must have been together in a previous life and we shall be together again. It may not be in India; it may be in Russia or Africa." This acceptance of reincarnation is manifest in the bearing of different caste groups. Members of serving castes and scheduled castes are deferential, *kachhis* independent. Most of the Brahmans have an air which ranges from self-assurance to arrogance. They know that they are on top, and they feel that they have earned this in an earlier incarnation.

Dharma is accepted in the village. Just as everyone in the family has a definite role, so every person in the village has a role in relation to others. Carpenters' sons are trained by fathers to be carpenters, *darzi* (tailors') boys are trained to be *darzis*. The same is true of others. Indian village society can be likened to chess, where each piece has a prescribed move or role. American society is more like checkers with every piece more or less the same.

The idea of *ahimsa*, non-injury to living things, permeates the lives of the village men and women. They are reluctant to take the life of any creature. Yet, they do not feed their dogs. They allow them to starve and become ferocious but will not kill them or drown puppies even though some are doomed to die early. The mother of my courtyard goes through the form of swatting at a fly, but I do not think that she has ever actually killed one. The children swat effectively and with zest. No adult in the family would willingly kill a rat. However, when my servant brought us a cat, they approved of the cat's prowess in obliterating the rats and thereby sparing a good deal of stored grain.

A number of religious practices, or practices which have been given religious significance, may have had a practical origin. For instance, every morning a *bahu* of my family freshly plasters the *chulha* and the ground around it with a paste of clay. This is regarded as a ceremony of purification. Also there is a low wall separating this space from the rest of the courtyard. No one enters the area except the woman assigned to cook the meal and perhaps one other to help her; and both of them are careful to wash their hands before they enter it. To us, the whole procedure seems a practical way of providing a clean surface and clean handling of food for the family, when all preparation must be done on the ground.

Eating by caste still holds. Few will accept food or water from anyone outside of the family or the caste. There are three exceptions to this rule. It is permissible to accept food from a member of a higher caste or to eat food fried under certain conditions by a member of a lower caste. High-caste friends of mine who decline to partake of any such food within the village, purchase it without question at a railway station when on a long journey. The third exception allows anyone of any caste to accept water from a member of a menial caste known as *kahar* in our area. *Kahars* are born to be water carriers as well as servants, some acting as cooks for *Brahmans* in large cities.

There has been criticism of caste by outsiders, but there are advantages to be noted as well. Where caste prevails every individual knows his function in the caste structure and knows what behavior is expected of him within his own caste and in his dealings with members of other castes. This in itself provides a sense of security. Also, if a man moves into a strange environment, he prefers to identify himself with his own caste group, where he feels secure and at ease.

Recently there has been a widespread movement in North India among certain scheduled castes and lower levels of *sudras* to raise their status by changing their caste names. No one expected anything so daring to occur in an ordinary village like Karimpur. Higher-caste men belittle the idea. However, before 1960 the *chamars*, most aggressive of our three scheduled castes, took the step upward. They became *jatav*, thus removing the stigma attached to *chamra*, hides, with which they had been traditionally engaged, from the skinning of dead animals to the curing of the hides by primitive, noisome methods. A few young *jatavs* went further and dropped the last part of the name, to make themselves *jats*, much higher in rank. And a few others softened the "j" and "t" to make the name *Yadav*, a caste only slightly below the *kshatriya*, the warrior caste.

More recently the carpenters, with the exception of one family, have made the leap from *barhai* to *maithil* and later to *ojha brahman* and have adopted the sacred cord. This ranks them higher than the *pande brahmans* who predominate in Karimpur. The *pandes* ignore the change and continue to address them as *barhai*. The *dhanuks*, a scheduled caste less ambitious than the *chamars*, have been invited to become *kataria*, a subcaste of *kshatriya*, but thus far have refused the offer. Likewise, the potters are content to remain *kumhar* rather than change to the higher status of *prajapati*. The *telis*, oilsmiths, are free to become *rathor*, a *kshatriya* subcaste; but only one young man has taken advantage of the opportunity. His father was able to finance the son's training as an expert tailor and later to set him up in Karimpur with a sewing machine. The son had no desire to become an ordinary *darzi* (sewing man), like his neighbors. Instead he skipped several castes, to become *rathor*. He alone speaks of himself as *rathor*. To others, including his own family, he is a *teli*.

Villagers accept without question the beliefs and traditions passed on to them by their fathers, just as they accept caste. These are universals, observed by all members of the village. No one now living has created them or considers himself responsible for them. However, the family is in a different position. Each man feels himself directly responsible for his own family and its security. His chief concern is its well-being. He has been taught this so firmly that he disregards the state of those outside of his immediate family, be they of another caste or of his own. He is not disturbed if they go hungry while he has plenty, because he can never be sure that the next harvest will provide enough for his own family's needs. His circle of interest may include those who serve him and for whom he is responsible as *jajman*, and he may help a close relative in a serious emergency. Beyond this he does not go. Buaji considers me unethical when I give a *dhoti* or food or school fees to anyone outside of her family, which she regards as mine.

In the joint family one finds the best possible security for a child. If a father dies, his children are treated by his brothers as their own. They are scarcely aware of their loss. If a mother dies, there are still aunts to care for the children, just as there were while the mother was living. In a courtyard which I do not visit regularly, I find it difficult to tell which child belongs to whom, unless one of them goes to a particular woman to nurse.

Weddings, as far as I have been able to observe, have not changed since I came to Karimpur. The marriage and the dowry are still arranged by elders of the two families without consulting the groom or the bride. Lower-caste families strain to have impressive weddings; and in the higher castes money is spent lavishly for a dazzling wedding that will confirm the family's prestige. A girl is married at the age of thirteen or fourteen, but she does not become a part of her husband's family until she is fifteen or sixteen.

She knows that she will be married to a boy from another village, and as a result her relationship with neighbor boys is free of romance. Parents of a girl favor an early marriage. They know that their daughter, when safely married, will be cared for by her in-laws should they themselves become indigent or helpless. A married girl's status depends on her husband's position in the family. She is called *bari bahu* (chief or eldest daughter-in-law) if married to the eldest son, or *majli bahu* (middle daughter-in-law) if married to the next son, and *chhoti bahu* (youngest daughter-in-law) if married to the youngest son. A young *bahu* in Karimpur leaves her mother-in-law's courtyard only to attend the annual fair, to get water from the nearest caste well, to perform tasks like shaping and stacking fuel cakes just over the courtyard wall, or to go at dawn to the nearest field to relieve herself. If she is the only *bahu* in the courtyard, she is lonely. If she is married into a large family, the courtyard life is rich and full. In rare cases there is companionship between a wife and her husband. For most young *bahus*, however, life consists of heavy work with little of the affection they have enjoyed in their own families. Each one looks forward to visits to her parents' home, where she is treated as an honored guest, relieved of customary duties, and waited on by a devoted mother. Also, each one can look forward to the day when she will be mistress of her own courtyard.

The wishes expressed by the young men at the close of 1960 have been met, at least in part. There are now two mills instead of the one mentioned. Many more villagers have houses either completely or partially of baked brick. The first threshing machine appeared in 1960, and now nine farmers own and use them and loan them to others. Two of the young men wear watches. The others have expressed no desire to own them except for prestige. A Hindi newspaper comes to the village daily. The young men and their friends have been playing volleyball for the past five years, whenever work is slack. Electric wires and poles have been waiting for current from the District Board for four years; and this summer we are promised not only enough for lights in the lanes but also lights in the few houses where they are wanted. Most families are still content with small oil lamps or lanterns. Block officers have not come oftener, as the young men hoped. But the Village Level Worker has responded to their requests for advice in handling new crops and new types of fertilizer. Fathers have allowed their sons to venture in trying new crops, although they have not granted the new degree of freedom the sons would like.

In their discussion the young men referred only to relations between peers. Thus far they have not shown concern over relationships with their wives or with other members of their own families. They express no interest in neighbors other than those who have quarreled with them or their fathers, or those who have attracted attention by achieving success or creating a scandal.

In the careers of two of the young men the Old and the New have met. One is Subedar, at that time *pradhan*, president of the village council, and the other is Ganesh, our first B.A.

For Subedar, trouble came when the Old tried to compete with the New. His father, Prakash, had dominated him, and he had remained a docile son in their traditional father-son relationship, throughout the years when he worked on the family plots and during his apprenticeship as tractor driver on a government project arranged by his father. And Prakash took for granted that the relationship would continue under new circumstances in which he placed his son. However, when he succeeded in maneuvering Subedar's election as *pradhan*, Subedar rejected his authority and looked to block development officers for instructions.

He became a regular participant in meetings held by the district magistrate and block officers for *pradhans*, and after each meeting he set out to implement the plans presented for the improvement of the village. First, he undertook the construction of new school buildings, which had long been needed. Later, he encouraged the digging of better compost pits. At one time, he gathered volunteers from among the younger men to construct a wide lane leading from the district road to the village proper. Everyone had complained of the state of the old lane. It was full of pot holes and ruts, but no one had thought of building a whole new road and no one had thought of volunteering to do it, until the *pradhan* made his proposal. Following this, he set out to improve the lanes within the village, each householder working on the lane in front of his house. He stocked the village pond with fish from the State Fisheries Department to be sold when full grown to provide funds for further improvements. He had poles and wires installed for electric lights along the lanes.

All of these plans were excellent, and he succeeded with a few: the compost pits, the construction of a large section of the lane from the district road, and two of the school buildings. The others failed partly because the block officers who had inspired him to improve conditions did not instruct him in the techniques of projecting new ideas. When he returned from a session with them, he was so convinced that the newest proposal was good that he expected others to accept it as he had. He made no effort to consult anyone, not even members of the village council; and no one had warned him that villagers must share in any innovation from the beginning. If they have even a slight suspicion that it is being forced on them or handed down to them, they do not cooperate. Subedar was too impatient.

The other reason for the failures lay not in him but in members of the council, men who were older than he and more adept in manipulating public opinion. They disapproved of the power he was gaining and set about weakening it as a means of augmenting their own. They were more concerned with the next local election than with the welfare of the village. In each monthly meeting of the council, they agreed to the *pradhan's* latest undertaking. They walked out from the meeting and immediately spread rumors that this particular idea was intended to win the approval of district officers who might visit the village. The *pradhan*, they said, was looking after his own interests, not those of the village. The reaction of most men was "why should we make this effort to help Subedar get ahead?"

The same council members aroused suspicion that proceeds from the sale of fish would go into the *pradhan's* pocket. As a result, villagers who were not strict vegetarians went fishing after dark. By the end of the year there were no fish left to be sold. When the building intended for the junior high school was three years old, the roof collapsed in heavy rain and Subedar was held responsible. One of his rivals reported that the delay in bringing electricity to the village, long after the poles and wires were installed, was due to the *pradhan's* holding the necessary funds for his own use. He was harassed at every turn. In spite of this, he continued to serve, not on a village scale, but in individual cases. He helped three oilsmiths, when oil mills appropriated their business, to procure small plots of land. They now can raise a crop of rice during the annual rainy season, and better still they have the satisfaction of owning land for the first time.

During his five years as *pradhan,* he maintained the dignity of his office and was treated with respect. Each morning he stepped out of the courtyard with his cycle, dressed in immaculate white homespun shirt and *dhoti* and white cap. When he returned in the evening and had been served his meal, he made a practice of sitting on my front verandah, ready to meet any man or men who might join him with requests or complaints. When his term of office was completed, he was prepared to return to farming. But the consolidation officers were moving in just then, and they arranged with the district authorities to have him retained. This proved his undoing. He gradually lost both his interest in his role as *pradhan* and his earlier zeal. He was now under the influence of men who had had experience with consolidation in other parts of the district and were well aware of the opportunities it offered for personal gain. He learned quickly and was soon in the thick of it. He was approached with offers on a large scale, especially from friends and acquaintances who saw in him an ally in securing the land they wanted. He ignored the urging of his father and mother that he share this new income with the family. However, they were able to exact one important favor from him. He had in his possession the map of all plots of the village. He was also in a position to influence the apportioning of fields and could give them preference. As a result, when consolidation was completed they were in possession of choice land in a favorable location. When others complained of the poor land received in spite of their donations, Buaji virtuously announced that they had not given a *paisa* to any officer. Everyone knew why.

He became reckless and more prodigal with his money. Then came the crash. As suddenly as he had gained power and riches, he was reduced to the depths of disgrace and poverty, entirely dependent on his family. Others who had set the pattern for him withdrew, and he was left alone.

During the past year he has grown old, his hair has turned white, and he walks with a stoop, the stoop of failure rather than that of age. His father treats him like a beggar. When he comes into the courtyard no one speaks to him. His wife, in whom he has never confided, serves him in silence. After his evening meal he sits alone, perched on the edge of the front verandah, looking out toward the fields where once he had worked in peace. Those who had courted his favor no longer have use for him, and those who were his friends seem unwilling to visit him. His brothers and their friends who gather at the other end of the verandah talk and laugh, and ignore him.

I was puzzled. Why had this happened to a man slightly over forty, who had shown promise of success? I knew that Prakash's disappointment was even greater than mine. Also I knew that Prakash alone could explain. One evening I broached the subject when he had finished his evening meal and we were sitting in the courtyard. Before I had finished my question, the bitterness, the anger, the humiliation he had suffered exploded in passionate sentences. "It is I whom he has ruined, I who have done everything for him. I taught him farming. I sent him for training as a tractor driver. I entered his name instead of my own as candidate for *pradhan*, and it was Buaji and I who won his election. I had him appointed to assist the consolidation officers." This last I had not known. He had not answered my question directly. But his few sentences and the tirade which followed made it clear that what he had done for Subedar was not for Subedar's benefit but with the expectation that Subedar would turn over whatever he acquired to his father as head of the family. He expressed no interest in the reforms that Subedar had introduced. When Subedar had worked under him, Prakash had given the boy what he considered that he needed, as a favor. What more could a son want? He had taught Subedar firmly, by precept and example, that his family must come first in reaping benefits. Instead, Subedar had repudiated him, the head of the family, and had transferred his allegiance to block officers and later to those directing consolidation, all of whom were outsiders. As I listened, the picture became clearer. Prakash was bound by tradition, and he had done his best to prepare Subedar for the way of life with which he himself was familiar. At the same time he had failed to provide his son with the inner resources or the direction needed to meet the unfamiliar situations in which he himself had placed him. As a result, he had damaged his own prestige and wasted money. Still more serious, he had sacrificed the future of his son.

Ganesh's adjustment to the New has been less eventful than Subedar's and, for several reasons, more successful. His father, Rajju, is as dogmatic as Prakash, but with ambitions that do not involve his son. He is one of the most orthodox Hindus I know, in the village or elsewhere. He is a highly qualified Sanskrit scholar and spends his days studying the Vedas and the Bhagavad Gita as well as the more popular epics. There are very few farmers in Karimpur who do not cultivate their own land. Rajju is one of them. As far back as Ganesh can remember, his father has let out their plots on shares, with the result that they have received half or less than half of the produce, depending on the reliability of the share-cropper. And their plots are small and few. To supplement his income, Rajju began giving lectures while Ganesh was still in high school. There were Hindus in larger cities so occupied with accumulating wealth that they had little time to devote to the sacred writings. And they were prepared to pay Rajju well for a series of lectures on selected texts. Rajju despised them, their caste and their unorthodox ways, but he needed the money they gave him. He himself is scrupulous in carrying out all ritual and strict in the observance of the rules governing personal conduct.

When he left home for a lecture tour he expected Ganesh to take his place as head of the family, and he left the burden of household management to Ganesh and his mother. Fortunately for Ganesh their family was small: his parents, himself, and one younger sister and brother. They shared the house with Rajju's farmer-brother and his wife and their family of small daughters. The two families had independent incomes and ate from separate *chulhas*, built at opposite ends of a verandah facing their common courtyard. When Rajju returned from a tour, always unannounced, he expected an accurate reckoning of all accounts. During his absence Ganesh had been obliged to make decisions that seemed right to him but which must also satisfy an exacting father.

Rajju had no definite plans for Ganesh. He expected him to prepare for some profession, perhaps a lawyer or a teacher. At the end of his second year in college, Ganesh failed in the final examinations. His father knew the circumstances that led to the failure, but he was merciless. His son had disgraced the family. He would provide no more funds toward the boy's education. By this time Ganesh knew that he wanted to continue his studies and refused to give up. By working in his father's fields when free from classes, by tutoring younger students and preparing his own meals in an *ashram* in Mainpuri during college sessions, he repeated the lost year and completed the next two years, earning the first B.A. in Karimpur.

Rajju arranged for Ganesh's marriage incidentally, during a series of lectures in Kanpur, a large industrial city. He did not inform anyone in the family, and the first inkling of it reached Ganesh when his father called him home from college to meet the father of the bride. Later, when he received orders to come at once to join his own wedding party, he obeyed without question.

The marriage might have ended in disaster. The bride was a city girl, openly scornful of village custom. On her first visit to his home she antagonized his mother and women relatives by her scorn of their dress and habits. She insisted that she and Ganesh live in Kanpur where her father knew of a job for him on the railway. Ganesh declined. He would live in the village and he would help her make the difficult adjustment to village life. He has succeeded in both. At the same time he and his father have found a number of common interests. In some ways Ganesh is as orthodox a Hindu as his father, though more liberal in others.

His goal was to teach in a school or inter-college near enough to Karimpur to make it possible for him to live at home. To get the necessary training he attended a college in Kanpur, leaving his wife and baby in his mother's care, and household affairs with his father. This was a new role for Rajju, but he accepted it with good grace. By this time he approved of Ganesh's purpose, and Ganesh had asked him for no financial help. This came from Ganesh's own peanut harvest, which was abundant that year, and a gift from his wife of some of her own jewelry.

He is now manager and teacher in a higher secondary school a few miles away. This allows him time before and after school to superintend work on his land and to enjoy Hindi literature, his favorite subject, and also to spend an evening hour with his wife and two children. The marriage, arranged in accordance with the Old, and precarious in the beginning, has become a love marriage in the best Indian tradition. He has no political ambitions and his father has none for him. He prefers to take his place among his peers as one of them, not as a leader. When he comes home from his teaching, he looks like a townsman, in bush-shirt and city-type trousers. But soon after his return he steps out in an old shirt and *dhoti*, ready to work in a field or to join his friends. He has opened a small library in his house and subscribes for a newspaper in Hindi, both of which are now being shared by other young men. He remains a villager from choice. Here he has land of his own, his own home, and his family. Here he has found life richer, more rewarding than that of the city. And he has discovered that it is possible to benefit from the New without sacrificing loyalty to the Old.

Postscript (1970)

Any coincidence has in it an element of surprise. One has just occurred that is so perfectly timed it is more than a surprise; it is startling. Early in 1961 as I was completing the manuscript of *Behind Mud Walls—1960* shouts outside my courtyard door heralded the arrival of the first ox-drawn thresher. Yesterday, early in 1971, just after I had posted the 1970 addition to the book, word was brought that a power threshing machine had been purchased by two farmers and was already functioning. It was at the far end of the village beside a tube well where power was available. Farmers gathered to watch, to make sure that it was actually doing what the owners had boasted it could do. And there it was, threshing the wheat and winnowing, all by electric current. No oxen were in sight, no men were tilting their winnowing baskets to remove chaff from the wheat. How far removed it is from the ancient method used by all of our farmers until the arrival of the simple ox-drawn thresher, ten years ago.

When a pair of oxen does the treading of the grain, the amount threshed in one day cannot be measured, because the whole process takes three days. For two days the animals, driven by one

man, go round and round over the stalks of grain spread out on
the threshing floor, breaking and cutting up the stalks into smaller
and smaller pieces until, by noon of the third day, the chaff is
loosened sufficiently from the kernels for the winnowing to begin.
All afternoon the winnowing goes on, one or two men tilting and
jerking their special baskets filled with wheat and chaff in the
breeze that blows the chaff away. In the absence of a breeze, a
sheet is flapped to create one. If there are two teams of oxen, more
grain can be added.

Men say that by this treading method they can thresh from
eight to fifteen maunds in three days. The ox-drawn thresher can
finish from twenty to thirty maunds in the same time. The power
machine, with three men to operate it, threshes and winnows forty
maunds of wheat in a day of eight hours. When farmers discuss
this new wonder machine they remind themselves that it had cost
more than a thousand rupees. The price will limit the number of
such machines in the village. But as I look down the lane to the
long rows of wheat stacked high by the harvesters, waiting to be
threshed, I feel sure that before very long there will be more
than one tractor and more than one power threshing machine.
This year's harvest is the best we have ever had. And abundance is
influencing attitudes. The owners of this new machine are sons of
two of the men who, in 1930, said to us, "We are uneasy when you
or our sons propose change."

We hear a good deal about the winds of change blowing over
India. The farmers of Karimpur have learned from their intimate
association with Nature that there is not just one kind of wind, but
three. There is the *andhi* that comes roaring over the countryside
when the temperature is highest, in June. It is laden with dust and
whatever else it has swept up from the ground on its wild rush.
Men and animals scurry to the nearest shelter when they see and
hear it approaching. Then there is the *luh*, the burning wind that
also comes in the hot weather, not so violent but steady and relentless, irritating the nerves and sharpening tempers. The wind that

my neighbors welcome is the *biyar*, the cool breeze that may come at any time, from spring to autumn, blowing over fields and through courtyards, when men and creatures most need relief from the burden of heat. It does not destroy. It refreshes.

Changes of the past ten years have been like this. They have not been a threat to tradition with its strong roots sustaining life as it is and as it has been. They have brought relief to many from the fear of hunger and from insecurity. And they have opened men's minds to the benefits of progress, preparing them for greater changes to come.

Gandhiji once said, "If the village perishes, India will perish. It will be no more India." Karimpur, an ordinary village of North India, will not perish while it is nourished by the best from its past and yet remains free to accept the best offered by the New.

The Village
in 1984

These men are working on their kerosene-driven tube
well. The availability of pump sets and bore holes met
a dramatic increase in water for irrigation during the
1970s and contributed to a general increase in
prosperity in the village and region. (1984)

CHAPTER XV

The Village in 1984

Susan S. Wadley

As our car sped down the one-lane road leading from the district town, I watched excitedly for the mound topped by the white shrine to the village guardian, Khan Bahadur, for that was always the first visible sign that we were indeed near Karimpur. Shona and Leela, aged seven and four, bounced on the seat beside me while their father sat in front to direct the driver. It was August of 1983, and after several years of planning we were returning to Karimpur for a year of research focusing on men's and women's life histories.

Our car rounded the curve at the next village, and finally we saw the hill with its shrine. We slowed down to pass the hamlets on the road, one inhabited by the leather workers and the other by members of the farming caste. At the bus stop we turned into the lane past the sweeper colony, then went around the pond and up to the door of the house built by the Wisers in 1960, long since taken over by Prakash's family. I had shared it with Prakash's family in 1968 and 1974–75, and although Prakash himself was now dead, his family was my family when-

ever I was in India. We were greeted with folded hands, em-
braces, and many stares, my blonde daughters awkward in those
first moments of meeting. I gave sweets and fruits to Prakash's
widow, Buaji, to distribute among her family. Although now
partially blind from cataracts, she remained the senior female in
the household, and it was her right to apportion the foodstuffs
among her children, grandchildren, and great-grandchildren. Tea
was offered, presents distributed to the children, and initial ex-
ploratory excursions made by my girls.

The back rooms of the Wiser house, built more than twenty
years earlier of mud bricks, had collapsed in the rains the year
before, and a new enlarged section was being built. Since only
the three front rooms were habitable and they were overflowing
with the family of Prakash's oldest son, we secured rooms in the
nearby town and commuted to Karimpur daily, staying over-
night for festivals and other special occasions. The erratic electricity and running water, as well as a bit of privacy, were other
welcome attractions of urban life, especially since even the pump
in Prakash's courtyard no longer worked.

For me, having lived in Karimpur for over a year some fifteen
years earlier, this return was a homecoming. Much was familiar:
the village lanes in the monsoon rains were as treacherous as
ever, and the school children crowding in our doorway to stare
at the foreigners were reminiscent of their now-grown aunts and
uncles, except that they were more numerous than ever. Yet
some things were clearly different: an electric wire ran by our
house, and five village homes actually had electricity. A motorcycle came by our door almost daily, bringing home a college
teacher, one of the village's first M.A. graduates. The women
were resplendent in orange, red, purple, and yellow machine-
made cotton saris, not the plain handlooms of 1968. On ritual
occasions, they donned saris of synthetic fabric, often elabo-
rately embroidered with sequins and worn "Delhi-style" with
the head uncovered. Brick dwellings were everywhere, and if a
whole house wasn't of brick, one room often was. And the "beep-
beep" of the pump sets providing water for irrigation echoed in

the quiet of the dark nights. The visible changes were material ones, signs of increased prosperity for some. The less visible changes, which became evident only months later, were in life expectations, family life, relationships between castes, employment opportunities, and ties to the government. In the following pages, I sketch my impressions of Karimpur in 1984, highlighting both the Familiar and the New, as they had evolved since Dadi had described it in 1970.

Changes in agriculture deriving from the Green Revolution and land consolidation had continued throughout the 1970s and early 1980s. These changes, combined with population pressure (by 1984 Karimpur had 2,048 inhabitants, an increase of more than 22 percent since 1975), contributed to new labor relationships and new employment patterns for many. In a human sense, the village had undergone dramatic changes in the 1970s.

The most important agricultural change in the 1970s was pumped irrigation water. Following land consolidation, and using easily accessible government loans, farmers started buying pump sets and boring tube wells to irrigate their crops. The new wheat seeds, which quadrupled their yields, required fertilizer and dependable supplies of water. Only one-third of the village fields had received water from the government tube well built in the 1950s, and the schedule created by the official running it was often unsuitable to a particular farmer's needs. Moreover, water went first to the rich and powerful. With their fields less scattered after consolidation, it was feasible for farmers to bore wells, attach portable pump sets and irrigate according to their own schedules. With their own pump sets and bore holes, all of the village fields could be irrigated. Farmers who didn't own a pump could rent one from a neighbor. Water was essentially available on demand; and by 1984, with thirty-nine pumps operating in the village, no farmer complained of a lack of irrigation water.

Mechanization, aside from water pumps, was less important. Two tractors were bought in the mid-1970s, but one was sold after the owner died. In 1984 only the headman had a tractor. Several large farmers had invested in the power threshing machines discussed by Dadi in her 1971 postscript, while several others used the oxen-drawn mechanical thresher first introduced in 1960. Yet others still used their oxen to thresh grain. For many, human labor was still abundant and cheap enough to be more cost-efficient than the new machines.

In addition to planting high-yielding varieties of wheat, by the mid-1970s Karimpur farmers had recognized the value of new cash crops for the local market. While the lack of a processing plant cut into sugarcane production, and cotton and peas had all but disappeared by 1984, peanut, garlic, fennel, and potato crops were expanding.

Meanwhile the value of land increased, and a lively land market developed, aided in part by the use of land as collateral for loans. Critically the average acres per household went from six in 1925 to three in 1984. The percentage of families owning over ten acres dropped from 21 percent to 8 percent, while the percentage of families with five to ten acres remained nearly stable. The percentage of landless families actually decreased from 1925, with a sharp decline since 1975.

The largest increase was in subsistence farmers: households owning fewer than five acres had increased by 333 percent since 1925, from 25 percent of the households (40 families) to 53 percent of the households (173 families). Many of those added to this category between 1975 and 1984 benefited from government schemes to redistribute village common lands to the landless or near landless. Thanks to the influence of the *dhanuk uppradhan* (assistant headman), the *dhanuk* caste during this period profited most from these schemes. The increase in families with fewer than five acres was most disturbing, however, because families with fewer than three to four acres were unable to subsist by farming alone. Aside from the landless, 50 percent of Karimpur families in 1984 had fewer than four acres. Adding in the landless, 255 Karimpur families (78 percent) had to seek other employment to live. (In 1925, 107 families [66

percent] were land poor.) Meanwhile, employment opportunities in agriculture elsewhere in the village declined as farm families, with their own population increases, specifically adult sons,
stopped hiring agricultural laborers and sharecroppers and began to farm their own land.

   In the sixty years since the Wisers first lived in Karimpur,
labor relations both within the village and within the wider region had changed dramatically. During the 1920s the labor environment of Karimpur was very inwardly directed. Brahmans
controlled the majority of the land holdings and were the *jajmans* who were served by the other members of the village
community. The economic life of the village centered on agriculture, and nearly all employment networks branched out from
a Brahman farmer-*jajman*. There were few options available to
those who were not fully employed in their traditional caste occupations or agriculture, and those very few available usually
involved the performance of a traditional occupation in a wage-
paying context. Although by the early 1980s Brahman control of
land remained strong, only a small proportion of the families
followed their traditional occupation. The *jajmani* system no
longer provided agricultural laborers, wage labor was more mo-
bile, and employment networks were more focused on the nearby
town where laborers were in constant demand and received daily
cash wages.

   Jajmani was much more than an economic relationship. In
1984 a Brahman leader and landlord summarized his view of
jajmani this way:

   We did not keep them as slaves. We had love for them. Even
   if you are my brother or grandson, you cannot quarrel with
   my *kamin*. We will give our life for him. There was no unjust
   force used against them. If you didn't have a *kamin*, then you
   can ask my *kamin* if he will work. I shall not let him be pres-
   sured into working [for others]. . . .

   We always used to feel our *kamins* should not have any
   sorrows. If they do not have grain in the middle of the night,

we will give. If no food, [we'll give] food. If police and other
people trouble them, we do not let them. If he steals your
sugarcane, I shall not give you permission to beat him. I will
beat him. I shall say, you can take of my field in exchange for
what he took. If my *kamin* is insulted it means that I am
insulted.

A group of low caste men gave their point of view to Derr in
a slightly different way:

They [Brahmans] say they kept us like *maa-baap* [like they
were our mother-father], that all we had to do was go to them
and we would receive. But to *maa-baap* one must show respect and humbleness, we would go with folded hands and
we might receive, if we were properly humble. They helped
us in the courts or with officials, surely. *They* could read, *they*
had time to go to school because *we* were working their fields
for them. By keeping us illiterate they could keep us unaware
of our rights—they could take advantage of us if we went against
them because they knew the workings of government, they
knew the officials, and they had the money to pay bribes.
They were *maa-baap,* and sometimes they showed the love
that *maa-baap* are to have for their children, but sometimes
they beat us just as *maa-baap* sometimes beat their children.

The turning point in *jajmani* appears to have been in the 1960s.
By 1968 only 71 of 246 families gave semiannual payments to
kamins, these payments being the primary payments for most
kamins. The reasons underlying the farmer-*jajmans'* decisions to
opt out of the system are many. Given the abundance of labor
in the late 1960s, a farmer no longer needed to maintain laborers who were obligated to work for him when called (and in the
1920s, a farmer could call any of his *kamins,* whatever their real
occupation, to work his fields when necessary). It was cheaper
to hire labor by the day than it was to maintain annual payments. Furthermore, the traditional grain payment had acquired a monetary value that exceeded the going wage labor

rate, and it was now cheaper for the farmer-*jajmans* to pay for labor in cash than in the traditional headloads of grain. As the poor also discovered, this shift made it harder to secure payment. Grain payments were made from the harvest at the end of the day: cash payments depended upon the whim of the landlord and often were not given until weeks later.

By the 1980s many services were simply no longer needed. Most rich farmers now had hand pumps in their courtyards, so the *kahar* water carrier was rendered obsolete. In a curious shift in behavior, most Brahman wives now used the fields as a latrine, obviating the need for the daily services of the sweeper (Wiser reports thirteen latrines in Brahman houses in the 1920s; none existed in the 1960s; a few were found in 1984). The traditional occupation of the oil presser was eliminated by the establishment of oil mills in Mainpuri. The richer farmers preferred the washermen in Mainpuri—with their soap powder, starch, and irons—to the Karimpur washermen, while their wives washed more of their own clothes with the water supplied by their new hand pumps and detergent purchased in the market.

In 1984 few *kamins* received regular semiannual payments. For weddings, childbirth, death, and yearly festivals, *kamins* continued to provide ritual services. But payments were for services rendered on specific occasions, not yearly subsidies. Moreover, few families used daily services—a half-dozen rich Brahmans still had a sweeper clean daily, while two or three households often used a water carrier to help the women scrub pots. The washerwomen visited the wealthier families every week or two, and the poorer ones only at childbirth or when clothes were polluted. One carpenter still had hereditary *jajmans*, while the others worked for cash customers. The tailors, now augmented by men of other castes who learned tailoring, no longer served traditional patrons but were chosen by need and skill.

Looking at the nonritual services that continued in Karimpur, one factor stood out: almost all were services primarily utilized by women or the poor—those who, for cultural or economic reasons, had little access to the services provided in the nearby market town. A few services, such as the barber's, were taken advantage of in the village by poorer men because it was less expensive than in Mainpuri and more readily available for those who had less need to visit town. But the rich farmers and their school-going sons got their hair cut, their carpentry done, and their clothes washed in Mainpuri. Their wives, however, were cut off from the services of the market economy by restrictions on mobility, and hence they continued to patronize village *kamins*. The midwives, sweepers, washermen, flower growers, water carriers, and even tailors all provided services accessible to the upper-class women in *purdah*. Thus, cultural norms for female behavior had been nearly as influential on modern *jajmani* practices as had the development of a market economy.

Contact with the district town of Mainpuri was now frequent, and many families had at least one male visiting every day. By the mid-1970s, bus service to Mainpuri was regular and reliable, with private buses picking up the passengers unable to fit into state-owned transport. Tongas were now regularly found at the Karimpur bus stop, with two owned by residents of Karimpur itself. Some rickshaws also went the distance, primarily in the morning or evening. The majority of households had at least one bicycle, used by schoolboys or their brothers and fathers. Only rarely did anyone walk.

Mainpuri is the market town for a district of 1.7 million people. Higher crop yields due to the Green Revolution demanded a wholesale market for the surplus, while larger incomes were expended on greater quantities of consumer goods. Hence the quantity of goods moving from the fields through the district markets and through commercial outlets into the hands of rural consumers had grown immensely. This commercial throughput was ultimately providing jobs to Karimpur men, not industrial jobs, but rather those of carrying and storing vast quantities of goods, including the grains funneled into the grain market and the potatoes stored in cold storage plants. With the development of a market for labor and a transportation system that made

Mainpuri a viable work locale, Karimpur men were rapidly shifting from agricultural labor to day labor in the marketplace. This contact with Mainpuri was male-dominated. Work for women was all but nonexistent in the marketplace of this north Indian town. Karimpur women visited Mainpuri either while passing through on trips to their natal homes or to take a sick child to a doctor. Rarely did Karimpur women shop in Mainpuri. Many women, especially the poor, claimed to go no more than once or twice a year. Certainly they didn't go for recreation, as the majority of women had never seen a film. Their primary recreation was a visit to the district fair held on the northern fringe of Mainpuri every April.

Farming remained the principal occupation of the majority of the men, but that majority had declined from 72 percent in 1925 to 51 percent in 1984 as reliance on other income sources grew. In the 1920s all but 14 families, landless or landed, derived the bulk of their income from agriculture, but in 1975 only 16 of the village's 106 landless families worked in agriculture. There was a diversification of jobs at all levels, with both rich and poor shifting from agriculture, though the landed continued to work their fields. Further, there was some caste specialization in the new occupations.

The number of workers whose primary income came from service (permanent regularly paid work, whether as a teacher, clerk, or factory worker) had risen from eight (1.0 percent of total population) in 1925 to fifty-four (2.6 percent of population) in 1984. Yet this minor rise in the percentage of population masked a crucial difference. In 1925 the service jobs were held by the poor—by the untouchable sweepers working in Calcutta. By 1984 new types of prestigious service jobs were the desired occupations of the wealthier families: there were fifteen Brahmans, nine water carriers, four accountants, and six farmers, in addition to eight sweepers and a variety of others, in service jobs. And another two dozen educated men were unsuccessfully seeking work.

Over time more and more people opened their own shops,

whether for cycle repairing, tailoring, or selling basics like soap and cigarettes. Responding to the increased consumerism of rural households, many landowning families saw shops as a way of employing educated sons while adding a small amount to the family income. For others, shops provided basic subsistence. Equally important, six men now had shops in Mainpuri—bicycle repair, radio, and bangle selling. Another occupation that showed a new orientation to the urban market was milk selling. Sixteen men, primarily shepherds and water carriers, now collected milk in Karimpur and nearby villages and sold it in Mainpuri. Some saw milk selling as a supplement to farm incomes; others regarded it as a full-time occupation. For those willing to work hard, milk selling was a lucrative business, and several had prospered. Milk selling had a detrimental effect, however, on village nutrition as more and more families now sold their milk to supplement family incomes rather than to retain it for family consumption.

Meanwhile the poor had shifted from agricultural employment to outside labor jobs. The number of men whose primary occupation involved labor outside Karimpur had risen dramatically since 1975, from two to eighty-four. These men drove rickshaws, carried bags of grain for mills, loaded brick kilns, unloaded trucks, worked in construction, or did any other of the many labor-intensive jobs that one finds in India. Even without an industrial base, Mainpuri provided jobs for those willing to seek them: having no land and no education, their bodies were their only resource.

Female employment in Karimpur had been affected by four trends: the decline in *jajmani*, the decline in male employment in agricultural labor, the mechanization of agriculture, and changes in cropping patterns. Karimpur was a community where the only acceptable jobs for women were those connected to traditional occupations or service jobs (only one woman, a Brahman schoolteacher, having such a job). Manual labor was not a choice for women and was pursued only by female household heads who had no other option.

Jajmani work was never purely male: many of the services were performed by females. The *purdah* system of north India demands that nonfamily men be denied regular access to women's quarters, so in those quarters, the duties of the water carrier, the sweeper, the washerwoman, the flower grower, and the barber were all performed by women. While a male water carrier might carry water from distant wells to a *jajman's* house, his wife also did so. Moreover, she was more acceptable as a household servant, helping the women to prepare dough, washing pots, or grinding grain. The *kaharin*, the female water carrier, was a critical functionary at weddings, funerals, and childbirth. It was she who often carried messages to other women of the village about rituals and songfests, and it was the *kaharin* who carried the offerings brought by daughters-in-law when they returned from their parents' homes. Likewise, the person actually cleaning latrines in Brahman houses was not the male but the female sweeper, who had access to female living quarters. The barber's wife, the *nain*, played a critical role in women's ritual celebrations, whether marriage, childbirth, or death. The flower grower bringing garlands for the ritual use of women was not the male but his wife or daughter. And the person serving as midwife was of course a woman. Thus *jajmani* largely aided women who were constrained by *purdah* from getting their own water, carrying their own messages, picking their own flowers. While *jajmani* is without doubt built on Hindu ritual needs, it is also built upon Hindu rules for appropriate female behavior.

With the decline of *jajmani* in the preceding two decades, many of the women who had made contributions to family income through their participation in it were displaced. Moreover, high population increases among the *kamin* castes created a surplus of women vis-à-vis the remaining *jajmani* demands. Many formerly *kamin* women were now jobless or only occasionally worked.

Females were also increasingly excluded from agriculture as their men moved into urban-based labor jobs. Women whose husbands were employed in agriculture were themselves involved in agricultural production, either in the fields or in post-harvesting activities, such as threshing. Even secluded women processed enormous quantities of agricultural produce. But women could only work in the fields when partnered by a male— a father, brother, or son. As men chose to work outside the village, their women were automatically displaced from agricultural participation since they were no longer properly accompanied. Further, men employed in the urban wage market were no longer paid with agricultural produce that the women had to process. Men who worked as laborers in the city did not buy raw grains with their wages, but ready-ground flour. Thus the women who were once employed in Karimpur through extended *kamin* ties were now unemployed. Many, in fact, had little to do, sitting idle throughout the day. But it was probably the loss of household voice that was most critical, for these women were no longer seen as contributing to the family income. One *dhanukin* put it forcefully: "Our men are earning more than before, but we have nothing!"

Mechanization of agriculture further inhibited women's work opportunities. The labor-intensive forms of irrigation, using Persian wheels or lifting water from tanks in leather bags, were replaced by pump sets. Women who had ground grain for rich families found themselves displaced by the grain mill located on the fringe of the village. Mechanical threshers often replaced the oxen traditionally used to thresh wheat.

Finally, changes in cropping patterns tended to emphasize crops that were less labor-intensive. Cotton, hand-picked by women and grown in large quantities through the 1960s, had disappeared. Peas, again requiring intensive field labor, were also gone. In most instances, these fields were now planted in wheat, a crop in which women played a minimal role. However, garlic, a popular cash crop in the 1980s, did demand women for planting and weeding and was grown primarily by the small landowners and sharecroppers of the *kachhi* caste of farmers whose women worked with the men.

Hence there were several factors affecting women's work, all producing a marked decline in employment opportunities for women. First, with the relative decline of male employment in agriculture and the shift of landless men to urban-based jobs, women who had worked in agriculture alongside their male kin were displaced. Second, women traditionally employed in caste-based occupations as servants through *jajmani* were no longer so employed. Third, mechanization had replaced female labor in a variety of arenas. Finally, changes in cropping patterns had made female help in the fields less necessary. These factors all contributed to the marginalization of poor women, giving them less voice in their families and ultimately devaluing them.

Both men and women in Karimpur had benefited from increased education, although male levels of education had grown more markedly than female. Three schools now served Karimpur and nearby villages—two primary schools, one for boys and one for girls, and a coeducational middle school for grades 6–8. Students attending high school (grades 9–10), intercollege (grades 11–12), or college still had to go to a nearby town. Forty-nine percent of Karimpur sons between six and ten years now attended school. An even higher percentage of those aged eleven through fifteen had attended school (74 percent). Only a handful continued to intercollege or beyond. Fifty-seven percent of daughters attended primary school, while 74 percent of those between eleven and fifteen had been in school: only two in the village were in high school or intercollege.

Education, particularly for girls at all ages and for sons past fifth grade, was not evenly spread through the village. Some 21 percent of Karimpur women were literate in contrast to 52 percent of men. Among the very poor, 4.1 percent of women and 14.3 percent of men were literate. Seven castes had two or fewer literate women, while another seven had no literate women. For the poor, school was still a luxury many could not afford,

even for sons. While tuition might be waived for those identified as scheduled castes, books and clothes were expensive, and
the income derived from the son's labor was lost. Further, it
was all but impossible—especially in the sciences—to pass the
examinations without private tutoring, adding further expense.
Karimpur sweepers were still forbidden to attend the village
schools, as they remained literally untouchable to their higher-
caste neighbors. While legally they had the right to attend, the
threatened walkout of other students had effectively barred them
from education. A few sweepers—one wife and five men—were
literate, having gone to school elsewhere, usually in Calcutta
while their fathers worked there. And two young boys were now
attending school out of the village.

At the other end of the educational ladder, Brahman men
were increasingly getting B.A. and M.A. degrees. Whereas in
1970 one man was working for a B.A., in 1984 fifteen men (ten
Brahman) had B.A.s and five Brahmans had M.A.s. No non-
Brahman had yet obtained an M.A. Further, all but ten Brahman men were literate, and more than half had gone to high
school or beyond. Only rarely did even a Brahman girl continue
past eighth grade, as families were reluctant to send a girl by
bus or cycle to a school six to ten miles away. In 1984 two Brahman girls commuted to Mainpuri for intercollege and one to
high school, while one five-year-old went to an English-language nursery school. Several girls had done high school courses
privately, and one recently married eighteen-year-old was doing
her B.A. privately—the first B.A. student among Karimpur
women, although several in-marrying wives had intercollege degrees.

Despite increased education among females, most Karimpur
women felt girls were sufficiently educated if they were able "to
write a letter home if there is trouble in their in-laws." (Parents
remained concerned about their daughters' treatment in their
husbands' houses, and literacy gave them a way of knowing the
circumstances there.) The result was that poor and landless
daughters either did not attend school or attended only through

second or third grade. In addition, because educated girls required larger dowries as families sought to find comparably educated mates for them (dowry demands increased with the level
of the boy's education), educating a girl was often economically
detrimental to a family.

Education was a key factor in changes in relationships among
the castes in Karimpur because it loosened the bonds of Brahman patronage. Brahman patronage extends beyond purely material benefits. If the police trouble a worker, for example, the
jajman will help. With education came the knowledge and ability to manipulate the bureaucracies that tied Karimpur to government agencies, whether those of the colonial government of
the British and the tax collectors of the Zamindars or the new
bureaucracies of modern India. Even in 1984, educated Brahman men, still linked to specific *kamin* families through old ties
of solidarity if not of actual employment, were called upon to
take their *kamins* to the government hospital, to a local doctor,
to find a lawyer, to arrange a tractor to convey a marriage party
to the bride's house, to accompany a man to the law court, and
so on. With the spread of local government agencies, cooperative banks and seed stores, development officers, and new medical facilities had come greater demands for help in dealing with
these agencies. For example, the forty-five-year-old head of a
carpenter family, no longer even working as a carpenter but still
attached to one particular Brahman family, insisted that the son
of that Brahman family, aged thirty-two but with wide experience in the district town and beyond, accompany him to Agra,
eighty miles away, to see a heart specialist about the palpita-
tions that he had been having. He was able to enter into the
world of modern medicine, itself remarkable, but only with the
support of his *jajman*.

Now, however, men from other castes with fifth- or eighth-
grade educations often felt able to deal with banks, lawyers, and
government development officers on their own: they no longer
found the Brahman intermediary essential. If a mediator was
needed, they could often find an educated caste-mate. Through

this dwindling of the need for patrons, the Brahmans were losing their ability to control the lower castes. Education played a major role in this process of "equalization" in Karimpur.

A variety of terms were used to describe the very real differences between social relationships in the 1920s and those in the 1980s. The village headman used the phrases "the time of domination" and "the time of democracy" for the respective periods. A group of water carriers saw it this way:

> [Earlier] the domination was of landlords and of the British. The English used to give allotments of land in the rural areas. As you became wealthy, you purchased a zamindari. So we were oppressed by landlords in the past. But now there is the domination of Indira. Now we are all on the same road. Neither you nor I are the landlord.

To this group, the changes had been positive, but not everyone saw them that way. A very poor woman of the midwife caste termed the past "the period of support." To her, the loss of support from *jajmans* was not outweighed by the political and economic freedom that other former *kamins* saw as so important.

It is the Brahman landlords who most regretted their loss of power. An old man from a rich and influential Brahman family described the past this way:

> At that time, they had no means of livelihood. We had everything—wells, gardens, fields, barren lands, desert, goats, buffalo, animals, grass. From every angle they were dependent upon us for money and goods. But now they have their own means. They have fields. They have land. Now they do not want our assistance. They do not need us, therefore they do not wait to do our work. This is reality.

He was later questioned by a younger Brahman who asked, "So the reason for *jajmani* was illiteracy and poverty." The answer, "What else?" A water carrier basically agreed, telling Derr:

They [the Brahmans] were powerful in both money and in education. They were educated men. We people were not educated. We were not able persons. Whenever a letter came, we had to go to them to read it. We were not educated because of poverty. We didn't have what they had. They had property and they had everything. Our lands were all with them.

He then proceeded to say,

Now the chief thing is that society has changed. Now the boys are educated and they have some knowledge and our power has also increased. Previously the Brahmans used to go to the Collectorate. Without a Brahman, I could not go there. But now they sit at home: I myself can do all the work at the Collectorate. . . . Previously these Brahman people used to say, "Do this work" and the old men used to go and do it. But nowadays the boys are educated, so they refuse to go. They are righteous.

Education, facilitated by government initiatives as well as by higher incomes resulting from increased crop yields and urban wages, had played a major role in the loss of Brahman dominance in Karimpur. But other factors were also critical. Many poorer families were no longer tied to Brahman moneylenders through loans because government loan programs provided for seeds and fertilizers, pump sets, and cattle. Families unable to pay off loans were bound to their moneylender, and even in 1984 those who used Brahman moneylenders found themselves called to do agricultural work at peak seasons. As one cotton carder put it, "Who would want to take a loan: even your grand-children would not be able to pay it off." It was also degrading to have to beg for food or even a piece of land to sharecrop. One farmer claimed that asking for land was like being a woman: it was demeaning and implied no self-respect.

A fundamental change occurring between the 1930s and 1984 was a growing sense of self-respect on the part of one-time *ka-*

mins. As the water carrier put it, "They [educated sons] are righteous [in not responding to Brahman calls for labor]." But the search for self-respect had a history. In the 1940s, the Karimpur *kamins* had gone on strike for six months. Later, probably in the early 1950s, they were allowed to sit on cots on a Brahman verandah and were no longer forced to rise from their own cots when a Brahman passed in the lane before their homes. A major breakthrough came when the Brahmans agreed, after much turmoil and many lathi fights, to greet the *kamins* at their homes at Holi, a time when all men of the village ritually greet one another. Brahmans also started sending representatives to *kamin* funerals rather than just demanding that *kamins* attend theirs.

The growth in urban labor was tied to these issues of self-respect as well as to the production changes in Karimpur. Urban labor was preferred to agricultural labor in Karimpur for two reasons: first, pay scales were higher, ranging from 15 to 25 rupees per day, while agricultural wages were 8 to 12 rupees per day. Second, payment was immediate, not up to six months later. Working for Brahman landlords continued to be demeaning because it still required repeated begging before wages were paid.

These changes in the relationships between former *jajman* and *kamin* were manifested in a variety of arenas in Karimpur life. While the *kamins* had a new sense of self-respect, the Brahmans saw themselves as losing power and the respect they had once had. Despite their own greater material prosperity, they saw themselves as worse off than they had been "in the time of domination." They also saw the government as clearly behind the poor and low castes and against them. In 1984, when a fire burned a large portion of the village, including many Brahman houses, they immediately said that if it had been a non-Brahman village, government aid would have been quicker and more plentiful. Moreover, the non-Brahmans of Karimpur were continually finding new ways to challenge the Brahman dominance, whether questioning the sequence in which different castes circled the

Holi fire, acquiring their own pump sets to have access to water, or forcing the Brahmans to greater levels of fraud in order to maintain their control of the *panchayat*. This is not to say that the Brahman community of Karimpur had lost its dominance, for they retained control of the cooperative bank and seed store, had significantly higher educational levels, and remained the primary moneylenders. But they were not the kings they had once been, and both they and their fellow villagers were well aware of this fact.

Just as relationships between farmers and laborers, Brahmans and *kamins* had changed, so had those in families, particularly as they affected women. Karimpur's population had increased by 120.4 percent from 1925 to 1975, from 754 to 1,753, then jumped another 22.2 percent to 2,048 by 1984. Much of this increase was due to lower child mortality. At the same time, fertility was high and increasing: the crude birth rate for 1969–75 was 41.8 per thousand, increasing to 47.5 per thousand for 1976–83. The population increase was not evenly spread among village social groups. Between 1925 and 1975 the population increase among the rich was 99 percent, while among poor it was 168.5 percent. These increases were matched by lower birth rates among the Brahmans (35 per thousand for 1969–74 and 40 per thousand for 1975–83) and markedly high rates among the poor (44.8 per thousand for 1969–74 and 47.8 per thousand for 1975–83).

Birth control was known to most Karimpur residents, but many women had no access to it. Birth control, like other forms of female health care, was unavailable unless permission was sought from husbands and/or mothers-in-law. Further, the method most strongly advocated by the Indian government was sterilization, particularly of women. The government health care system focused much of its attention, energy, and finances on family planning. Medical camps for mass tubectomies were common in the rural areas, and government medical personnel such as the government-appointed midwife resident in Karimpur had to meet yearly quotas for sterilization. The government provided cash subsidies for women who underwent tubectomies, and this enticement could be alluring. But the results could also be devastating. One Karimpur widow, aged about forty and not truly eligible because of her marital status, finally agreed to sterilization because she really did need the money (100 rupees, about $8). Unluckily, her operation resulted in a serious infection, which the government did not pay to cure. She ended up losing many weeks of work (her only income) as well as running up debts to the local moneylender. Stories such as these deterred Karimpur women from taking the risk of an "operation."

Other factors contributed to the relative lack of family planning practiced in Karimpur. Sterilizations, with its closing of options for further childbearing, was a choice made only when sufficient children were alive to reassure the family that a viable number would reach adulthood (two sons being the minimum desired family). Many young women would have liked help in spacing their children, but family planning choices for them were less available. The midwife was supposed to have supplies of birth control pills, but didn't. Men often refused to use condoms, sometimes available in the market. Meanwhile the rising birth rate provided verification of what older women continually told me: "These young brides have their children too quickly and too close together." The ideal used to be a child every three years; now many children were spaced closer to two years apart. It appeared that the desire for family planning to space children was not being met by government programs.

In addition to a large population increase, there was a change in the sex ratio for both adults and juveniles, from 866 adult females per 1000 adult males in 1925, to 814 in 1984. The change in the juvenile sex ratio was more marked, from 900 females per 1000 males in 1925 to 790 in 1984. These changes could be attributed to an increase in female-specific child mortality. As an outsider, I found the increasing female bias in child mortality to be particularly disturbing, for it marked an increasing devaluation of females in Karimpur. What was most troublesome was the increasing disparity between male and female child deaths in certain groups. Poor women in Karimpur were attempting to ensure family welfare by using high fertility and sex-specific child mortality to maximize the number of surviving males. Sons could now get laboring jobs in the surrounding areas, whereas women's work opportunities had declined. More sons and fewer daughters optimized a family's welfare: dowries were saved, more income was generated, and sons remained with the family after marriage.

There was no doubt that child mortality was a frequent occurrence in Karimpur. Sixty-six percent of all mothers had had a child die. Of those mothers who had had two or more live births, 81.6 percent had suffered at least one child death. There had been a continual decline in Karimpur child mortality since the 1930s, from 458 per thousand in the period 1932–51 to 250 per thousand in the period 1972 to 1984. This decline was due largely to an increase in health care, particularly protection against tetanus (especially in the period 1952–71) and the eradication of smallpox prior to 1975. Deaths of female children were heavily weighted toward those illnesses most attributable to "neglect," particularly malnutrition and kwashiorkor. More girls than boys also died of fever, diarrhea, and chickenpox (and formerly smallpox), suggesting a lack of medical attention for sick daughters.

The ratio of male to female mortality had declined from 84.8 in the period 1932–51 to 74.5 in the period 1972–84. That is, female children had a 10 percent less chance of surviving than their brothers in the early 1980s than they had had in the 1930s and 1940s. This skewing of the male/female mortality ratio in favor of male survival was attributable solely to shifts among landless laborers and subsistence farmers, for the rich in this community had begun to favor female children. The ratio of male to female mortality among landless laborers and subsistence farmers had declined from .88 during the period 1952–71 (.84 for the period 1931–51) to .70 during the period 1972–84. Meanwhile, the ratio of male to female mortality among the rich

had increased from .72 in the period 1931–51 to .84 for the
period 1952–71 to .91 in the period 1972–84.

In the neonatal period, male mortality was greater than female mortality. At a time when biological factors were the dominant cause of death, this was what we would expect. But after
the first month of life, when factors such as quality of life, environment, and care were more critical to life chances, female
deaths exceeded those of male deaths. These factors could be
controlled by human agency and thus reflected pervasive socie-
tal values that led to discrimination against female children. What
girls were most susceptible to childhood death? In Karimpur,
the daughters of the poor were now at greater risk of early death
than their brothers.

Karimpur mothers, especially the poor, verbalized little clear
son preference, often saying, "Whatever Bhagvan [God] gives,
we will have." Others would cite the government slogan of "two
sons and one daughter." In this community, where fertility control was largely unknown and mortality still high, clearly artic-
ulated preferences for family size were largely lacking. Behav-
iorally, however, preferences were being shown.

Karimpur residents were blatant in their discrimination against
female children. A toddler about to topple off a cot onto a brick
courtyard wasn't prevented from falling as the grandmother
commented, "Let her, she is only a girl." In one instance, a
young mother of three daughters induced a late-term abortion,
almost killing herself, convinced that the fetus was yet another
girl. Births of daughters were not celebrated unless it was the
first child born to that woman, and sometimes not even then.
None of the birth songs honored the birth of a daughter. The
auspicious head-shaving ritual was often eliminated for daughters, especially in poorer families. Daughters were breast fed
for shorter periods, contributing to the malnutrition noted above,
as mothers shortened the interval between pregnancies to get
the desired son. It was not uncommon to find three- and four-
year-old girls so malnourished that they were unable to walk.
In the one case of male and female twins that survived infancy,

at age one the boy was fat and glowing with health while his sister was scrawny, with yellowed hair.

Not only did mortality data and behavioral patterns show a continual, often overt, discrimination against female children, but also this discrimination seemed to be increasing within the context of generally lowered mortality rates. As women were increasingly marginalized, they were seen as being of less value to parents. Among the poor, male children continued to be an asset to parents, but female children no longer were. Rather than curtailing fertility, poor families were maximizing surviving male offspring. High fertility in conjunction with a decline in mortality increased both the number of female children who could be "neglected onto death" and the population of sons who might eventually obtain jobs and hence increase family prosperity. Through high sex-specific mortality, parents had greater control of household composition than they would by controlling births alone.

Another demographic change with marked consequences for family structure was a decline in the widowed population. In 1925, 15.9 percent of the population was widowed; in 1984 only 5.6 percent. Additionally, in 1925 there were a large number of unmarried men, especially Brahmans. A variety of factors contributed to this phenomenon, with poverty, bad reputations, and lack of females the most commonly cited. But whatever the reason, the large numbers of widowed adults and unmarried men were factors in household composition, since both demanded that household structures accommodate an "extra" person.

The data on mortality, fertility, and widowhood suggest that the building blocks of Karimpur households were not the same in the 1920s and in the 1960s and 1970s, leaving aside variations in the socio-economic context. In the 1920s high child mortality combined with (relatively) low birth rates meant that families were small and that there were few living sons with whom to form joint households. High adult mortality, seen in the widowed population, combined with a large number of unmarried adult males to further limit the potential for either nuclear or joint families, both dependent upon a living married couple. By the 1960s, child mortality declined, sons were alive as adults, and parents were living longer. These demographic factors had major consequences for Karimpur household structures. Nevertheless, in both time periods, the ideal remained the joint family. The prevailing ethic was that a powerful family was a large family.

There were several reasons for the preference for a joint family. First, a joint family demonstrated the effective control of a strong leader and family unity in village politics. Second, it provided women with companionship and enabled them to maintain *purdah*. Third, a family workforce could be mobilized for agricultural operations, while employed sons provided a steady source of income to compensate for the vagaries of seasons and crops. Finally, a joint family often freed a male from everyday agricultural chores so that he could pursue the patronage activities necessary to maintain a strong voice in Karimpur politics.

A major focus of discussion in Karimpur was the breaking up of families. When separation occurred, it was a sign that the men could not reach consensus on economic issues and that the daughters-in-law were fighting. Ultimately, separation was a blot on a family's honor. Since honor was continuously sought after and fought about by Karimpur men, the pressure to remain in a joint family was great.

Despite the political and social desirability of a joint family, for many, but especially for the poor, a nuclear family was more rational. In some cases, men or women just did not get along. When shares in crops from land were not an issue and when resources were scarce, the tensions involved in sharing unequal incomes were great enough to lead to separation. So, despite the social approbation, separation took place. Nevertheless, the ideal remained: to Karimpur villagers, a big family was a powerful family.

Karimpur families had become larger over time, and this was particularly evident among the richer landed groups and among the higher castes. The toll of death and disease in the early twentieth century, for adults and children alike, contributed to a significant number of subjoint and subnuclear families, as well as to other "fragmented" family structures. Despite the ideology, only 15.5 percent of families in 1925 were joint. In 1984, 43.7 percent of Karimpur families were nuclear, while 27.8 percent were joint. In terms of actual population, only 34.7 percent of residents lived in nuclear families, while 41.8 percent were in joint families.

Only after 1968 did the poor begin to manifest a significant decline in joint families, although even now the percentage of joint families among the poor was markedly higher than in 1925. As the poor and landless shifted away from agriculture, nuclear families became more rational economically. Even after 1968 landed families with over five acres continued to demonstrate an increase in joint families. The landed were following a dual strategy for economic survival: participating at a high level in agriculture *and* diversifying through the process of educating selected sons for outside employment. In these families the regular income of an employed male, combined with the security of land and the need for two or more adult males to farm successfully, made joint families desirable and possible. Moreover, the political advantage of a large family, especially one with underemployed adult males who could offer patronage, remained a critical factor in family composition strategies.

At the same time, education had affected familial relationships, giving more emphasis to the "couple" as opposed to the hierarchy of the joint family. In 1968 only Ganesh and his wife had their own room. His bride, from a nearby city, had demanded this arrangement, to the great disapproval of her mother-in-law. By 1984 many couples had rooms specifically allotted to them and were free to make their own sleeping arrangements, whereas formerly the mother-in-law had nightly allotted beds and private rooms, effectively regulating the potential fertility of her daughters-in-law. These changes might have contributed to the increased fertility rates among all groups in the 1970s.

Dowries were increasing for all, whether rich or poor, and

while bride-price marriages among the poor were never common, they were exceedingly rare by 1984. One oil presser girl was married at age ten or so, and her father took money for her. (If a family needs female labor, it is willing to pay for a bride.) Throughout the year, she was pointed out to me with the derisive comment, "Look at how young she is: see, she even dresses like a grown woman [in sari, instead of the tunic and pants worn nowadays by most ten-year-olds]. And her father even took money for her."

In addition to marriages requiring dowry or bride-price, a third kind of marriage was prevalent among the poor. In these marriages the groom's family paid all the wedding expenses, and the ceremony itself occurred in his home. These marriages were no longer performed and had been replaced by dowry marriages, with the bride's family bearing most of the wedding expenses. Hence older women in poor families often had marriages that cost 1 or 101 rupees for dowry, in addition to a modest feast. Now their daughters could not be married for less than 2,000 to 3,000 rupees, and more if they were educated. Brahman weddings in 1984 averaged 50,000 rupees (about $4,500), with 20,000 to 30,000 rupees or more in cash, plus additional goods and the costs of lavish feasts and entertainment.

Another change in marriage practices affecting family life was the increasing ages of bride and groom. Girls as old as twenty remained unmarried, often because their families could not afford a dowry. Education played a major role in late marriages, as it was considered inappropriate for either bride or groom to remain in school once married. As one parent put it, "The boy will no longer think of school once he is married." This rule was adhered to strictly for girls but less rigidly for boys. Nonetheless, grooms in their early to mid-twenties were no longer uncommon, and many girls of richer families remained unmarried past sixteen. Among the poor, marriages were now common between ages thirteen and sixteen for both males and females, and younger marriages were exceptional, although the mothers of both rich and poor were married by thirteen. Thus, in one generation there had been a significant increase in age of marriage. One result was older educated daughters-in-law in families with an illiterate mother-in-law, altering the power structure in the joint family more in favor of the daughter-in-law. Women were divided on the desirability of an educated daughter-in-law. Some preferred someone that they could raise and train, while others appreciated the worldly knowledge and skills of sewing, knitting, and cleanliness that often came with better education. One Brahman family with sons who all passed high school had illiterate daughters-in-law, while another with sons with B.A.s actually had a daughter-in-law who finished intercollege.

Later marriages had not so significantly changed the age of first child. Marriage per se was a ritual event, uniting two families as well as a couple. But marriage in the ritual sense did not mean that the marriage was consummated. Consummation involved a second ceremony, one that usually took place after the girl reached puberty, often three or more years after the marriage ritual. Then it might be a year or two before the girl had her first child, at age sixteen or seventeen. With later marriages, the interval between the ritual and the consummation ceremony had shortened, and if the couple was well over sixteen, sometimes the two occurred together. For others, it occurred within a year or so, rather than two or three years later. One result was that the age of first child had barely increased over time, with most girls having a child by age seventeen.

The composition of the village population had also changed markedly since the 1920s in another group: widows. In 1925 widows were 30.4 percent of the adult female population, whereas in 1984 they were 13 percent. In Karimpur, only Brahmans, Rays (a low Brahman caste), and *kayasthas* (accountants) forbid widow remarriage. Widows from other caste groups could remarry. In 1984 there were sixty-nine widows living in Karimpur, as well as ten widows who had remarried. Women widowed in their teens remarried if possible: the only widows who lost their husbands while teenagers and did not remarry were

Brahman (excluding one shepherd girl who was only eighteen and a candidate for remarriage).

Sons and land, either in the widow's own name or in a son's name, were critical factors determining a widow's future. Sons provide access to the normative patterns of the north Indian male-dominated system. Land provides the material resources necessary for survival. Two cases highlighted the role of sons and land in remarriages. A young *kachhi* man of a landowning family died of cholera in 1984, leaving a teenage wife. Both the girl's family and the village community felt the family should marry her to the younger brother, but her in-laws refused, despite a caste *panchayat*. She had no claim to land, and they could get a large dowry for the younger son if a new bride was sought. Later, a twenty-five-year-old water carrier died of tuberculosis, leaving a wife, infant son, and a claim to his father's land. Since he had a son, the claim was greater, and that family was planning to marry her to his younger brother.

Women without land remarried to avoid the dire poverty of a landless single woman, and would do so even at older ages. While most widows lived with their sons, whether adult or juvenile, some were forced into other choices. Women with only daughters often faced difficulties, especially if their daughters were young and there were no sons-in-law to provide assistance, whether legal, financial, or physical. In the absence of aid from her husband's lineage, one *kachhi* wife with a daughter of about ten had moved in with her neighbors. Her husband had owed them a considerable sum, so in exchange for his remaining land, they cared for the woman and had arranged her daughter's marriage. With the land gone, she was totally dependent upon her neighbors' generosity. A Muslim widow with two young daughters survived by begging. Two or three times a week she made the rounds of Karimpur and nearby hamlets, getting enough handfuls here and there to feed her small family for the next few days. This household lacked a cot to sleep on or a quilt for the winter cold. When her older daughter was married, twenty or so Hindu villagers contributed food and goods for the ceremony and necessary (but small) feast. This family was surviving, but barely.

Landless women with small children often returned to their parents. Those widows with children and some land remained in Karimpur, for the land would undoubtedly be taken by others if they left. One *kachhi* woman with two children owned one-and-a-half acres; but since her son was only ten, it had to be let on shares. The 50 percent (or less) that she received left her family in dire poverty, even though the young son tried to help by selling vegetables in the village. Yet a woman with sons and land would think carefully before remarrying, for it might be detrimental to her son's inheritance if she did: if there was sufficient land to allow her to survive until her son was old enough to earn income, she could remain unmarried.

The story of Kali's wife illustrates a woman's difficulties in earning a livelihood for herself and her children. It also highlights issues of female work and the barriers that prevent women in rural north India from seeking more equality with men. Kali's wife was a water carrier by caste. She was considered by many the poorest person in the village. Her own mother had been widowed young and had remarried after five or six years. Kali's wife lived mostly with her maternal grandparents, where her mother had returned after her husband died. Kali's wife had been married young—at eleven or twelve—in a simple ceremony in 1962. Her marriage was consummated a year later, and she had her first child within a few years. Of her six pregnancies, two children lived, a boy about ten and a married daughter.

Within two years of her moving to Karimpur, Kali's wife had been kicked out of her in-laws' house—she said that her husband had taken her to bathe at the Ganges and her mother-in-law had not given her approval, so a separation took place. Meanwhile, her husband started to gamble, as had his father. Kali's wife was soon forced to be concerned about feeding her small family. Her husband shared in one acre of land with his father and two brothers, but there was little food from this and he took whatever household money there was for gambling. He also beat her regularly. She said, "I did not know the love of my husband. All I knew was that God has given me two hands and I have to work with them to earn a living." When asked how she felt about her husband's death, she replied, "Sister, what can I tell you about my sadness. I had problems from the start." She started making cow dung cakes to earn enough to feed her children, but her husband would search the house and find the hidden money. Somehow they managed until her husband's death in 1982. Six months earlier their one daughter was married. The family was poor, but they borrowed 900 rupees to pay for the wedding. Since her husband died, she had paid back 600. Now her daughter lived with her husband in Panjab, where he did field labor.

Her husband's brothers and father also died about 1982, leaving the three young widows alone. One had since married a distant relative from Karimpur and gone to live in the nearby town; the other had returned to her parents. Only Kali's wife remained in the village, with no close relatives to aid her. After her husband died, she reestablished connections with her brother, whom she hadn't seen in years: her mother was dead, and her stepfather had no love for her, so this one brother was her only potential source of aid. For a while her son lived with his uncle, but Kali's wife missed him dreadfully and brought him back to the village, despite her difficulty in feeding and clothing him and her inability to supervise him while she worked.

Unlike most village women, Kali's wife had earned trifling sums before her husband's death, as she tried to protect (and feed) her family while he gambled. But even though she had been earning, widowhood forced her into new income-generating activities. She could no longer survive by making and selling cowdung cakes, a woman's activity that was often expanded for income. Since her husband died, Kali's wife had sought other employment of various sorts. Changes in Karimpur had denied her the traditional work of widows fifty years ago: then most grain was ground on large stone-grinding stones in each house,

often requiring hours of female labor per day. With the advent
of grinding machines, most richer families no longer ground their
own flour, and poor women were denied a source of acceptable
employment. For a year Kali's wife worked in the nearby district town, earning her food and two to three dollars a month
washing utensils or storing garlic. But this work was poorly paid,
and she didn't have her son, so she returned to Karimpur, where
she tried to raise two goats and did field labor during the harvest and planting seasons. For this she earned 4 to 6, sometimes
8 to 10, rupees per day. Altogether, she worked three to four
months a year on a regular basis. Food for herself and her son
cost 2 to 3 rupees per day (bread, oil, spices, and a meager
quantity of vegetables), so she had to stretch her money. Her
clothes were torn and filthy. Her few cooking pots were worn.
Her house had only one cot and a torn quilt for the winter.

Kali's wife was known throughout the village as being honor-
able and hard-working. No one laughed at her as she did work
mostly done by men. People respected her efforts to feed herself and her son. But it was a hard life, for even though she
came from a caste in which the women traditionally worked in
others' homes and where *purdah* restrictions were minimal, she
was working harder than almost any woman in the village and
at jobs not normally held by women. Her labor came cheaper
than men's, and with no one to argue for her, landlords regularly took six months to pay her.

Kali's wife's story reflects why a widow would want to remarry: a woman with no land and with a small child has few job
opportunities, and those that do exist are laborious and poorly
paid. She refused to leave her son with her brother, saying "I
brought him back here because of the festival. I had celebrated
Holi and Diwali alone, now my affection for my son started
growing. So I have brought him because of Holi. I could not
celebrate Holi nor even eat if I was alone." Yet her son did not
attend school in Karimpur, but instead ran wild with the neighborhood boys. And she had to feed him. But without him, her
life was too miserable. Yet work she must, and she refused to

survive on loans. She once told me, "I'm scared to take loans. That's why I earn. If I can't earn, then I stay hungry."

Her caste status allowed her rather free mobility, and her widowhood increased that. Yet she said that women who worked only in their homes were happy and comfortable. "They are in pleasure. There is only the work of the house. They don't have care of anything. They don't have the worry of clothes to cover their body. When I don't work, where will food come from?" Kali's wife would have gladly traded her mobility, her control over her life, and her power over her son for the seclusion and apparent lack of power that came with village women's middle-class status.

Another widow, one who had taken advantage of modern opportunities, was Ram's wife, whom I called Caci (Aunt). Ram was a Brahman landlord of Karimpur who died very suddenly about eight years earlier. His wife was about fifty at his death, but his sons were still young, as no children arrived until she was in her late twenties. At the time of Ram's death, the household contained three unmarried daughters, aged seven, thirteen, and sixteen; a son of twenty-one and his wife; and a son about nine years of age. Ram's oldest son had completed tenth grade and, like many educated Brahman boys, had resisted working in the fields with his father. His father's death changed that, but the shift was slow. Initially, Caci took over responsibility for the fields, turning them over to sharecroppers. The land in the younger son's name was still sharecropped. For some years Caci was the sole leader in their house: she married off two daughters, arranged the marriage of the second son, organized the fields, supervised the sharecroppers, and so forth. Outside of her sons, she had no close male kin in Karimpur who could act on her behalf. Moreover, turning responsibility for the land over to even close male relatives could be disastrous, as one landless Brahman widow had learned. Caci had little choice but to act herself.

Finally, the older son, abetted by his wife, separated his small family, now including a young daughter. His move was partially financial: there remained two marriages, both likely to be a major drain on the family resources. By separating his land and household, he was no longer responsible for the marriages of his brother and sister. His brother's land would have to bear that burden. Also critical was the fact that Caci and her son's wife were both articulate, forceful women. The feuding continued, but often silently, as the two women refused to speak to each other for long periods of time.

Widowhood to Caci meant a drastic alteration in her way of life. She had fields to supervise—fields that she had never before seen. There was a tractor to sell, as it was not a viable investment with the fields being sharecropped. There were potatoes to store in the cold plant. And daughters to marry. She quickly moved into almost solely male spaces and activities. Moreover, she added politics to an otherwise busy life, becoming leader of the local women's nonformal education group.

The Women's Circle had twenty members per year. Its main function was to provide a week's training in childcare and nutrition at the block headquarters. Each member received 5 rupees per day for attending. All caste groups were supposed to be represented, but in fact most members were Brahman. No untouchables belonged. The first year many village daughters attended, but Caci was given orders to have few old women and no young girls in the future. Young women with children were of course the most difficult category to entice into joining, even if their mothers-in-law or husbands would give permission. Even in 1984 only three members were under thirty-five years of age.

Caci had much visibility in 1984 when smokeless cooking hearths were once again introduced into the village. Those given in 1960 had disappeared long ago. Pipes and fittings were brought by the block, and Caci was given authority to choose the lucky recipients and install the stoves. She relished the power and awarded those who supported her. The stoves were not, however, a success with the women who used them. The pipe carrying smoke away was welcome, but no one was used to cooking on two openings at a time. Moreover, they used more fuel than

the traditional stoves. Within a year, all were torn out and replaced by the traditional stoves.

In the late 1970s Caci joined the Congress party, in which
she campaigned actively for Indira Gandhi, being rewarded with
trips to Lucknow and Delhi to meet national leaders, including
Mrs. Gandhi herself. By 1984 Caci was known as "the village
Indira," an appellation given her, so some said, because she
stuck her nose in other's people's business and acted like a man.
One old Brahman woman said that she had no honor left—that
her mobility and activities showed that she had no shame. Yet
one middle-aged wife spontaneously named her as the village
woman with the most honor. She then added that it was because Caci knew people at the block and in the district town.
Caci had connections that no other women and few men had.
These connections were valued, and Caci herself was rewarded
when her younger son got a job as a peon in a government
office.

Caci forcefully claimed that her political activities would not
have occurred if her husband had lived. Until his death she was
a proper Brahman housewife, living a rather secluded life and
ruling over her family. And while she relished her many political activities, she claimed that the life of a widow is a sad one
and that she would gladly return to being a wife with a living
husband.

A third widow whose story can enlighten us about women's
roles in Karimpur is Masterin (literally "female Master," schoolteacher). Masterin was in her late fifties, and her mother herself
was widowed when Masterin was an infant. Her mother had
natal kin who fought court battles for her so that she retained
her husband's land. Masterin was sent to school by her mother's
family, and she eventually got a job as a schoolteacher. She didn't
marry until her late twenties and remained in her mother's village to protect the land. She had five children, all but one married. The sons were all well educated but jobless. The youngest
daughter was attending intercollege in Mainpuri. Masterin walked
five miles to school every morning and returned in the late

afternoon. She was a quiet woman who had worked hard to support her family but had done so unobtrusively and without fanfare. Although she was the only upper caste woman in Karimpur who had ever had a job, no one criticized her, for her behavior in all other ways was circumspect. She played no political role in the village, nor did she use her standing to fight the system.

Widowhood forced some women to enter spheres of activity normally reserved for males and thus highlights for us the obstacles faced by all Karimpur women as they began to seek a wider voice in their community. *Purdah* acts to cut women off from those who have power in a community and prevents them from joining together to advocate their rights. It is a primary obstacle to change for women in rural north India. Karimpur women regularly told me that they'd like to be men because then they could "go anywhere." Only later was I able to decipher this statement. They did indeed desire to move about but could not do so as women, hence they wanted to be men. The value was placed on mobility: they might not really want to be men, but they did want to go to town as they wished, hence they must be men. Yet *purdah* remained entrenched in Karimpur. For women the winds of change blew very slowly.

I am often asked if the village is better off than before—whether it is better than in the 1920s, in the 1960s, or in the 1980s. Certainly the Brahmans think conditions have declined. The headman told me, "But the condition of our [Brahman] people was better [in 1925]. Now the village people are not so good. . . . But theirs [the condition of other castes] was bad, their condition has improved. Only ours has become worse." But his view is that of a group which has lost political and economic power.

There is no doubt that the standard of living in Karimpur was better in 1984 than in 1925 or even in 1968. If we look at health care or mortality rates, quality of housing, source of water, quality of clothing, educational levels, or consumer goods (watches, radios, cycles, etc.), the village had prospered. Yet there were many whose families had seen none of this increased prosperity. Their standard of living was comparable to that of their grandfathers in the 1920s, and some might have been even hungrier. As one elderly leather worker stated, "The condition of our house is the same as before. There is difficulty all the time: there is no rest."

Part of the paradox of change in Karimpur is that in the 1920s the rich ate better than the poor and certainly had political and economic clout over the poor, but otherwise everyone shared in a poor standard of living. Now everyone in fact probably ate less well (e.g., the lack of milk). But the rich lived in brick houses while the poor still had mud huts; the sons of the rich received M.A.s while the poor remained illiterate; the rich daughters wore 200- and 300-rupee saris while the poor were still in tatters. There was a greater visible disparity between rich and poor than before.

There had been a decline in families owning large amounts of land, as land had been apportioned among numerous sons, a factor affecting primarily the Brahman landlords. And Brahmans now controlled only 58 percent of the land, whereas before it had been more than 80 percent. Meanwhile, many landlords were heavily in debt, having overextended themselves with easily accessible government loans that they could not repay. But they had brick houses, well-dressed daughters-in-law, and educated sons and daughters.

The Brahmans of Karimpur were used to comparing themselves to the farmers, water carriers, and other *kamins* of Karimpur as well as to their kin in nearby villages and urban areas. They saw their economic control of the old *kamins* eroded. One Brahman family used to feed the whole water carrier caste at Holi: this was no longer possible. They also saw their political superiority melting away, as the lower castes, having no economic ties to the Brahman landlords, no longer abided by their political wishes. In addition, the disproportionate population growth of the poor had given them a greater voice in Karimpur

elections. Further, the educated sons of the rich were not able
to find jobs suitable to their degrees, so they remained at home,
refusing to farm but unable to work. Not surprisingly, the most
desirable attribute for a family seeking a boy with whom to marry
their daughter was that he have a job.

At the same time, increasing contact with urban areas had
made the Brahman families aware of the possibility of an even
better life-style, one filled with gas stoves, videos, and cars.
Some of their daughters cooked on gas stoves, others had relatives with large houses in Agra. The Karimpur Brahmans were
caught between the economic and political challenge of their
old *kamins* and the disparity between themselves and the urban
middle class. Despite their increased material prosperity, they
saw themselves as having lost ground.

The poor also saw a loss, a loss of community and of a village
that was in some sense united, even if it was united through
ties of servitude and fear. For many of the poor, educational
levels were up, new employment opportunities were developing, health care was keeping more sons alive. Yet they too saw
a loss of the old moral order in which a Brahman landlord would
feel obligated to support his *kamin* in times of crisis. I was constantly told that people no longer cared for one another, that
there was no longer any love in the village. The Brahman may
have been an authoritarian father figure but was also a loving
one.

In April of 1984 a massive fire swept through Karimpur,
burning twenty houses and killing six people and twelve animals. In the days that followed, the village was factionalized by
groups competing for the government's minimal largesse. When
a doctor representing the Rotary Club came from Mainpuri to
provide help, he left in disgust at the petty fighting and total
refusal to provide aid for one's bereaved neighbors.

A year later, a clear consensus had developed about the cause
of the fire: it was blamed on the Brahman community generally
and its corrupt leaders, like Prakash's son Subedar more specifically. One explanation for the devastation wrought by the fire

was the accumulation of sins in the village itself, especially those of past leaders. These leaders, people felt, had written a bad fate for the community as a whole. That the Brahmans suffered most was only expected, for they had sinned the most while ruling the village. When a friend asked two young non-Brahman men about the fire, they responded, vehemently, "But they sinned." With the Brahmans no longer in firm control, it was easier to see the rifts in Karimpur society. As ties outside of the village gained in strength, the sense of community that was once there was declining.

As Karimpur enters the last decade of the twentieth century, material and social changes seem to be accumulating at an unparalleled rate. As I write, a letter has come saying that almost no one threshed grain manually this year. A non-Brahman from an adjoining hamlet won the recent election for headman. And there are now seven television sets in the village. New ideas from agricultural experts, education, government agencies, and urban relatives have all contributed to the major socioeconomic changes of the 1970s. Mass communication, especially television, heralds a whole new set of ideas. How they will affect village life remains to be seen. Karimpur will still exist in the year 2000, but the extent to which the social fabric will remain Familiar is questionable.

The Village
in 1998

This Muslim daughter-in-law was posed by her
mother-in-law before the Koran to document the
fact that she was literate. Even today, less than half the
females in Karimpur are literate, and literacy amongst
the Muslims is particularly low, making this
girl's literacy valued. (mid-1990s)

CHAPTER XVI

The Village in 1998

Susan S. Wadley

Once again I was in a car, this time with only my youngest daughter, Leela, driving toward Karimpur. If it had not been for the white shrine of Khan Bahadur atop the hill by the village, rebuilt after it was destroyed in the communal (Hindu-Muslim) turmoil of the early 1990s, I might not have recognized the turn into the village proper. The bus stop, once a tree with a shrine to the goddess as its main marker, is now a thriving commercial area, with fifteen shops including a tea stall, a sweet shop, a barber, a cycle repair shop, and an electrical store, all vying for the business of the passersby. It was late September 1998, and I was in Karimpur for a month-long stay. Although I had visited the village almost yearly since 1984, this was my first extended visit since then, as well my first one in many years during the fall festival cycle. Like a child, I eagerly awaited my favorite festivals, including Divali, the annual festival of lights in which the goddess Lakshmi is worshipped as the bringer of prosperity; Siyao Mata, or Lampblack Mother, when the women worship for the welfare of their male kin; Gobardhan, or Cow Dung Wealth, in honor of Krishna's protection of family and community; and Bhaiya Duj, or Brother's Second, when daughters worship their brothers and are rewarded with gifts. If I was lucky, the men might also perform the Ram Lila, the story of the god-hero Rama that is often enacted in villages and cities through northern India every fall.

I did celebrate the festivals, and did see Ram Lila, but during that visit Karimpur had other agendas for me, ones that represent the changes facing this still-rural village as it approaches the twenty-first century. I learned of motor scooters and television sets, as well of malaria and new forms of tuberculosis. Brick houses were all around, the numbers of mud walls far fewer; and electrical lines ran everywhere. As I reflect back, it is clear that increased globalization and the economic liberalization that have occurred in India in the past decades have increased the disparity between rich and poor in Karimpur. Yet new consumerism and a greater awareness of the world outside abound among all classes. A sign for computer education can be seen in the town a hour away, though only one person in Karimpur had ever seen a computer. Television sets are found in about 20 percent of Karimpur's homes, bringing with them new demands for products unheard of twenty years ago. These contradictory pressures of globalization and increased disparity in numerous realms of social life (family life, education, health care, consumerism, religion, and politics) lay the groundwork for the twenty-first century.

Population and Migration

I began learning of the changes that had occurred over the past fifteen years by taking a census, a process that took me to every house in the village and reacquainted me with it many hidden corners. The population did increase—from 2,048 in 1984 to 2,581 (excluding 381 people who migrated out) in 1998, though the percent of juveniles remained almost constant (see table 1). Many families have five or six children, but some have only two or three. Probing more deeply, I found some thirty-six women, mostly higher caste, who had had a tubectomy to control family size. Many in the landowning castes have clearly made an effort to contain their population. This is especially true for families with parents under forty years, for it wasn't until the mid-1980s that tubectomies became prevalent in the region. One Brahman family illustrates this trend clearly: the older two brothers, both with tenth grade schooling who are now in their late forties and early fifties, were married to women without any education, in the hopes that these women would be more easily integrated into the large joint family of a major landowner. Each has six children. The third brother, now in his late thirties, was married to a girl with an eighth-grade education. They have three children—and she has had a tubectomy.

Data on family structures (see table 4) reveal that contrary to the models of modernization created on the basis of the evolution of Western society, the number of joint families in Karimpur is actually increasing. Joint families (defined as two married couples and their children—either a father and his son(s) and their families or two or more brothers and their families) are particularly prevalent among the landowning and farming families, where several adult men are needed to work the fields and the family's financial status is strong enough to mitigate against the competing demands of sons and their wives and children. Nuclear families are most common among the non-farming poor. Many families, both rich and poor, had a widowed parent or other relative living with one son and his family, forming supplemented nuclear families. It is clear that the value placed on being a joint family, especially by the upper castes, has not declined, despite the influences of the media and "Westernization."

The census also revealed that there was a major out-migration from the village, with 381 individuals (or almost 13 percent of what would have been the total population) from more than 100 different households moving more or less permanently out. A few wealthier and educated men were even selling off their family holdings, both houses and land, to purchase housing in Agra or Delhi or some other city. The financial advantage of selling land is related to current prices: one family was selling seven acres of land for 1,225,000 rupees (approximately $30,000): as one relative commented, you could put it in a bank and live off the interest for years. (A lower-middle-class urban family living in a major city needs 7,000 to 9,000 rupees per month.)

Families currently selling land realize that their children, raised and educated in an urban area, are not likely to return to farming, nor do they have the skills to do so. The sons could not even cut fodder or feed livestock, while the daughters only knew how to cook on gas stoves, not the village hearth with its cow-dung cakes as its primary fuel. Moreover, village homes with their earth-packed floors require frequent replastering with cow dung, something the urban daughters refuse to do. When I asked one teenager raised in a nearby town what she would do if she married into a village and had to cow dung the floor, she replied that if her father didn't marry her into a house with cement floors, she would refuse to marry, for to her this once-sacred dung was now "shit."

Two generations ago, the sons were raised to be farmers, though families hoped that an educated son might get a job in government service. Nowadays, government jobs are rare, and most men seek private employment in the cities. This out-migration has also taken a disproportionate share of the educated men: those with master's degrees, in particular, seldom remain in the village. But contact with Karimpur was not cut in these moves: relatives constantly visit their kin in urban areas, where the better hospitals, schools, and stores are located; and the brighter children are boarded with urban relatives to attend more prestigious schools.

Moreover, there are caste-based patterns of migration, based in part on kin networks, but also on caste cultures and attitudes toward work and work opportunities. Two castes, middle-ranked by both education and landholdings, illustrate this difference. The farmers, or traditional vegetable growers, are almost all still involved in farming: of eighty-six families, sixty still have farming as their primary occupation, while only seventeen have men working out of the village (three in the nearby town of Mainpuri and fourteen in Delhi or farther). The caste of shepherds, who were also farmers for most of the last century, provides a strong contrast: of the twenty-one families, only eight are still farmers; nine men work in security forces in Bombay and Surat and another four men work in Delhi, while two are in the local police force (and two sell milk). The shepherds moved into these other jobs, I think, for a variety of reasons. First, in 1984, the farmers had about 0.4 acres of land per person and the shepherds 0.2 acres per person. This basic land shortage could have propelled the out-migration, though some other poorer castes do not have such a large out-migration. Also contributing to this pattern is that the farmers have close connections with the Brahman landowners as sharecroppers; these ties support farming their own land because their sharecropping duties allow them to access the resources necessary for farming, such as animals for plowing and water for irrigation. The shepherds, in contrast, were only minimally tied into the old patron-client relationships of *jajmani;* they had far fewer connections to the Brahmans and have more consistently challenged Brahmanical superiority, thus making their connections to the village itself less stable and easier to dissolve. Finally, the shepherds developed a connection to Bombay about ten years ago through an affinal relative and have been slowly able to obtain jobs for other kin from Karimpur. Both shepherds and farmers, however, have a larger portion of male-only migration than the richer Brahmans.

Another group of men, these better-educated Brahmans, has moved into the market for labor contractors in Delhi: as middlemen between general contractors and laborers, they provide labor for given sites. But this work is risky, for if the job doesn't meet the required specifications of time and quality, they must eat into their profits to make up the lack. Yet these men earn enough to be considered lower middle class: they might own a motor scooter, and though they and their families all live in one room in the high-rent urban squalor that is Delhi, they have amenities such as a TV, a refrigerator, and a fan. Their children are well-dressed, and they attend schools that are far better than those in the village. The disadvantages are that women are cut off from their female kin support groups, and the benefits of fan and electricity do not necessarily outweigh their living and cooking in one room, with no courtyards or other open spaces available to them. Whether schoolteachers or labor contractors or other government servants, the

Brahman migrants, being better able to afford urban housing and
wanting the advantages of urban schooling for their offspring, are
most likely to have their wives and children with them.

Those who remain in the village are also shifting their employment, though most remain farmers or farm laborers. Several men
run a flour mill; another has an electrical shop; a half dozen have
government jobs (one, for instance, is a clerk in the nearby court;
another is a tube well borer for the government). Several men work
in the state police force, while a couple are in the military. In
marked contrast, only two women, one the wife of a young Brahman man and the other the wife of a man from the accountant
caste, have paid jobs: one is a schoolteacher and the other a nurse.
Neither resides full-time in Karimpur.

Education

Closely tied to the increase in migration is a significant increase in
education for both males and females, and for most caste groups.
In part this increase is due to new educational opportunities: a
paved road now runs around the pond at the edge of the village and
crosses the fields to the small town of Bichwan on the Grand Trunk
Road (the major highway across northern India), two miles away.
Since it is only two miles, Bichwan has become a prime receiving
locale for high school and intercollege (eleventh and twelfth grade)
students. For those who are often needed as household labor, this
proximity means greatly reduced travel times. It also opens up the
possibility of going to Bhongaon, further down the Grand Trunk
Road, for college—whether B.A. or M.A. Moreover, the numbers
of students are now great enough that girls can travel in groups, for
safety and protection. And for those seeking urban education
for their very young, a private bus funded by a local doctor takes
primary school children to his private (religion-based) school in
Mainpuri.

Despite a greater focus on education, in 1998 only a third of
Karimpur's female population was literate, while a mere 53 percent
of the men were literate. Looking at education by caste, the range
is from almost total literacy among the accountants to almost total

illiteracy among the potters and sweepers. Nowadays, all the caste groups send students to primary school, though the potters send no girls and have no literate women. Most castes send some boys through high school, but female participation in schooling declines rapidly after grade 5, with only half of the twenty-two caste groups sending girls to high school (grades 9 and 10), and only five (of twenty-two) sending girls to intercollege (grades 11 and 12). Currently one young woman and seven young men are studying for their M.A. degrees.

The most significant increases in education have taken place among the Brahmans. Of the group of women over fifty-five years of age, only seven of twenty-four are literate. In contrast, only two men and five women between the ages of five and thirty are illiterate, and this includes one couple where both are mentally handicapped. More important, however, most Brahman girls and boys are in school through high school, with equal numbers of males and females in intercollege (six young men and seven young women). The effects are particularly evident in higher-caste, three-generational families: the grandmother, now in her sixties or seventies, is illiterate. Her daughters-in-law (and daughters) received fifth or eighth grade educations. Her teenage granddaughters will certainly finish grade 12 and perhaps go on for a B.A. Intrafamilial relations are strained because the younger generations of women have access to knowledge long denied their elders. It is difficult for a mother-in-law to retain authority over a daughter-in-law whose knowledge is now valuable to the larger family endeavor.

The rationale for the push for education is unfortunately all too clear: I was told again and again by Brahman men and women that intercollege was now necessary for girls to get a good marriage. Education is not for the sake of education, but for the marriage market. Girls are not expected to seek employment: rather, they should be well educated so that they can train the next generation. Here the expectations are even higher: daughters married into urban families are sending their children to English-language schools starting with first grade. These schools have considerably higher standards and demands than the village schools, and it is the woman's job to help the children study and prepare their lessons. The more education the mother brings, the greater the chances that her offspring will succeed in the all-important school race that so consumes many middle-class Indian families. So while most mothers in Karimpur are barely involved in their children's education, those daughters who have married into urban families are finding new roles as tutors and advocates for their children. Since many Karimpur Brahman families are now marrying at least one daughter into an urban setting, everyone is fully aware of the need for education.

I should also note one peculiar pattern for the Brahmans, and that is the education of only daughters. Three families have an only daughter who will inherit the family's land: one daughter is now nearing seventy, one is in her fifties, and one is nineteen. All three are among the best educated of their peers. The oldest is a retired schoolteacher whose mother fought in the late 1930s to get her daughter educated. The one in her fifties, also married and living in Karimpur, has an eighth grade education, highly unusual for her age and obtained by staying with relatives out of the village. The third, now nineteen, is the first female in Karimpur to seek an M.A. These women's odd positionings as only children and heirs have given their families the ability to make unusual educational decisions for them.

For the poorer families, education for males transfers to employment irregularly: one of the poorest village families, from a group where the women were traditionally midwives, educated two sons past high school, only to have one drive a rickshaw and the other pack clothes for an exporter in Delhi. A third well-educated young man from this caste group remains in the village, farming his father's land, greeting me sadly on each visit with his hopes that somehow he can break this cycle. Lacking connections and know-how, these lower-caste families are seldom able to convert education into any kind of decent employment.

Those educated men who do not migrate use education to circumvent the old Brahman patronage system within the village and with the local government. But even then, help is often needed for medical crises and other tragedies. With sons not getting jobs, and with few marriages into urban areas or into families where an educated bride is expected, there is no need to educate sons or daughters, certainly not at the higher levels. If a girl can write a letter home, that is sufficient. So it is not surprising that among some of the poorer caste groups, such as the water carriers, less than half of the school-age boys are in school, and less than one-third of the girls. Although the water carriers make up one of the largest castes in the village, with a population of 333, they have only five men and one woman over age thirty who are literate.

So the educational picture in Karimpur is complex. Some groups, like the Brahmans, are rapidly shifting their expectations of levels of education, whereas others such as the midwives/mat makers and water carriers are still choosing to keep half their sons out of school. The costs of education still appear overwhelming to many, since books, paper, pens, and a decent set of clothes are necessary. With their elders unsuccessful in finding decent employment, there is little incentive for poor youths to move beyond basic literacy, if even to attain that.

The ramifications of education, or lack thereof, are many. As with the Brahman family described above, the better-educated women are more likely to use birth control. Equally important is a shift in the age of marriage. While marriages before puberty are now exceptionally rare, the marriage age remains well under twenty for both males and females among the lower castes. Yet among the Brahmans, marriages now almost always take place after age twenty, often in the mid-twenties, reflecting the felt need to complete education before marriage as well as the need for the son to be employed in order to attract an educated wife with a reasonable dowry. But there is a downside: the better educated the girl, the higher the dowry demands from comparably educated boys. For village Brahmans, the family of a girl with a twelfth grade education can expect to spend 80,000 rupees in dowry (about $2,000 where the wage rate for an unskilled laborer is $1 per day); if the girl has a B.A., the demand will be 150,000 rupees; and if she has an M.A., "hundreds of thousands" (since in each case, a comparably educated groom must be found).

Some women have been able to profit by their education and

have both mobility and access to resources that were unheard of one generation ago. In the 1960s, a woman only rarely went to the nearby town, and then almost always was escorted by male kin. The men knew the locations of the doctors, the stores patronized by her family, the schools, and so on. Nowadays, a few better-educated women have gained knowledge of the city and its ways and have become patrons, much as their menfolk were and still sometimes are. Most critical is knowledge of the medical options and how to maneuver among them. For example, one Brahman woman in her mid-forties knows how to get malaria tests, when to bribe the technicians to make sure the slides are read correctly, what to take for a hospital stay (bedding and a jug for water), which doctors are best for different illnesses, and so on. Various members of her husband's extended family rely on her and her knowledge, and she moves around the city, and between city and village, freely. Other women travel to town with sick children or to shop, or commute between their husbands' towns or villages and their parents' without the escorts once required for women. Education thus provides some women with opportunities to gain yet other kinds of useful knowledge that allows them to negotiate the complexities of life in modern India.

Mobility and Consumerism

Everyone's mobility, and with it access to new markets and ideas, is eased by the numbers of vehicles now plying the roads. In Karimpur itself, two families own jeeps, another ten have tractors, several own trucks, one owns a bus, and numerous men have motor scooters. A call from the one telephone in the village can bring a taxi from Mainpuri, eight miles away. Numerous buses ply routes that once were walked. Travel by bullock cart is almost unheard of, as tractors can be hired for any long-distance trip, such as attending a wedding or carrying grain to the market.

In addition to Karimpur's residents moving out to the city to work or to shop, there is a corresponding movement of urban ways into the village, especially via television, radio, and movies. Some eighty families have television sets, though the erratic electrical supply (often missing for a week at a time, otherwise available only a few hours a day) means that these are less dominant than we might otherwise think. A few families have a battery that can be charged to run the TV when the electrical supply fails. On Sunday morning children were likely to run to a neighbor's house to watch the latest installment of one of India's religious epics on TV.

One result is a rampant consumerism, even among those who can barely afford it. Consumer goods from toothpaste (where once a branch of the *neem* tree sufficed) to sweets for the children to polyester saris and shirts and pants are bought. Cotton, once the fabric of choice, has been replaced by polyesters, especially among women and upper-caste men (who rarely wear traditional cotton clothing unless they are presenting themselves as politicians, where the accepted garb is starched white traditional cotton clothing). Along with the shift in fabric is a shift in style: men prefer Western trousers and shirts to cotton "pajamas" (worn in India outside of the bedroom) or the even more traditional *dhoti*. Although women still wear saris, they are no longer plain white or blue, but vividly colored and often worn "Delhi style" with the drape over the left shoulder and down the back, rather than in the village fashion with the drape coming up over the right shoulder and across the front of the wearer. While *purdah*, or the seclusion and veiling of women, is still enforced in the village and before one's husband's older male kin, these restrictions are eased in the city. They in fact remain most prominent on ritual occasions, when propriety demands adherence to older rules. There is no doubt, however, that *purdah* rules are desirable in the village. One day I was sitting with my landlady on her verandah when a jeep pulled up near the path to the village, and two well-dressed women got out. Since it had been raining, they couldn't drive to their house, but had to walk the final three hundred yards. As my friend stared, she commented, "But that is X's wife. And her head is uncovered!" She went on to say that it is acceptable for the schoolteachers and nurses who come from town to walk through the village without their heads covered, but a wife of the village, even if she lives in town, should follow *purdah* rules when in the village.

Girls' clothing is also changing. Since I have been going to Karimpur, the shift from schoolgirl, or girl not old enough to be married, to marriageable woman has been marked by a shift in clothing from a long tunic and baggy pants (*silvar-kurta*, or "Panjabi suit") to a sari. Girls under ten or so would wear dresses, or frocks. As the marriage age has moved up, the length of time that a girl will wear the Panjabi outfit has increased. Moreover, for teenage schoolgirls, a new outfit has emerged: a skirt (about mid-calf length) with an overblouse. Among the upper castes, this skirt and blouse outfit will often be worn until the girl is close to twenty or until her schooling ends, whichever is first. Then she will shift to a Panjabi suit until her marriage is arranged. Only when married, perhaps as late as her mid-twenties, will she begin wearing a sari.

The new consumerism is not necessarily all good, especially when combined with family-planning practices. One result is what I term the "only son sugar syndrome." As families limit their children, having one or two sons and one daughter (ideally), an only son is likely to become very spoiled, especially in view of the few limits put on small children in many Karimpur households. Further, having disposable income means that a family can buy sugar. And because Karimpur mothers believe that their children will not drink milk unless it is highly sweetened, only sons receive, at their demand, an inordinate number of their daily calories from sugar, and as a result suffer from malnutrition. This evidence of malnutrition among boys runs counter to the older patterns where daughters regularly received less food, and less good food, than their brothers and hence were often severely malnourished. Girls actually benefit in this new schema, as they do not get as much of the highly sugared milk (and other sweets) as their brothers. Among the better-off, this higher quality of care for girls is manifested in long, healthy hair—something their mothers and grandmothers and aunts were never able to achieve.

Health and Health Care

Further complicating the treatment of illness is the multiplicity of treatment options. In both village and town, there is a range of alternatives for medical care. In the village, you can seek treatment through traditional means such as possession rituals, or you can seek to ward off evil spirits by using lampblack on a baby's eyes, or you can call the local man who worked as a peon in a nearby hospital and who now considers himself a trained medical worker ("doctor"); he will gladly give you an injection or set up an intravenous drip bag of glucose if you have had a fever for some days.

A patient thought seriously ill, or an only son, might be taken to town. Mainpuri has a government general hospital where malaria and TB tests are done and serious cases taken, as well as a woman's hospital for obstetrical patients. There are also numerous private hospitals and clinics, some little more than storefronts and others with x-ray and sonogram equipment, as well as beds for the truly sick. Many of these urban doctors have MBBS degrees in medicine, but many do not, for medical practice is not strictly regulated, and many self-educated "doctors" are found in cities and villages alike. Some clinics specialize in homeopathic cures, following ayurvedic practices used in Indian medicine for thousands of years. And, as noted below, because the treatment of illness is often complicated, and the causes unclear, the town offers yet other choices for traditional cures via possession or similar means.

Unfortunately, the choice of treatment is often largely determined by sex and age. Men are more likely to get treatment, or more expensive treatment, for themselves than they are for their wives. And boy children are more likely to get treated by the town doctors than their sisters, for whom the family calls the self-trained "doctor" resident in the village. Unaware of the most standard antiseptic rules, the village "doctor" cleans his needle (for an intravenous glucose drip or an injection of an antibiotic) with well water. He can treat a fever with aspirin or an antibiotic, as well as give intravenous drips, but has neither the training nor the ability to diagnose the underlying cause; as a result the patient often becomes seriously ill before he or she is taken to the hospital in Mainpuri. In the short time I was in Karimpur last fall, one such "doctor" contributed to a serious malaria case described below through not diagnosing it properly; gave a shot to a woman who was seven months pregnant that may have led to her having the baby a few hours later (the child survived—at least through its tenth-day naming ceremony—but was not bigger than my hand); and perhaps led to the death of a young girl with a stomachache whom he treated with a shot. This three-year-old was dead a few hours later. Even if the shot did not kill her, the misdiagnosis most probably did. But the "doctor" is not alone in erring, for this same girl's younger brother had been taken to town the day before for a minor earache. But when his sister fell ill with diarrhea and a stomachache, her family chose not to take her to one of the reputable doctors in town, but instead called the untrained village "doctor."

Other health issues present a picture of impending crisis for Karimpur. The most immediate are increases in malaria and TB. Since DDT spraying has been stopped, the mosquito population has increased dramatically. Further, the strains of malaria present across northern India are increasingly quinine-resistant, making treatment more expensive and more difficult. To diagnose malaria, a blood test at either the government hospital or a private clinic is necessary, requiring that the often very sick patient be transported to town, eight miles away. The next difficulty is getting the blood tests read correctly, for not only must malaria be identified, but the technicians must test for the quinine-resistant strain. This doesn't usually happen without a bribe in addition to the small fee demanded by the government hospital.

I knew one family that took two very sick women, one in her seventies and one only thirty (and pregnant), for the malaria test. The results supposedly showed that the older woman had malaria, but the younger didn't. Both returned to the village, one with quinine and one not. Three days later, the younger one was rushed by taxi to Agra, four hours away, with cerebral malaria caused by a quinine-resistant strain. Her relatives commented that they had erred in not paying two bribes when they initially took the two women to the hospital: the result was only one careful screening of the slides.

Once malaria is identified, it is easily treated unless the case has progressed so far that serious complications have resulted—dangerously high fevers, enlarged livers, malnutrition, and dehydration. In such a case, the options in Mainpuri are poor, and families prefer to seek out the government hospital in Agra. In addition to the expense, going to the hospital requires a relative who knows how to manipulate the hospital system and gain the care that is needed for his or her relative. This was particularly true in the fall of 1998 when the halls and wards of the hospitals were literally packed with patients, most with malaria. Moreover, some adult must remain with the patient throughout his or her hospital stay, to provide food, water, and other care not given by the hospital staff. It is even worse if a family does not have a spare adult and if the hospital is in another town where there are no other relatives to take food to patient and caretaker and to provide some relief for the caretaker.

Chances of getting malaria can be reduced in part by using mosquito nets in sleeping areas and for protecting small children, especially since most people sleep outside or on verandahs during the hot rainy season, when malaria is most prevalent. Screening windows is not effective under these circumstances. Yet mosquito nets are almost never used in Karimpur, except by the anthropologist and her family. Further, a second mosquito-borne fever, dengue, is also increasingly prevalent in northern India; and whereas the kind of mosquitoes carrying malaria tend to bite at night, the kind carrying dengue bites during the day.

TB, also with new drug-resistant strains, presents other complications. TB tends to be recognized only after the disease is well established, when the patient gets a constant fever and serious cough, often involving the coughing up of blood. By this time, the whole family (and school, if the victim is a child) has been exposed for some time to this highly infectious disease. Diagnosis requires an x-ray; treatment is a combination of drugs that must be taken for at least six months; in addition, extra milk, fruits, and vitamin supplements are also prescribed. Unfortunately, all too often the family stops the treatment before the end of six months, as the patient seems cured and the expense may seem enormous to them (about 6,000 rupees, or $150).

Complicating this scenario is the as-yet absence of AIDS in Karimpur, though the probability of an AIDS outbreak there is now high. Factors contributing to an impending AIDS crisis are the numbers of men who live in the cities, the spread of allopathic medicine with the resulting belief that the only good treatment is an injection (often given with unsterilized needles), and the increased incidence of AIDS in India generally.

As these examples show, the management of illness is not an easy matter, for it involves a multitude of cultural decisions about who is ill, what the problem is thought to be (and how serious the family deems it), the family's financial status, the range of options available to that family that they think relevant to the illness, and so on. Some treatments, such as ritual ones, are often highly effective as cures for illnesses that involve mental health. Others, such as a glucose drip with a dirty needle for malaria, are very dangerous for anyone so treated, if not now, then in the future. But in a community where people have been taught that Western medicine is now better than their traditional cures, and where the best way to obtain Western medicine is through an injection, the possibility of abuse—and eventually the spread of AIDS and the emergence of drug-resistant strains of bacteria—is enormous.

Another result of modern medical care, though not openly discussed, is the new means of determining the sex of one's unborn child. In a country where female children, especially babies, have higher mortality than boys, and where sex selection of the fetus is becoming more common, it is not surprising to find sex selection of a fetus now an option in Karimpur. A storefront clinic near the government hospital in Mainpuri advertises a "two-minute blood test" to determine the sex of an unborn child (a test unknown to Western scientific medicine). But the most common method of sex determination of a fetus is now a sonogram. I found that women from better-educated and wealthier families are now given a sonogram as a regular part of prenatal care (it cost about 400 rupees, or $10, in the fall of 1998); and while this is certainly appropriate in terms of caring for an unborn child, it suggests that the possibility of terminating pregnancies where there is a female fetus is ever-present. The juvenile sex ratio (age fourteen and under) in Karimpur, a very low 790 females per 1000 males, suggests that it is possible that there is now selection for male children before birth as well as after.

Politics and Religion

A final significant change in Karimpur relates to village and national politics, with associated changes in religious practice. Without doubt, the Hindu-Muslim communalism of the 1990s has affected the village. Although Karimpur, and the whole district, remained free of Hindu-Muslim riots in 1990 when much of the surrounding area was not, the shrine to Karimpur's Muslim guardian saint, Khan Bahadur, was destroyed. The government acted quickly to repair it, and as one of the landowning Brahmans commented, no one in Karimpur would have caused the damage. The Hindu women of the village continue to visit the shrine on Thursdays to seek the protection of Khan Bahadur and to ask for his aid in such endeavors as getting jobs for their sons or good marriages for their daughters.

At the same time, issues of Muslim identity are more noticeable. Muslim women, who used to be indistinguishable from their Hindu neighbors in their cotton saris, now wear a *silvar-kurta* and even don a *burqa* when leaving the village. Muslim houses are decorated with tiles in Arabic and with glass, and the men sometimes gather for an outdoor *nimaz*, or prayer meeting, in an open space near their houses. But the most prominent Muslim in the community, a man now in his forties, has left, taking his family to the Muslim conclave in Mainpuri, where he owns a watch and radio repair shop. Only his mother regrets leaving the village, for she had enjoyed a freedom of movement and decades of friendships there that are impossible in town.

The state of Uttar Pradesh, where Karimpur is located, has also had a series of political leaders who, among other things, have designated that only lower castes can be elected headmen in some villages. Karimpur is so designated; and in the last election for headman, an illiterate water carrier was elected *pradhan* against an opponent from the shepherd caste, leaving the old Brahman leadership of the village to work behind the scenes on the village council. Meanwhile, the Brahman community is active in national politics, and leaders from the Brahman community represent the two main contenders for power in the village—the BJP, a Hindu fundamentalist party (which retains its leadership of India as I write), and the Congress, for many decades India's ruling party. As the representatives of the national parties in the local elections, these men are able to spend thousands of rupees and add to their roles as patrons.

Although the Brahmans still wield the most power in local Karimpur politics, despite no longer having control of the *pradhan*, their sense of control has eroded significantly. The *jajmani* system of patron-client relationships has all but ended, with a few castes providing ritual services at weddings and funerals, but with none receiving semiannual payments. Thus the Brahmans, as the primary patrons, have lost a major source of control of the rest of the community. The decline in tenancy and sharecropping has had a similar effect of eroding Brahman control of lower castes. As men move into jobs outside the village, they no longer need to respond to the Brahmans' demands—whether for respect or votes or services. My middle-aged research assistant, himself a Brahman, commented that the young man in his twenties (from one of the most important Brahman families) who was also assisting me at times "did not remember what it was like when we had control" and hence did not act appropriately superior to the lower castes.

The Hindu fundamentalist movement with its focus on the birthplace of the god-hero Rama in Ayodhya also revived and added to the village Ram Lila traditions. Every year in villages and communities throughout northern India, the story of Ram is sometimes portrayed in a ten- to thirty-day drama. In Karimpur, it generally took ten days and was organized by the Brahman community, with Brahman actors. But through much of the 1980s, Ram Lila declined, only to be revived with the rallying cry of "Ram rajya" (Ram's kingdom) as a political move by the Hindu fundamentalist BJP party. By the early 1990s, the Brahman community had revived its Ram Lila performances, and in 1994 I had aided them by buying a backdrop and costumes. More recently, a second Ram Lila performance has been organized by the middle-ranked farmer caste. The respective merits of these two performances are hotly discussed, with the Brahmans, in particular, disparaging the others' performance, claiming that it is too much "dancing" and not enough "religion." But in fact, the Brahman performance too highlights dancing and music in its attempt to draw an audience.

Globalization and modern media have affected other religious traditions. One example is the extensive worship of the goddess Santoshi Ma, who bestows peace and benevolence. Gaining popularity though pamphlets and a feature film in the 1970s, Santoshi Ma benefited from the new media of film and television, as well as recordings and printed materials. Moreover, Santoshi Ma protects women whose husbands are away; and as more and more men migrated, usually without their families at least initially, her popularity increased. A noticeable change in religious practice is the almost complete loss of the girls' ritual of Simara-Simariya, which took place during the period of Navratri, the nine nights of the goddess, every fall. Through the mid-1980s, images of a male and female made on the walls of the courtyard were worshipped early every morning by the teenage girls of the family to aid them to obtain good husbands. On the ninth day, a lavish marriage of this pair (also made as stand-alone clay figures) was held: one of the brothers would act as priest; the girls would make clay pots and other utensils as "dowry" as well as elaborate figures for a marriage procession. The ceremony would conclude with a meal cooked by the girls in the courtyard and shared among their kin. But in 1998, I found only one household still making the Simara-Simariya figures, for most of the girls had adopted the more mainstream and prestigious goddess rituals brought to Mainpuri (and hence to the village) from Calcutta and its environs. Instead of worshipping the Simara-Simariya on their walls, these young women were taking their pots and trays of offerings to the goddess shrine near the bus stop for the nine days of Navratri.

Karimpur at the end of the twentieth century is certainly not the isolated village first studied by the Wisers almost seventy-five years ago. It is more prosperous than ever before, with amenities such as electricity and vehicles not thought possible even when I first studied there in 1967. Through migration, it is increasingly connected to urban areas throughout northern India, from Calcutta to Bombay, with men of every caste group leaving for jobs elsewhere. A slow process of raising educational levels is under way, with substantial changes for the girls of wealthier families, changes that are reflected in changing roles for women. Women's education, in particular, also marks the growing disparity between those better-off and the very poor. But despite more prosperity and modernization, numerous health care crises foretell problems for every family. And finally, both materially and religiously, Karimpur is being affected by the globalization processes at work around the world. Whether it is men in Delhi packing clothes for the export market or girls wearing an adaptation of Western fashions, the global economy and global culture are increasingly important to this still-rural village.

What will Karimpur's story be in another fifteen years? Certainly, it must include an increased globalization of culture, increasing issues of identity for those of different castes and religions, new religious practices encouraged by television and film, more extensive migration out of the village for employment elsewhere, and new family structures with their changing roles for both men and women. Hopefully, it will also include more education that includes greater portions of the community's children, as well as better health care.

Appendix:
Demographic Tables

These women are preparing the cow dung figures for
the ritual of *govardhan,* literally "cow dung wealth."
Celebrated in honor of the god Krishna's protection of
his childhood village, the dung figures recapture that
story where Krishna held the mountain govardhan over
the village on his finger when it was faced with an
unstopping rain storm sent by the god Indra. Figures of
all the family members are placed in a square marked
off by mountains (toward the front of the photo):
Krishna is represented by a head, hands, and feet
surrounding the square. In the evening, the family
worships the completed ritual construction. (1974)

APPENDIX: DEMOGRAPHIC TABLES

Table 1. Basic Facts in Karimpur's
Demographic History

	1925	1984	1998
Total population	754	2,048	2,581
Number of families	161	327	385
Average family size	4.7	6.3	6.7
Percent literate			
Male	21	34	53
Female	4	23	37
Adult sex ratio (F/1000M)	866	814	847
Juvenile sex ratio (F/1000M)	900	790	790
Percent juvenile (under 15 years)	35.0	43.0	41.5
Percent over 55	6.5	9.1	7.3

Table 2. Population, Families, and Land by Caste in Karimpur, 1925–1998

	Total Population			Total Families			Total Land[1]	
	1925	1984	1998	1925	1984	1998	1925	1984
Best off								
Brahmin (Priest)	188	443	507	41	62	67	721.02	562.90
Better off								
Lodhi (Rice Grower)	6	14	13	1	2	2	11.75	10.00
Ray (Bard)	15	16	27	2	2	4	1.72	10.00
Banya (Shopkeeper)	14	38	54	3	5	9	0.28	39.90
Kayastha (Accountant)	6	25	30	1	3	3	3.54	7.60
Poor								
Kacchi (Farmer)	152	414	532	26	59	87	150.26	167.14
Bhurji (Grain Parcher)	10	29	38	1	4	5	0.00	5.60
Mali (Gardener)	17	20	34	1	3	5	4.95	5.46
Garariya (Shepherd)	26	107	133	6	20	19	1.28	23.10
Sunar (Goldsmith)	11	—	—	2	—	—	0.00	—
Very poor								
Dhanuk (Midwife)	28	167	248	7	30	36	3.79	43.30
Darzi (Tailor)	21	28	20	5	4	3	1.09	3.00
Kumhar (Potter)	9	10	11	3	3	3	0.00	0.50
Kahar (Water Carrier)	83	236	333	19	45	52	36.01	45.92
Barhai (Carpenter)	42	76	113	8	11	18	16.81	14.00
Teli (Oil Presser)	10	55	85	4	11	12	0.00	10.80

Poorest

Thakur (Landowner)	—	6	1	—	1	1	—	0.00
Chamar (Leather Worker)	29	96	137	8	16	17	6.51	12.80
Bhangi (Sweeper)	35	118	118	8	19	18	3.21	3.40
Manihar (Bangle Seller)	10	24	36	2	5	6	0.00	0.00
Dhuna (Cotton Carder)	9	38	27	1	5	4	0.00	3.00
Dhobi (Washerperson)	6	9	20	1	3	3	0.04	0.00
Faqir (Beggar)	22	71	64	8	13	11	7.14	0.12
Nat (Entertainer)	—	7	—	—	1	—	—	0.00
Tawaif (Dancing Girl)	3	—	—	1	—	—	0.00	—
Nai (Barber)	2	—	—	1	—	—	0.81	—
Total	754	2,048	2,581	161	327	385	970.51	968.54

¹Figures for 1998 are unavailable.

Table 3. Size of Land Holding and Number of Families in Karimpur

Holding Size (acres)	Number of Families (percent)			
	1925 (n = 161)	1968 (n = 246)	1975 (n = 282)	1984 (n = 327)
0.0	73 (45)	99 (40)	121 (43)	92 (28)
0.01–4.99	40 (25)	94 (38)	102 (36)	173 (53)
5.00–9.99	15 (9)	29 (12)	31 (11)	36 (11)
10.00–	33 (21)	24 (10)	28 (10)	26 (8)
Total	161	246	282	327

Table 4. Family Types in Karimpur

Type	Number of Families (percent)			
	1925	1968	1984	1998
Single person	13 (8.1)	9 (3.7)	7 (2.1)	13 (3.3)
Subnuclear	33 (20.4)	11 (4.5)	26 (8.0)	23 (6.0)
Nuclear	36 (22.4)	107 (43.5)	143 (43.7)	159 (41.3)
Supp. nuclear	42 (26.1)	33 (13.4)	58 (17.7)	60 (15.6)
Joint	25 (15.5)	81 (32.9)	91 (27.8)	130 (33.7)
Other	12 (7.5)	5 (2.0)	2 (0.6)	0

APPENDIX: PHOTOGRAPHS

Prakash was the Brahman farmer that became the Wisers' best friend in
Karimpur. He loaned them the land on which they built in 1960 and later
his family shared the house with first Charlotte Wiser and then Susan
Wadley. He died in the mid-1970s. (1972)

This Brahman woman is giving Charlotte a cooking lesson. Since the kitchen area of a Hindu house is sacred space, this lesson is taking place in the family courtyard. (1920s)

The Wisers' car is loaded for a trip to town, about 8 miles away. (1920s)

Two of the Wisers' sons are pulled by a village boy on their homemade wagon. The tent in which they lived while in the village is in the background. (1920s)

Charlotte standing in the doorway from the cattleyard to the verandah, gazing at the road and fields beyond. (1968)

With a plow on his shoulder, a farmer heads to the field with his bullocks. Even in the 1990s, most farmers use animals (bullocks or water buffalo) for plowing, rather than tractors. Although they must grow fodder for the animals, they also get valuable manure and cooking fuel in return. (1984)

Hand pumps in the women's courtyards have cut into the work available for the poor, and have pretty much eliminated the need for water carriers who used to have a hereditary relationship with their patron families. They also make women's work much easier. (1972)

This group of young students is off to the elementary school, each carrying their wooden slate. Children start attending school when their parents feel that they should, sometimes at ages three or four accompanying their older siblings.

They languish in first grade until they have learned enough to pass on to second. (1970s)

This group of girls is diligently completing their homework. While the older ones write in copy books, the younger use a wooden slate and chalk to practice their letters and spelling. The fact that the girls, still in school, are wearing saris dates this picture to the late 1960s. Nowadays school girls wear frocks or a *silvar-kamiz* (a long tunic top with baggy pants). 1968 marked the first year that girls completed 8th grade in the village junior school. (1968)

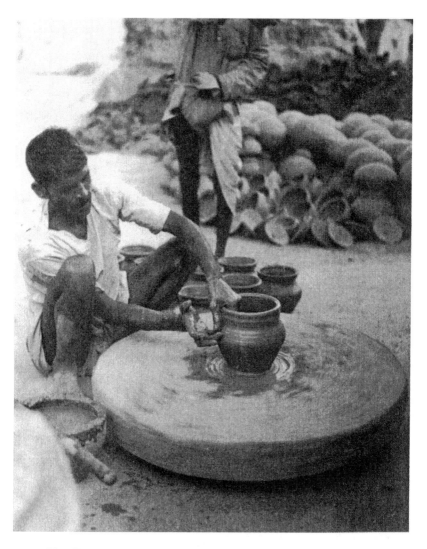

The village potter at his hand-operated wheel. Behind him is the kiln—
pots piled into a large pit dug into the ground. Cow dung cakes are
interspersed amongst the pots, and later the mound will be covered with
straw and ashes and set on fire. Plastic and aluminum goods in the
market have cut into the demand for clay pots. (1975)

This woman is preparing breads for her family at a hearth set on verandah. The rains had made her normal cooking space unusable. Since men are around, she has pulled her sari over her face to keep *purdah*. For fuel, she is using wood and dried cow dung cakes. (1998)

This family gathered for one last picture of a dying relative. This woman suffers from TB, which is reaching epidemic proportions in India. Drug-resistant strains of TB have made the battle against it even harder. (1994)

The village priest is preparing a letter detailing the arrangements for the wedding of a Brahman girl in her mid-20s. Except for the older age of the bride, and the higher dowry, this ritual is little changed from the 1920s. (1998)

These four women, all married into the same family, mark changing styles of dress. On the left is the oldest, wearing her cotton sari in the traditional village style. Next is a sister-in-law who lives mostly in Delhi: she wears her sari 'Delhi' style, and with less of her head covered. Her younger sisters-in-law to the right both live in the village, but have adopted the Delhi style of wearing their saris. The youngest, at the far left, is wearing a polyester sari decorated with gold threads—her wedding sari. (1994)

Although *purdah* (the covering of a woman's face) is declining slowly, it is still mandatory on ritual occasions. Here, before an all-female group gathered to celebrate a wedding, the young woman dancing must cover her face. (mid-1900s)

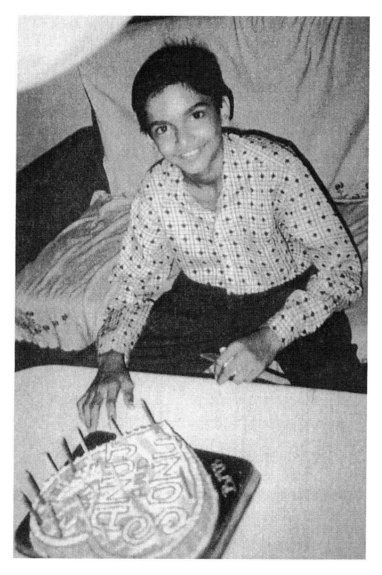

Although birthdays are only rarely celebrated in Karimpur, this young man had a 'cake' for his twelfth birthday. His cake was made of carrot halva, an Indian sweet, decorated with whipped cream frosting. The local town nearby does not have a bakery, nor could this Brahman family eat eggs in a more western "cake." (1998)

BIBLIOGRAPHY

Bibliography

Derr, Bruce W.
1979 *The Growing Abundance of Food and Poverty in a North Indian Village: Karimpur, 1925–1975.* Doctoral dissertation, Syracuse University, Syracuse, NY.
1981 Sharecropping in Karimpur: Contemporary Forms and Tendencies. In *Proceedings of Second International Symposium on Asian Studies, 1980.* Hong Kong: Asian Research Service.
Wadley, Susan S.
1975 Folk Literature in Karimpur: A Catalogue of Types. *Journal of South Asian Literature,* 11: 7–17.
1975 *Shakti: Power in the Conceptual Structure of Karimpur Religion.* University of Chicago Studies in Anthropology: Series in Social, Cultural, and Linguistic Anthropology, no. 2. Chicago: Department of Anthropology, University of Chicago. (Reprinted by Munshiram Manoharlal, New Delhi).
1976 Brothers, Husbands and Sometimes Sons: Kinsmen in North Indian Ritual. *Eastern Anthropologist,* 29: 149–170.

1976 The Spirit "Rides" or the Spirit "Comes": Possession in a North Indian Village. In A. Bharati, ed., *Rituals, Cults and Shamanism: The Realm of the Extra-Human*, pp. 233–251. The Hague: Mouton.

1977 Power in Hindu Ideology and Practices. In K. David, ed., *The New Wind: Changing Identities in South Asia*, pp. 134–157. The Hague: Mouton.

1978 Texts in Contexts: Oral Traditions and the Study of Religion in Karimpur. In S. Vatuk, ed., *American Studies in the Anthropology of India*, pp. 309–341. New Delhi: Manohar.

1981 Women as Mothers, Wives and Daughters in North Indian Folklore. *Asian Thought and Society*, 6: 4–24.

1983 Dhola: A North Indian Folk Genre. *Asian Folklore Studies*, 42: 3–26.

1983 The Rains of Estrangement: Understanding the Hindu Yearly Cycle. *Contributions to Indian Sociology*, 17: 51–86.

1983 Vrats: Transformers of Destiny. In V. Daniel and C. Keyes, eds., *Karma: An Anthropological Inquiry*, pp. 147–162. Berkeley: University of California Press.

1986 The Katha of Sakat: Two Tellings. In. A. K. Ramanujan and S. Blackburn, eds., *Another Harmony: New Approaches to Indian Folklore*, pp. 195–233. Berkeley: University of California Press.

1989 Choosing a Path: Performance Strategies in a North Indian Epic. In S. H. Blackburn, P. J. Claus, J. B. Flueckiger, and S. S. Wadley, eds., *Oral Epics in India*, pp. 75–101. Berkeley: University of California Press.

1989 Female Life Changes in Rural India. In *Cultural Survival Quarterly*, 13: 35–39.

1989 (reprint) Women's Family and Household Rites in a North Indian Village. In N. Falk and R. Gross, eds., *Unspoken Worlds: Women's Religious Lives in Non-Western Cultures*, pp. 72–81. Belmont, CA: Wadsworth Publishing Company.

1991 Why Does Ram Swarup Sing? Song and Speech in the North Indian Epic Dhola." In A. Appadurai, F. J. Korom, and M. A. Mills, eds., *Gender, Genre and Power in South Asian*

Expressive Traditions, pp. 201–223. Philadelphia: University of Pennsylvania Press.

1993 Beyond Texts: Tunes and Contexts in Indian Folk Music. In B. C. Wade, ed., *Texts, Tunes, and Tones: Parameters of Music in Multicultural Perspective*. New Delhi: Oxford and IBH Publishing Co.

1993 Family Composition Strategies in Rural North India. *Social Science and Medicine*, 37: 1367–1376.

1993 The Village Indira: A Brahman Widow and Political Action in Rural North India. In P. Johnson, ed., *Balancing Acts: Women and Social Change*, pp. 65–87. Boulder: Westview Press.

1994 *Struggling with Destiny in Karimpur, 1925–1984*. Berkeley: University of California Press.

1995 No Longer a Wife: Widows in Rural North India. In L. Harlan and P. B. Courtright, eds., *From the Margins of Hindu Marriage: Essays on Gender, Religion, and Culture*, pp. 92–118. New York: Oxford University Press.

1995 *Women in India: Two Perspectives* (with Doranne Jacobson). Rev. 3d ed. Delhi: Manohar Book Service.

1998 Women to Woman: Charlotte Wiser's Srimati. *Manushi*, no. 107, pp. 16–23.

Wadley, Susan S., and Bruce W. Derr

1978 Introduction. In *Four Families of Karimpur*, by Charlotte V. Wiser. Foreign and Comparative Studies Program, Series in South Asia, no. 3. Syracuse University, Syracuse, New York.

1988 Karimpur Families over Sixty Years. *South Asian Anthropologist*, MSA Rao Memorial Issue, 9: 119–132.

1989 Eating Sins in Karimpur. *Contributions to Indian Sociology* 23: 131–148.

1989 Karimpur, 1925–1984: Understanding Rural India Through Restudies. In P. Bardhan, ed., *Toward a Dialogue Between Anthropologists and Economists: Understanding Socioeconomic Change in Rural India*, pp. 76–126. New Delhi: Oxford University Press.

1993 Karimpur Families over Sixty Years. In P. Oberoi, ed.,

Family, Kinship and Marriage in India, pp. 393–415. Delhi: Oxford University Press.

Wiser, Charlotte V.

1929 A Hindu Village Home in North India. *International Review of Missions,* July. London.

1936 *The Foods of a Hindu Village of North India.* Allahabad: Superintendent, Printing and Stationery, United Provinces.

1978 *Four Families of Karimpur.* Foreign and Comparative Studies Program, South Asian Series, no. 3, Syracuse University, Syracuse, NY.

1980 Time Perspectives in Village India. P. Reining and B. Lenkerd, eds. *Village Viability in Contemporary Society,* pp. 123–159. AAS Selected Symposium 34. Boulder: Westview Press.

Wiser, William H.

1933 *Social Institutions of a Hindu Village in North India.* Doctoral dissertation, Cornell University, Ithaca, NY.

1958 *The Hindu Jajmani System.* Lucknow: Lucknow Publishing House.

GLOSSARY

Glossary

ahir	a man of the cowherd caste (sudra)
arhar	a species of pulse (*cytisus cajan*)
aryuvedic	traditional Hindu system of medicine, essentially based on ancient scriptural knowledge and practiced widely in India
baithak	a sitting place outside the house, where men gather, fodder is cut, and visitors are entertained; usually a broad, unroofed veranda (or raised platform) of packed earth
batasas	a sweet, common in North India, used ceremonially as part of a blessing
bhagat	an exorcist or shaman whose power derives from devotion to a tutelary godling
bhajan	a hymn
bhangi	a man of the sweeper caste (untouchable); in Karimpur, the only Christians are converts from this caste

brahman	a man of the priestly (highest) division (or varna) of Hinduism
chamar (chamain)	a man (or woman) of the untouchable leather-working caste (*see also*: jadav)
chaprasi	a messenger
chaukidar	a watchman
chilam	the upper part of the hukkah (water pipe), made of clay
chulha (or chula)	hearth or cooking stove, horseshoe-shaped, usually made of earth, 12-18 inches high
darzi	a member of the caste of sewing men or seamsters (sudra)
dhanuk(in)	a man (or woman) of the untouchable mat-makers caste, now usually laborers
dhobi(n)	a man (or woman) of the untouchable washerman caste
dholak	small barrel-shaped drum, struck rhythmically with the fingers at one end and the palm of the hand at the other
diwali	the festival of lights, held in mid-November; characterized by illumination with small mustard-oil lights
ekka	horse-driven two-wheeled cart, with the passenger accommodation high off the ground
fakir	an untouchable Muslim beggar
Gandhi ashram bandar	retail store for distribution of handicraft products (especially handspun, hand-woven cloth) under the auspices of an organization founded by Gandhi
ghat	a landing place on a riverside
ghi	clarified butter
gram sathi	village-level worker in the Government of India community-development program
gur	unrefined brown cane sugar
hakim	local medical practitioner, usually untrained

Hindi	the vernacular in North India, spoken by Hindus, written in Devanagari script
Hindustani	dialect combining Hindi and Urdu, the lingua franca nearly in all India, written in Devanagari or Arabic script
holi	spring festival held at the full moon in February-March
jadav	new, more prestigeful name adopted by the chamar caste
jajman	the patron in the system of hereditary relationships between artisans and patrons
kabaddi	a boys' game, not unlike hockey
kachhi(n)	a man (or woman) of the vegetable-gardening caste (sudra), now general farmers
kahar(in)	a man (or woman) of the water-carrier caste (sudra)
kankar	loose fill of stone, chipped brick, or hard earth used for roads
kaura chaut	a day in October-November when women fast in order to bring prosperity to their husbands and sons
kshatriya	the second of the four main divisions (varnas) of Hinduism; the warriors
lathi	a long stick, often bamboo, used as staff or weapon
lekhpal	new name for village record-keeper (formerly known as patwari)
lota	small, pot-bellied brass jar used for water or milk
mahajan(i)	a man (or woman) of a vaisya caste of shop-keepers and traders
mali	flower sellers (sudra)
mantras	verses from the sacred scriptures
maulvi	a man learned in Persian and Arabic
memsahiba	term of respect given to ladies of rank and European women

namaskar	traditional Hindu greeting, consisting of palms folded together and raised to the forehead
nazarana	a fee or present given by tenants to visiting landlords or other superior persons
neem	the tree *Azadarichta indica*
panchayat	an assembly of arbitrators (usually five) who settle petty village disputes
patwari	official record-keeper of the village
peepul	a large fig tree, *Ficus religiosa*, which Hindus regard sacred
Petromax	trade name for a pressure-operated kerosene lantern, which has become a generic name; costing 50-100 rupees, while the ordinary hurricane-type kerosene lamp costs 3-6 rupees
pradhan	popularly elected head of the village council (panchayat)
pundit	a person learned in the sacred Hindu books
purdah	a screen; used to denote the custom of secluding women
purdahnashin	a woman who remains in seclusion
Rama	incarnation of the Hindu deity Vishnu; hero of the Ramayana
Ramayana	great epic poem recording the exploits of Rama, the perfect ruler, husband, brother
Rawan	the demon king of Ceylon who carries off Sita in the Ramayana
sadhu	a religious person; a Hindu ascetic
sahib	term of respect for gentlemen of rank and European men
sari	traditional garment worn by Indian women, draped around the body
Shiva	one of the gods of the Hindu triad of Brahma, Shiva, Vishnu—the creative, destructive, preservative principles
Sita	the wife of Rama in the Ramayana

sudra	a man of the fourth division (varna) of Hinduism; a worker
swarajist	a person who works for home rule
tahsildar	a subcollector of revenue
twice-born	a member of one of the three highest varnas, permitted to rebirth, following religious education and initiation in early adolescence
Urdu	Hindustani as spoken by Muslims, written in Arabic script
vaisya	a man of the third division (varna) of Hinduism; a trader
wajib-ul-arz	village customs which are recorded and legally recognized
zamindar	landlord

INDEX

Index